Jeffrey Tayler is the author of *Facing the Congo* and *Siberian Dawn: A Journey Across the New Russia*. He writes for such publications as *Condé Nast Traveller, Spin, Harper's Magazine* and is a correspondent for *Atlantic Monthly*. In 2000 two of his essays were selected by Bill Bryson for the inaugural edition of *The Best American Travel Writing*. Jeffrey Tayler lives in Moscow.

VALLEY OF THE CASBAHS

A Journey Across the Moroccan Sahara

Jeffrey Tayler

ABACUS

An *Abacus* Book

First published in Great Britain in 2003 by Little, Brown
This edition published by Abacus in 2004

Copyright © Jeffrey Tayler 2003

The moral right of the author has been asserted.

All quotes from the Qur'an are taken from Arthur J. Arberry's
1983 translation, Oxford World Classics edition

A CIP catalogue record for this book
is available from the British Library.

ISBN 0 349 11536 2

Typeset in Imprint by M Rules
Printed and bound in Great Britain
by Bookmarque Ltd, Croydon, Surrey

Abacus
An imprint of
Time Warner Books UK
Brettenham House
Lancaster Place
London WC2E 7EN

www.TimeWarnerBooks.co.uk

To my wife, Tatyana

Cette vie est un hôpital où chaque malade est possédé du désir de changer de lit. [This life is a hospital where every patient is possessed of a desire to switch beds.]

Charles Baudelaire

CONTENTS

ACKNOWLEDGEMENTS

I would like to express my deep gratitude to and admiration for Wilfred Thesiger and Philip K. Hitti. Had I not come across their writings, I might not ever have become enamoured of the Arab world or ended up travelling the Drâa, and my life would have been immeasurably poorer. I would also like to thank Ali Daimin of Zagora/Mhamid and the sands beyond for arranging my expedition and for finding my guides and cameleers; Charles Benjamin, longtime resident of the Drâa and Dadès valleys, for his hospitality in Morocco, his regional knowledge and his valuable source materials; Alison Humes, features editor, and Thomas J. Wallace, editor in chief, of *Condé Nast Traveler* (where the article from which this book grew was first published) for supporting me in a trip I made around the Drâa in 1998; and, as always, my agent, Sonia Land, for her faith in me and her tireless efforts. Finally, I am indebted to Jamil M. Abun-Nasr for his *A History of the Maghrib in the Islamic Period*, and C. R. Pennell for his *Morocco Since 1830: A History* – two superb and seminal scholarly works that provided me with much information useful in writing this book.

To protect the privacy of certain people in the book, a few names and minor identifying characteristics have been changed.

NOTE ON TRANSLITERATION

Owing to the French colonial past, a tradition persists in
Morocco of transliterating Arabic placenames into the
Latin alphabet following the French 'system', which
comprises little more than employing maddeningly
inconsistent conventions of orthography to produce
divergent spellings for the same sounds, as a glance at
road signs and maps in Morocco will tell the befuddled
(and frequently lost) motorist. To wit, the name of the
valley down which I travelled has been variously written
as Dra, Draa, Drâa (the most common French version
and the one used in Morocco), Dr'a. Dir'a and Dra'a.
All this and the pronunciation is the same: 'd' followed by
a rolled 'r', the retching laryngeal sound of the Arabic
letter 'ain, and finally the short vowel 'a'. For 'ain (and
the glottal-stop diacritic, hamza) there are no English
phonetic equivalents, but they are often represented by an
apostrophe, a practice I have followed here. In writing
the name of the valley, I have opted for Drâa, since it is
the version the Moroccans themselves use.

If accepted English versions exist for other place-names, I have used them, or I have used the conventional French – whichever is simplest, most common and most accurate. (If the conventional French is wrong, or convoluted, I have replaced it with a corrected English version.) The Michelin maps of North Africa have served as my French standard. If there is no accepted French or English spelling, I have transliterated place-names using a simplified English system, ignoring differences between long and short vowels, and using apostrophes for 'ain and hamza. I have thus preferred the English transliteration of the Arabic 'wadi' (seasonal river bed) to the French 'oued'. For personal names, I have reproduced the transliterations Moroccans themselves use. Thus, for the king of Morocco (and other Moroccans) I write Mohammed, but the name of the prophet of Islam appears as Muhammad, the most accurate rendition of the Arabic in the Latin alphabet.

I have transliterated the names of Drâa tribes and peoples following simplified English conventions, and in most cases used the Arabic plural – as in Ruhhal (the singular is Rahhal); 'Arib (the singular is 'Aribi); and Haratin (the singular is Hartani). For the Arabic words appearing in the text I have chosen to reflect the Moroccan colloquial pronunciation if the word belongs to dialect, or the classical Arabic pronunciation if it does not. Finally, I have used the English 's' plural where Arabic broken plurals would be puzzling or incomprehensible for readers without a knowledge of Arabic.

I ask the reader's indulgence for any inconsistencies that may occur.

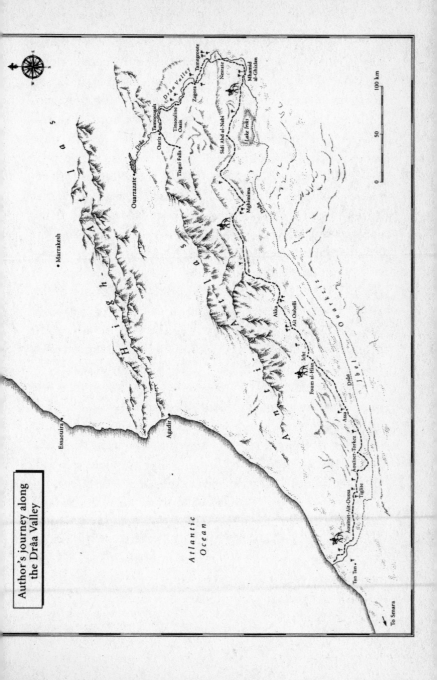

Author's journey along
the Dráa Valley

Atlantic
Ocean

Marrakesh

H i g h - A t l a s

A n t i - A t l a s

Dráa Valley

Essaouira

Agadir

Ouarzazate

Dráa

Ouriz

Tamnougalt

Tinzouline
Oasis

Tigzui Falls

Zagora

Sidi Abd al-Nabi

Tansikht

Tamegroute

Lake Iriki

Mhamid
al-Ghizlan

Mhimima

Dráa

Alka

Aït Ouabelli

Icht

Foum al-Hisn

Aqa

Amtoudi

Aoulnet-Torkoz

Tiglite

Aoulnet-Aït-Oussa

Jbel Ouarkziz

Tan Tan

To Smara

100 km

0   50

N

PROLOGUE:

A Long Way From Home

WADI SASI, THE Moroccan Sahara. A scorching wind is driving a blinding assault of sand and salty dust off the dead lake, over the blackened, basalt-shard steppes and scattered thorny acacias above it, shrouding the looming, shark-tooth buttes of the distant Madwar mesa in tawny brown and ash-grey. My one-humped Arabian camel is couched on the cracked earth, famished and braying with exhaustion, refusing to rise, no matter how hard I tug on his rein. Shouting commands drowned out by the wind, Mbari, one of my two Bedouin guides, kicks his camel in the rear. The camel, encrusted in dust, baring his yellow teeth and bellowing, struggles to stand, but his lame leg gives way and he collapses. '*Guf! Guf!*' Mbari yells, kicking him again and again. Finally he clambers to his feet.

We turn our eyes to Hassan, my other guide and the leader of our expedition, who has managed to rouse his weary camel and is now walking away from us into the whirling clouds of dust. He is tugging his camel by a rope looped through a hole bored into its left nostril, which stretches like an ever more tenuous rubber band. Hassan does not look back, for it is the habit of the Bedouin to face ahead when on the move, lest they intrude on the bathroom activities of fellow tribesmen.

I choke on the blowing sand and grow dizzy from the heat. I slump to the earth beside my camel and cough up a ball of grit. Mbari, also stricken by the heat, clutches his turbaned head and leans on his camel. Shouting over the wind, I ask him how he's doing.

'Praise be to God!' he yells. 'How are you?'

'Praise be to God!' I croak, inhaling more sand and turning away to retch.

We are both happy: we have only three hundred miles of desert left to cross.

OTHER LIVES TO LEAD

The Road to the Drâa Valley

IN 1986, WHILE in graduate school writing a master's thesis on famine in the Soviet Ukraine, I discovered two books that pointed me toward transformational peregrinations in the Arab world. The first was Wilfred Thesiger's *Arabian Sands*, the great British explorer's account of his postwar travels on foot and by camel with Bedouin tribesmen in the Empty Quarter of the Arabian Peninsula. Though hired by the Middle East Anti-Locust Unit to search out locust breeding grounds, Thesiger pursued a personal quest while in Arabia, a quest intimately related to the nomads with whom he lived: he hoped to 'find the peace that comes with solitude, and among the [Bedouin], comradeship in a hostile world'. The spirit of the Bedouin, he wrote, 'lit the desert like a flame'. Traversing much of Oman and Saudi Arabia in their company, he at first felt like 'an uncouth and inarticulate barbarian, an intruder from a shoddy and materialistic world'. So poor were the Bedouin that they wore only smocks, loincloths and daggers, yet they never stole from him. Indeed, they proved themselves paragons of desert virtue, and during the five years he spent roaming the sands as their guest they became his closest friends. Thesiger emerged from the Empty Quarter hardened by heat, hunger, thirst and tribal raids, and for ever after felt himself a stranger in 'civilised' company. He had, in sum, found what he was looking for among the Bedouin, and it had transformed him.

When I read *Sands*, I was studying Arabic, having had an inkling that adventure – another life, even – awaited me in the Arab world. *Sands* introduced me to the Bedouin, who were masters of terrain in which one needed stamina and courage to survive. I read and reread the book, dreaming of journeys in the Empty Quarter, but Arabia had changed much since Thesiger's day, as he himself had written. In the 1970s he had revisited his old haunts and found them an 'Arabian nightmare' of oil money and skyscrapers, of Bedouin who had abandoned their camels for Land Rovers. *Sands* was really an elegy, a travelogue that would, he hoped, remain a 'memorial to a vanished past, a tribute to a once magnificent people'.

Soon after finishing *Sands*, I came across the other book that fired me with passion for the Arab world: Philip K. Hitti's *History of the Arabs*. Every word of *History* rang with the author's love of Arab civilisation, the Islamic era of which began in the seventh century with the eruption of Arab armies, largely composed of Bedouin tribesmen, out of Arabia. In the name of Islam the Arabs conquered all of North Africa; in Europe they overran Spain and reached France; in Asia they made it to China. 'Around the name of the Arabs', Hitti wrote,

'would gleam the halo that belongs to world-conquerors.'
To the Bedouin, 'the Arabian nation is the noblest of all
nations (*afkhar al-umam*). The civilized man, from the
Bedouin's exalted point of view, is less happy and far
inferior. In the purity of his blood, his eloquence and
poetry, his sword and horse and above all his noble ancestry (*nasab*), the Arabian takes infinite pride . . . The
phenomenal and almost unparalleled efflorescence of
early Islam was due in no small measure to the latent
powers of the Bedouins, who, in the words of the Caliph
'Umar, "furnished Islam with its raw material."'

From Hitti I learned that the Bedouin were not only
the archetypal wanderers, but the co-originators of
Islamic civilisation, which was once one of the most pro-
gressive civilisations on earth. From the eighth to the
thirteenth century, while Europe recovered from barbarian invasions and suffered seignorialism and feudal rule,
Córdoba of the Umayyad dynasty and Baghdad of the
Abbasids rivalled Constantinople in splendour. While
Western Europe was largely illiterate, the Arabs were
conquering the Middle Eastern and North African terri-
tories of Byzantium and absorbing Hellenic culture;
Arab caliphs were reading Aristotle; and Arab thinkers
were syncretising Hellenic and Islamic philosophies and
transmitting Greek scholarship to Europe, thus eventually fostering the Renaissance. During the Middle Ages
Arabic became a language of science and literature, and,
by way of medieval Latin, contributed to English a
plethora of now-common words, among them alcohol,
algebra, syrup and coffee. From the eastern realms of
their empire, the Arabs brought back Hindi ('Indian',
later called 'Arabic') numerals and passed them on to

Europe; the Indian concept of zero permitted the birth of modern mathematics and science. The Arabs kept alive the ancient Greek notion that the earth was round, and, through a work in Latin, delivered it to Columbus, thus aiding his discovery of the Americas.

Hitti's work taught me that the Arabs were the exponents of a civilisation that differed fundamentally from that of the West. Whereas in the West commercialism and multitudinous creeds, religions and philosophies flourish and in their cacophony offer no single answer to our existential quandaries, in most of the Arab world one religion, Islam (which translates as 'submission' – to the will of God), dominates all aspects of life, demanding of its followers discipline, self-abnegation, and the observance of ritual. In the concept of *Umma*, the Islamic Nation, is a refutal of Western individualism, and an antidote to loneliness and alienation. Moreover, and this was crucial to me as a traveller, the cities that gave birth to this civilisation bore some of the most exotic and alluring names (Baghdad, Marrakesh, Damascus) that I had ever heard.

After reading Hitti, I threw myself into the study of Arabic, spending six hours every day learning grammar, listening to tapes and meeting with my Jordanian and Palestinian instructors. A year later, in 1987, I quit graduate school, flew to Portugal, and sailed from Algeciras in southern Spain across the Strait of Gibraltar to Morocco, from where I intended to make my way east across the entire Arab world, my destination Baghdad.

This was a grand idea that owed more to rash enthusiasm than planning. A few days after arriving in Morocco, beneath the soaring minarets and earthen ramparts of

Meknès, I ate a bad kebab and it nearly killed me with a fortnight of nausea, vomiting, dizzying headaches and diarrhoea. Food poisoning was but one of the impediments that confronted me. Darija, the Arabic dialect of Morocco, proved almost completely unintelligible to me, bearing little resemblance to the classical Arabic I had been studying. I thus found myself able to recite chapters from *A Thousand and One Nights* while having trouble understanding directions to the bathrooms I so often needed. There were also *faux guides* who set upon Nasranis ('foreigners', or more exactly, 'Nazarenes', 'Christians') in the streets. Day after day, as I staggered out of my hotel to buy yogurt and Lomotil, I was accosted by unemployed youths demanding I hire them as guides for tours of the medina. Few took kindly to rejection. One youth whose services I declined grew irate. 'You won't hire me! Then you'll rot in a Moroccan prison!' He turned to passers-by and shouted, while pointing at me, 'Drug dealer! Drug dealer! This Nasrani's trying to sell me drugs! Police! Police! Drug dealer!' There were no police about, though, and I slipped back into my hotel, shaken up and uncomprehending. More incidents like this followed.

Previous travels in Europe and Turkey had not prepared me for Morocco. Still sick, I gave up and staggered aboard a plane in Casablanca, bound first for Rome and then for familiar haunts in the eastern Mediterranean. My plans for the Arab world would have to wait. I would have to prepare myself better if ever again I attempted to tread in Thesiger's footsteps.

After seven months of rambling around Italy, Greece and Turkey, my money ran out and I returned to the

States. I pursued my Arabic studies at a language insti-
tute in Washington, DC, and wondered what to do next.
Having no other ideas, but wanting to return to an Arab
country (any Arab country but Morocco, that is), I
applied to join the Peace Corps, and was called in for an
interview. The Peace Corps occupied an old building in
the centre of town. Fans chopped the air above desks
cluttered with amulets and native trinkets from West
Africa and Central America; posters of smiling African
children and Bolivian peasants in colourful shawls hung
on yellowed walls. There was an earnestness about the
besandalled employees there that I found disagreeable.

The recruitment officer to whom I spoke was a perky
young woman in a frumpy dress. Scribbling and hunched
over a mess of papers, she asked me to explain why I
wanted to be a volunteer. I sensed that I needed an altru-
istic motive along the lines of Thesiger's locust research
to win her over, so I said something about wanting to
help people in developing countries better their lives.
This platitude elicited smiles and comments about how
my undergraduate degree in psychology (a discipline I
had renounced) would suit the Peace Corps just fine.

She scribbled away. 'Sooo . . . is there any place you'd
prefer to go?'

'Since I speak Arabic, I'd like to go to Yemen or
Tunisia.' I paused. 'The only place I don't want to go is
Morocco.'

'Peace Corps is not a travel agency,' she said, in a tone
that sounded like it portended my imminent disqualifi-
cation. 'You can't choose your country of service.'

'Then why did you ask me where I wanted to go?'

'You can state your preference, that's all. You should

be ready to serve in whatever country we offer you for the good of the people.'

A few weeks later she called me. 'We have an opening.'

'Where?'

'In Morocco.'

'But . . . You have nothing else?'

She told me that Morocco was all they had available in an Arab country at the time, and reminded me that if I turned her down I might lead her to believe that I saw the Peace Corps as a travel agency. I thought it over for a few minutes. My money had run out, and I had no other prospects for employment. I accepted her offer, and was soon on a plane to Morocco.

After three months of instruction in Moroccan Arabic and culture in Rabat I was given a two-year assignment in Marrakesh working with a school for the blind and with the parents of handicapped children. Dating from the eleventh century, Marrakesh is an imperial city of souks and snake charmers and hash-scented alleys largely enclosed in earthen walls on a burned-out plain, beneath the snow-mantled peaks of the High Atlas. I took up residence in the casbah (from the Arabic *qasaba*, or citadel) district, far from other volunteers; I adopted an Arabic name, Jelal, because I found that few Moroccans could remember my own. There were no Bedouin in the casbah or elsewhere in Marrakesh, but there were many *faux guides*. Now that I was a long-term guest in their country, I was compelled to reach a sort of modus vivendi with them. I could not escape them, and they were, after all, just poor youths in a country where there was little work. But I never allowed them to intimidate me as they had the previous year. When necessary, I adopted their blustering tactics and threatening postures to use against them. The only time I have ever hit anybody was while I was a Peace Corps volunteer in Marrakesh.

In any case, I discovered a distraction that brought me closer to Moroccan life than any job with the Peace Corps ever would: Moroccan women. The first year I didn't dare engage them; the second year I found I couldn't resist. They glided down Marrakesh's alleys of dung-leavened dust, their kohl-daubed eyes alert, their breasts swinging under the silk of flowing djellabas, their hair glinting with the warm tints of henna. The prospect of marrying an American (and thereby gaining access to his relative riches) made me attractive enough, as did the chance to dabble in pleasures of the flesh with a forbidden Christian; and they knew that a Nasrani would not despise them as whores for sleeping with him.

This was new territory for me. During training, Peace Corps instructors had warned female volunteers of the trauma they could expect to suffer in adjusting to the second-class status Islamic society would impose on them, but they said nothing to male volunteers about the magic Moroccan women practised to trap a mate (though they did warn us that irate brothers and knife-wielding fathers made 'dating' an exceedingly dangerous business). The instructors said not a word about the evening paseo, during which single men and women strolled the downtown avenues, arranging trysts after exchanging little more than stares and smiles. They certainly didn't mention *sbagha* (painting), the practice whereby a Moroccan woman, desirous of maintaining her virginity yet determined to get off with her lover, vigorously 'paints' her clitoris with the tip of his erect penis. Nor did they tell us anything about the prevalence of prostitutes, often veiled, who worked the crowds of big cities at dusk, searching for clients as the call to prayer sounded. The word *qahba* (whore) was not even in the Peace Corps manual of Moroccan Arabic, though it was one of the more frequently used words in the language.

So I did my time in Marrakesh, conducting trysts, evading brothers, reading Arabic literature, and yearning for even more adventure, more escape, something along the lines of what Thesiger had described in *Arabian Sands*. Then, at the very end of my tour, Iraq invaded Kuwait. Just as I was preparing to travel to the Middle East to try to start a career in photojournalism, another volunteer told me of a valley in Morocco's remote south called the Drâa. The Drâa was, he said, the desert waste-land from which, in the sixteenth century, warriors of the Saadi Dynasty had emerged to halt the advances of the Portuguese and the Ottoman Turks. In a shivery flash of insight I saw that the Drâa was what I had been searching for all along: there, gazelles gambolled and oases of palms shimmered like seas of emerald; there, Morocco ended and the no man's land of the Sahara, vast and ready for exploration, began; and, most impor-tant, there dwelled Bedouin, unspoiled Bedouin who knew nothing of the pampered lifestyles of their oil-rich brethren in the east. Whereas much of the Arab world had been modernised, even radicalised, beyond recog-nition since the end of the colonial era, the Drâa, from what I could tell, had remained a sort of ur-Arab paradise.

As I packed to leave Morocco I read up on the Drâa. The valley begins 150 miles southeast of Marrakesh, on the Saharan side of the moonscape crags of the Atlas, where the red clay wadis (seasonal river beds) of Ouarzazate and Dadès converge. Watered by underground springs and the April melt of Atlas snows, the Drâa River cuts its way for 160 miles southeast across the 6500-foot-high Saghro massif (an offshoot of the High Atlas), and enters the Sahara proper through Beni Slimane Pass in Jbel (Mount) Bani to reach the oasis village of Mhamid. From Mhamid the Drâa veers west and snakes for 375 more miles through the desert, along the base of the Anti-Atlas, to debouch into the Atlantic. The six palm oases of the Drâa's upper reaches (from Ouarzazate to Mhamid) rest on fertile loam and support ancient agricultural communities dwelling in elaborate, towered casbahs and walled villages known in Darija as *qsars* (from the classical Arabic for palace), made of ochre-hued adobe bricks hewn from the river's banks. The French dubbed this part of the valley the *coude du Drâa*, a metaphor hinting at the origin of the Drâa's name: a corruption of the Arabic word *dhira'* (arm). About the lower expanses of the valley beginning at Mhamid and extending to the Atlantic I could find no information.

From the ninth through the fifteenth centuries, the Drâa served as one of the main caravan routes between Europe and Timbuktu. The desert-wise Bedouin, or Ruhhal (from the Arabic *rahala*, 'to wander from place to place') in the Arabic dialects of North Africa, were the master navigators of this 1100-mile channel across the sea of sand. After making the two-month crossing of the desert, lengthy, plodding caravans arrived in the Drâa bearing ivory, gold and slaves. The last of these were among the most profitable of the caravans' commodities:

the Africans whom Ruhhal traders bought from dealers in Timbuktu for fifteen to twenty talers could fetch ten times more in Marrakesh. In exchange for slaves and gold, the Ruhhal took to West Africa leather goods, textiles and, eventually, guns; they also spread Islam in the Sahel, which is Muslim to this day. The last slave caravan, it is said, crossed the Sahara in the 1950s.

The valley was, historically, a wilderness not only of sand and rock but of raiders and rebels. The Drâa belonged to the *bilad al-siba* (the land of dissidence), the domain of anarchy and tribal rule where the writ of Moroccan sultans held little sway, and where local chieftains known as *qa'ids* and *sheikhs* reigned in qsars and casbahs, suffering frequent attacks from Ruhhal tribes. The Ruhhal of the Drâa, especially the 'Arib tribe, earned themselves a formidable reputation as warriors. The 'Arib subdued the indigenous Sanhaja Berbers, whom they terrorised into payment of tribute. They eventually crossed the Atlas Mountains and penetrated the Sous Valley, and for a while even raised a revolt against the sultans of Marrakesh.

'*Bilad al-siba*,' I repeated to myself. The Land of Dissidence. Intrigued by this history of battling tribes and desert warriors, I left Morocco for the Middle East, vowing to travel through the Drâa one day.

In 1996 I visited the Drâa – and made a serendipitous error that nearly cost me my life. Accompanied by a teenage Ruhhal guide, I drove my Peugeot eleven miles off the cracked tarmac of the Drâa's only road on to a *piste*, or desert track, to camp for the night on the dunes, near a tent owned by a Ruhhal named Ali Daimin. At midnight a wind (called a Shirgi, I was to learn – among the Ruhhal every wind has a name) howled in from the torrid wastes of Algeria to the east. By sunrise the Shirgi was flaying the entire valley, blowing sand at ninety miles an hour and raising temperatures to 120 degrees; it covered the *piste* and disoriented my guide on our drive back to the tarmac. Having no water, food, maps or radio with us, and suffering a punctured radiator as we bumped over stony tableland in search of the road, we could have remained lost and died of thirst. But five hours later we ended up back where we started and came upon – indeed, nearly ran right over – Ali's tent. He took us in. When the wind subsided he guided us back to the tarmac. I offered him money as compensation but he refused it.

Ali impressed me. Not only did he know the desert, but he radiated modesty and had an inherent dignity that I would later come to associate with the 'Arib. He was in his mid-thirties. He was high of brow and aquiline of nose; his features hinted at Yemeni ancestry. (The 'Arib claimed to be descended from Yemeni Bedouin who arrived in the Drâa in the twelfth century.) Like most 'Arib, he wore a black turban called a firwal, and a white smock known as a fouqiya. He tended flocks of camels and goats and preferred the peace of life on the sands to the tumult of the cities, but unlike most of his tribesmen, he was educated: he had studied history and geography at university in Marrakesh. His intellect and pride in his Ruhhal heritage marked him as someone with whom I wanted to keep in touch, and I left the Drâa understanding I had made a friend who would one day play an important role in my life.

Two years later Ali arranged and accompanied me on

my first real expedition in the Drâa – a two-week trip by camel and on foot in the *coude* region, ending just to the east of Mhamid at the dunes of Shgaga. This outing gave me a glimpse of the valley's unsettling beauty, but most of all it whetted my appetite for more. Under the red sky of dusk, standing atop a dune at Shgaga, I conceived a desire to push on to the Atlantic – a distance of some 350 miles. I asked Ali to research the possibility of my making a descent of the entire valley at another time. He agreed, but did so cautiously. From Shgaga to the Atlantic was Ruhhal land, yes, but wells in that distant stretch of valley were said to be days of walking apart, the routes between them known only to a few. Without the protection of the Saghro range, the heat and Shirgi-driven sandstorms would be terrible in that part of the Drâa (which bordered the open Sahara), and both Westerners and Moroccans had lost their way and died of thirst there. Literature on the lower part of the valley was scant: French colonial officers stuck to the *coude* and had little reason to travel into the wastes beyond it.

There were other reasons for caution. After 1912, when the French established their protectorate over most of northern and central Morocco, the country's far south remained undemarcated *bilad al-siba* where thousands of spirited Ruhhal rebels fought the colonialists in vicious desert wars. Only in 1934 did the French manage to subdue the Drâa. It was not until 1956 that the French, in an attempt to prevent Algerian independence fighters from basing themselves in Morocco, built a series of fortresses from Figuig in eastern Morocco along the Drâa to Tarfaya, on the Atlantic, thereby making the valley Morocco's *de facto* if not *de jure* southern border.

Morocco and Algeria never recognised this makeshift border. A dispute soon developed between them (and Mauritania) over the 100,000 square miles of phosphate-rich desert to the south of the frontier. This land, now known as the Western Sahara, had belonged to Morocco from the 1500s until the Spanish seized it during the colonial era. When Spanish dictator Francisco Franco died in 1975, King Hassan II of Morocco launched a march of 350,000 civilians across the border to 'reclaim' the Western Sahara, and his army occupied the region. The Ruhhal of the Western Sahara, aided by Algeria and Libya, formed the Polisario (the National Front for the Liberation of the People of the Western Sahara) and took up arms against the Moroccans. A long guerrilla war ensued. Although the Polisario and Hassan II concluded a truce in 1991 stipulating that Morocco allow the conduct of a referendum on the Western Sahara's future, no vote had been held, and periodically the frustrated guerrillas threatened to take up arms again.

The Drâa border region thus remained a potential locus of conflict, and in places it had been mined. One part of the valley, in fact, was said to be a forbidden military zone where the Moroccan army hunted guerrillas and smugglers, and allowed no one, whether Moroccan or foreign, to enter.

Despite these risks, the Drâa exercised a pull on me, and I was as determined as ever to travel through it. Whereas most of Thesiger's Bedouin had settled decades ago, Drâa Ruhhal still roamed the sands, and questions arose in my mind. Was there any valour left in their way of life, or had it become an anachronism? The Drâa Ruhhal regarded herding animals as their cherished occupation, and considered agriculture and trades the work of 'inferior' villagers and townsmen. Now that animal products were mass produced on farms, were the Ruhhal degenerating into parasites of the people they disdained? A drought had afflicted southern Morocco since 1997. How was it affecting the Ruhhal, who depended on fragile desert vegetation to pasture their herds? Could lack of rain move the Ruhhal off the sands as oil money had prompted Thesiger's Bedouin to settle?

During the autumn of 2000 Ali sent word to me in Moscow (where I live) that my expedition would be possible in the following winter and spring (when the weather would be relatively cool). It would certainly contain risk, but now all my time in Morocco and trips to the Drâa suddenly seemed like a prelude to the chance to realise a dream I had nurtured for fifteen years, ever since reading *Arabian Sands* and *History of the Arabs*.

DEPARTURE FROM TIZGUI FALLS

FROM A LIMPID turquoise sky the February sun fell over the rock walls and slag-covered ledges of the gorge, showering amber light on their umber surfaces, surfaces that still held the cold from the winter night. A breeze sifted down the staggered footpath descending to the base of the gorge, near where I stood, bringing a shiver to the fronds of the palms above me. Ahead, the gorge narrowed and rose into a crevasse, down which water trickled into an oval-shaped pool at my feet; there, green-gold fish flitted under the liquid crystal of snow melt, water that had come from somewhere in the Atlas Mountains to the north. The pool drained into a brook a foot or two wide that wound away down the gorge toward the Drâa. This trickle was Tizgui Falls.

There was a voice speaking French behind me. 'Please, *monsieur*, come have tea with me.'

I turned to confront a tall black man in an embroidered beige skullcap and a yellow djellaba. He was barefoot, and his long toes gripped the stones on which he stood. His voice was deep and kind. I responded to his greeting in Arabic, to which he switched with some relief. He turned and walked toward a bamboo hut built next to the wall of the gorge, and I followed him.

'I'm Omar, the caretaker of Tizgui Falls,' he said, stopping to let me enter the hut first. 'Really, they're called Drâa Falls, you know, but the government changed the name.'

The hut's walls were porous to the breeze, and it was draughty inside; the ground was strewn with coarse wool carpets of the kind woven in mountain villages to the north. He puttered around with tea glasses and a kettle, and lit a burner atop a steel-blue canister of Buta gas. 'I've been here seventeen years, and I remember when there was much more water. Tizgui doesn't look like a waterfall now, does it? It's this drought we're going through.' He put a wicker stool behind me and asked me to sit. 'You're Tunisian?'

'No, American.'

'Oh, an American once signed my guest book.' After handing me a glass of tea, he drew a battered black cardboard album from under his stool. The writing on one of the pages was in French. The author thanked Omar for taking care of the falls, and said something about enjoying this *petit coin de paradis* – a cliché, but as I sipped the warm tea, with the breeze rustling the palms, and the light filtering in through the bamboo, it seemed an accurate one.

I told him that his guest had been French.

'Oh, I thought that was English,' he said. 'I can't read. I taught myself to speak some French so I could talk to

the Nasranis who come here. I'm alone here. I want
Nasranis to visit me, but hardly any come.'

'Why?'

'Our government doesn't tell the world about the falls.
No one in the government helps me. I built this hut
myself, otherwise I'd just be sitting in the sun all day,
with no place to invite my guests.'

Omar told me that he was from Tizgui, the first village
of the Upper Drâa, a half-mile down the gorge where
the 'falls' drained into the river. There were no Arabs in
Tizgui, he said; it was a Berber village. His first language
was Shilha, short for Tashilhait, the Berber dialect
spoken in the mountains of southern Morocco.

The Berbers were the original inhabitants of North
Africa. From Morocco to Libya they call themselves
Imazighen, the Noble or Free Born. (The English
'Berber' comes from the Arabic *barbar*, which itself is an
adaptation of the Latin *barbarus* or 'barbarian' – that is,
one who did not speak Latin. The Arabs borrowed the
word and used it to signify 'uncivilised' people; i.e. those
who did not speak Arabic.) The name 'Imazighen' was
probably coined during the time when the Berbers
migrated from the lowlands to the mountains to escape
invading Arabs, who took over their farms. The Berbers
have never been united as a people, but rather have been
divided by their dialects (speakers of Tashilhait identify
themselves as Shluh), which are for the most part unwrit-
ten. About a third of Moroccans speak some Berber at
home; most Berbers are bilingual in Arabic, which they
need to trade and get by in the towns and cities.

Although for at least a thousand years before the birth
of Christ the Berbers governed their own kingdom on the

territory that is now Morocco, their origin is uncertain. Ethiopia has been suggested by at least one ancient explorer, who found the Drâa inhabited by what he called 'inhospitable Ethiopians living on land full of ferocious beasts'. (The 'beasts' were probably crocodiles, the last Saharan specimen of which a French colonialist proudly exterminated in 1929.) The Berbers of northern and central Morocco suffered the Arab invasions of the seventh and eighth centuries and became subjects of the Arab Idrisid Dynasty; the Berbers of the deep south ruled the Drâa oases until the twelfth century, when the nomadic Arabs of the Bani Ma'qil tribe arrived and subjugated them. There has been much mixing of blood. If Omar was black and Berber, Berbers of the Sous Valley (who also call themselves Shluh) and the Rif Mountains are pale, with high cheekbones and straight black hair; a few are fair and some are even blond. Egalitarian Islam has always encouraged intermarriage.

This was all history an illiterate man probably would not know. In any case, Omar had more immediate concerns, as he told me when I asked him how life was in Tizgui.

'We have no running water or electricity, so we have to draw water from wells. We don't even have a road, so if one of the elders gets sick we have a problem getting him to the hospital. If an elder . . .'

He looked down abruptly and turned his head away, his voice hoarse with pain. He collected himself and changed the subject. The women in Tizgui spoke mostly Berber, he went on to say, learning not much more than prayers and greetings in Arabic.

It was time for me to go. I thanked him for the tea, left

him a tip, and set out into the sunshine for Tizgui village, where Ali and my guide, Noureddine, were supposed to be waiting for me.

For an hour just after a frigid clear dawn that day, a creaking Suzuki pick-up truck had rattled up a hairpin *piste* branching off the road running along the eastern edge of the Drâa. At a pass high above Tizgui the truck had deposited Ali, Noureddine and me, plus our gear, supplies and one mean-eyed horse. As the truck lumbered back down the *piste*, we looked around, our arms folded against the cold. Mountains of the Saghro massif, all burnt umber and dusty taupe, treeless and scarred with horizontal serrations, jutted up in every direction, recalling the red planet Mars. Somewhere far below were Tizgui Falls, the village of Tizgui and the Drâa River.

Our horse had clumpy whitish hair and his ribs stuck out. Feeling sorry for him, I moved to pet him, but he bared his teeth and his eyes blazed with a sort of malicious stupidity. Noureddine flashed me a gap-toothed smile, as if apologising for his animal's manners.

While I was still in Moscow, Ali had explained the plan for my expedition. I would descend the first ninety miles of the Drâa, from Tizgui to the town of Zagora, in the company of a horse and his master, Noureddine. (I would begin at Tizgui because the gorge starting from the Mansour Eddahbi Dam – the actual head of the Drâa, a few miles north – is too steep to hike.) The mountain trails from here to Zagora were too rough for camels; in the uppermost segment of the valley horses and donkeys served as pack animals. In Zagora, where the desert began, I would part with Noureddine and exchange the horse for two camels led by two Ruhhal 'Arib guides. They would take me seventy miles south to Ali's tent at the dunes of 'Irq al-Yahudi, near the village of Mhamid, where I would rest, buy provisions and pick up a third camel for the 375-mile journey to the Atlantic.

I had never before travelled with a horse in Morocco, but I had hoped for a more elegant animal than this. Hitti described the Arabian thoroughbred as 'the most noble of the conquests of man . . . renowned for its physical beauty, endurance, intelligence, and touching devotion to its master', no less than 'the exemplar from which all Western ideas about the good breeding of horseflesh have been derived'. This horse was clearly no thoroughbred. I tried to pet him again but he pulled away.

'Noureddine, what's wrong with this horse?'

He smiled nervously. 'Pardon me, but this a mule.'

The long ears and stout build, to say nothing of the rancour in his eyes, should have told me this. Noureddine examined a gash the mule had received above the tail from bouncing against the Suzuki's rear door latch. He tore a piece of dangling flesh the size of a thumbnail off the wound and tossed it to the ground. The mule didn't flinch.

'Mules are much stronger than horses,' he said. 'No one would use a horse in these mountains.'

'This is true,' Ali said, adding that he had not thought to tell me that I was getting a half-ass instead of a thoroughbred; he assumed I would have figured it out. Ali would come with us for only a short while; he had business to attend to in Zagora, so he would leave us at Noureddine's home village of Ouriz, a two- or three-day walk away.

Ali's black firwal announced his desert descent, as did his satiny blue caftan and blue sirwal, Ruhhal trousers that are baggy until the knees, but tight from the calves to the ankles. Noureddine, in contrast, looked thoroughly if depressingly urban in a threadbare brown sweater, bald-kneed jeans and mud-caked sneakers. He was not an 'Arib or a Ruhhal, but a member of the Awlad Yahya (the Sons of Yahya) tribe that had renounced wandering the desert and settled some time ago. In his early thirties, Noureddine was a livestock trader who had hiked almost every footpath and visited almost every village in the upper part of the valley in search of sheep and goats; good qualifications for a guide to Zagora.

Noureddine's smile was broad and quick, but his two upper front teeth were missing, which, along with his crewcut, made him look like an overgrown schoolboy. His hands were callused; his grip, as I had learned painfully when we shook hands, could crush pig iron; and the muscles bulged under his sweater. That he had led a settled life was clear: no Ruhhal would be so burly. From the rigours of desert life nomads tended to acquire the gaunt look possessed by Ali.

After tossing a two-basketed packsaddle over the mule's back, we began loading our gear and provisions: sacks of rice and semolina; two plastic crates of vegetables (tomatoes, onions, carrots, cucumbers and potatoes); a box containing tea, canned peas, blocks of sugar, packets of saffron, salt and pepper; a burlap bag with three round loaves of bread (which we would replenish in villages along the way); a canister of Buta gas and various jerry cans for water; pots, pans and cutlery; a two-man tent for me and a four-man tent for Noureddine and Ali; plus blankets, three foam mattresses, and my and Ali's back-packs. The mule snorted and teetered until all this was properly balanced on his back.

Aside from sturdy walking shoes, about the only gen-uinely expedition-worthy item I had brought with me was a dual compass–thermometer attached to my Swiss Army knife. I had brought along a firwal, but on my last trip I had found it suffocating, so I covered my head with a broad-rimmed straw hat of the kind worn by oasis farmers. There were few health risks associated with the trip, aside from water-borne diseases such as dysentery and other gut infections. I could find no water-purification tablets in Moscow and Ali had none here, but since I had drunk well-water without harm during previous trips, I was not particularly concerned.

'We are going to have some great talks about religion, you and I,' Noureddine said, winking at me and yanking the ropes tight around the mule, who grimaced and snorted with his exertions. The load, now rising three feet from the mule's back, swayed and teetered. It looked like an awful lot for such a skinny animal to carry, and my face must have shown concern.

'Oh, his old owner beat him and didn't feed him,' Noureddine said. 'That's why he's complaining. But this will be good exercise for him. God put this beast on earth to serve us. The Qur'an says it. I'll be teaching you all about that.' He cited the relevant sura (chapter from the Qur'an), and then tossed more ropes over and under the beast. Ali grabbed the other ends, and the two of them yanked and knotted, knotted and yanked.

I turned to the pristine valley of rock and palms below and revelled in the soft sun from above. I inhaled deeply, finding the air so pure and bracing that it dizzied me.

Noureddine pulled the mule around to face the descending *piste*. '*Bismillah!* [In the name of God!],' he pronounced, and prodded the mule's haunches with a short steel rod. The animal started staggering down the *piste*. Noureddine followed just behind him, and Ali and I brought up the rear. Our mood was light, the walking easy, and none of us felt like saying much.

A few hours later, after a lunch of salad and sun-warmed bread near the valley floor, we split up. I hiked to the falls; Ali and Noureddine proceeded to Tizgui village.

After leaving Omar at the falls, I trekked down the wadi to Tizgui village and the Drâa River, which here meandered dark green and ten yards wide from behind the gorge walls on to the broadening, white-stone valley floor. By the river's flat banks I found my crew waiting for me, and we set off into the village. Tizgui was all scattered boxy stone houses with mud-packed straw roofs; people lived in one room, goats and chickens in another. The houses might have been the same a thousand or even two thousand years ago. Only a Javel bleach bottle here or a rusted pump there reminded us of this century.

By the entrance to the village a few barefoot tots in tiny djellabas stood and stared at us, half-chewed pieces of bread in hand, something between fear and curiosity in their eyes. Strolling by with laundry piled on their heads were slender black Berber women of Amazonian stature, with high cheekbones and long noses. Their black, ankle-length skirts trailed behind them, as did their black shawls, which were embroidered with blue-silver beads and floral loops at the edges. The shawls covered their hair, but not their faces.

A couple of the women hailed us with bemused calls of '*As-salam 'alaykum!* [May the peace be upon you!]' With their leonine grace and slender builds they did resemble Ethiopians. Whatever their origin, the people of Tizgui were Haratin, the mostly black Berbers who had lived on the land since before the Arab invasion. Farther south in the Drâa, the Haratin had sharecropped for nomadic overlords (the 'Arib among them), but up here distance and the mountains protected them from desert raiders. I couldn't help thinking that the easy smiles and cheer of these women accorded with the peace of the valley in which they lived.

Laughter broke out in the village as we left it: our presence had drawn a small crowd of well-wishers who shouted goodbye and safe journey. We re-emerged on to the valley floor. As evening came on, the cappuccino escarpments of Saghro darkened to mocha; the white rock plain around us seemed to glow, as if exuding sunlight absorbed during the day. Beside us the Drâa flowed south, shallow, silky and now silvery blue, between crooked swards of grass and patches of mossy gravel. We encountered a shepherdess swathed in many layers of wool and cotton, with only her eyes showing, moving her flock of black goats toward Tizgui, tossing rocks to their right and left, and clucking at them.

Then we were alone. Not a bird fluttered, not an insect stirred. The cliffs rose empty around us, and the sun, now set, cast paling light on to the lambent scrim of sky above.

At a crook in the valley we espied the village of

Tamanroute – a cluster of squat adobe and stone houses
dominated by a mosque and its rectangular, white-
trimmed minaret. Well away from the village we halted
on a patch of sand to set up camp. Noureddine unroped
the upper storeys of the load and disassembled it, and he
and Ali hoisted the saddlebags off the mule's back. The
mule, freed, shook himself and stomped his hooves, and
then wandered off to graze on the grass along the banks
of the river. We set up our tents, and tossed our foam
mattresses on the sandy earth.

After gathering firewood, Ali hollowed out a depression in the sand and filled it with a clump of twigs. He lit
them and tossed on a handful of thicker branches.
Keeping one eye on the flames, he poured water and tea
leaves into a tiny blackened Ruhhal kettle. The fire soon
dwindled into embers, among which he nestled the kettle.
The tea he was preparing, the tea of the Ruhhal, would
be bitter and brown, unlike the syrupy green mint brew
drunk in the north of Morocco. As it bubbled he lit the
Buta gas burner and began heating a pot of water. Then
he started peeling cucumbers for tagine.

After placing my things in my tent, I pulled a foam
mattress close to the fire and lay down on it, tired from the
hike, and contemplated the purpling sky. Here, I thought,
there were only elements: earth, fire, light from the sun,
wind from beyond the Saghro – a dry, serene purity.
There was, most of all, peace. I foresaw the months ahead,
wandering through a desert of peace, letting the peace
settle over me, permeate me, transform me. Peace.

Noureddine thrust his face inches above mine, blocking out the sky. He was smiling, his tongue showing
between the gap in his teeth.

'Caves, fires, a playing field and a forest filled with beasts!' he announced and giggled.

'What?' I exclaimed, taken aback by his sudden proximity and odd declaration.

'Caves, fires, a playing field and a forest filled with beasts!' He made a poking motion toward his eyes with his fingers, then wiggled them over his head. 'Come on. Guess the riddle! Come on, think! What has caves, fires, a playing field and a forest filled with beasts?'

'I . . . I'm a bit tired. I haven't any idea.'

'Oh, come on! Play along, won't you!'

He again poked toward his eyes, and I caught on. The eyes were caves with their fires. He stroked the playing field of his forehead, patted his crewcut forest. 'Get it?' He burst out laughing. 'Get it? The beasts are lice! Lice!' With his two fingers he mimed a louse skittering across the top of his head. 'Get it?'

I slipped sideways out from under his face and sat up. Ali was slicing tomatoes in dignified 'Arib silence, paying no attention.

Noureddine was beaming. 'Okay, okay, what makes beautiful sounds and lives between two cliffs and a ditch?'

'Well . . .'

'Think! What makes beautiful sounds and lives between two cliffs and a ditch?'

'I don't know.'

'A tongue! Get it?' He stuck out his tongue and showed me his teeth and throat, and then ululated as Arab women do at weddings. 'Isn't that clever?'

I said it was. But was he always so cheerful and energetic after a hard day's hike?

His tongue flapped between his teeth. 'Tell me some of your own riddles.'

'Riddles? I don't know any.'

'What do you mean, you don't know any? What do you talk about around the fire at home?'

'We can't light a fire in our apartment. We'd burn down the building.'

He gave me a stunned look. 'It must be *very* warm where you live.'

Ali glanced up from his vegetables. 'What crosses the river but doesn't get wet?'

Noureddine held out his hand as though to keep me from blurting out an answer, but I had no idea. He massaged the bridge of his nose, looked at the sky, studied the ground.

'A shadow,' said Ali.

'Oh, I was just about to say that, really! You didn't give me a chance!' He turned to me. 'That's not fair!'

Ali poured us tea. I found it more bitter than I had remembered, and hard to swallow. Noureddine slurped his tea and kept his eyes on mine, still beaming.

An hour later the fire flickered goblins against the rock wall behind us and a moon silvered the cliffs above. Tamanroute was dark (it had no electricity), but we heard singing, raucous Berber chants and hand-clapping. Ali took the pot off the burner and set it on the ground. He then broke bread, distributing shards of the heavy round loaf. The tagine was steaming in the chill air; each of us would scoop up meat, vegetables and gravy with the bread from his own third of the pot.

'*Bismillah*,' said Noureddine.

We dug in. The stew was hearty and nourishing, and I

felt its ingredients replenishing strength I had lost during
the day's hike.

'"He who does not share his food is not one of us,"'
said Noureddine with a full mouth, quoting the Qur'an.
He looked at me and swallowed. 'May I tell you something? I decided to guide you for one reason, and one
reason alone: my brain. I want to improve my brain and
learn about the Nasrani's world. I have so much to ask
you.'

'Well, I'm very happy to meet you, too. I'll—'

'You see, I'm not the kind of guy who goes around
repeating things women say. I study things. I base my
knowledge on facts. I exercise my brain. Always. All the
time. That's why I like riddles. Most people here just
sleep and eat. But not me. No, not me.'

Smiling, he kept his eyes on mine and chomped away
on his tagine.

After dinner I retired, exhausted, to my tent.
Noureddine and Ali talked, or rather Noureddine talked,
until well into the night. Around two in the morning I
awoke to silence, shivering. My sleeping bag, which was
supposed to keep me warm to five degrees below zero,
was failing at six degrees. Soon, from mountain to moon-
lit mountain, the valley rang with the yelps of jackals. I
moved to the door of my tent and looked out, but I could
see no animals.

The racket grew louder and then subsided, over and
over again. The stars twinkled brilliantly in the icy air.
After a while, a low chanting of Qur'anic verses arose
from Noureddine's side of the other tent, and grew
louder and louder . . .

The sun mounted a cold, pearly sky, its beams inching

their way down the serrated slopes of the Saghro massif. Given the divagations and abrupt turns in this part of the valley, twenty minutes of hiking put Tamanroute out of sight. We had decamped early, Ali and I aching and silent, Noureddine brimming with vim, humming as he saddled the mule. The soreness in my calves seemed to increase in direct proportion to the rise in volume of his humming; the intensity of his brimming made only more exasperating the memories of the night I had passed shivering, listening to him chant the Qur'an, and waiting for jackals to tear through my tent wall.

In tacit alliance Ali and I allowed Noureddine to lead and eventually slip out of earshot. I noticed Ali's eyes were bloodshot. 'You didn't sleep either?'

'Sleep? Didn't you hear him reciting the Qur'an in the middle of the night?'

Noureddine halted, turned toward us, and waited for us to catch up. 'Thought of any riddles?'

'Not yet,' I said. 'I didn't sleep well.'

'Well, I want to solve some riddles. Riddles improve my brain. Please think of a riddle, *please*. If you tell me a rid—'

Ali cut in. 'What is interminable and has no shadow?'

'Wait, wait, let me guess! Umm, um . . .'

'This trip,' I answered.

'Close, very close. A road.'

Noureddine snapped his fingers. 'You say you don't like riddles, but look how good you are at them!' He shook his head and stabbed the mule in the rear with his rod.

A few hours later we were trudging beneath cliffs over-hanging masses of scree that looked like it might break loose at any moment and bury us. What could have left so much stony detritus so high up on the mountainside? Since Ali had studied geography I thought to ask him about this, but Noureddine caught me glancing at the rocks. 'You're looking at those caves up there, aren't you?'

'What caves?'

He pointed. Every hundred yards or so there was a cave in the face of the mountain.

'See? I've hiked up there.'

'You're kidding! Up all that loose rock?'

'Yes. A very powerful tribe called the Portuguese built those caves. You walk in the cave and walk and walk. Twenty metres inside, there's a pit. It's very dark. If you don't know the pit's there, you fall in and die. It's to catch the enemy.'

'But', I said, 'the Portuguese never got to the Drâa. They were mostly along the Atlantic. And they aren't a tribe. Furthermore, they didn't live in caves.'

'The Portuguese were a great cave-dwelling tribe. I told you, I've been up there and seen the caves. Only a very advanced tribe could build such caves.'

I turned to Ali, who was rewrapping his firwal around his head. He affirmed that the Portuguese had never made it here, and they didn't live in caves.

Noureddine was implacable. 'But I've *been* in the caves, and you *haven't*. I *know* it's true. This isn't something I heard from women. I've studied all about caves.'

He jabbed the mule with his rod and shook his head at our ignorance.

Around noon a village appeared on Saghro's eastern slopes, built in such a way that it appeared to be frozen in mid-tumble down the mountain. Many-storeyed adobe houses rose in confusion; watchtowers of ochre stood against a firmament of deep azure. This was the village of Insay. Since Ali needed cigarettes, we began marching toward it.

Noureddine grew animated. 'When I see such a view it inspires me to poetry. We must immortalise our passage down the valley in verse!' He flourished a walking stick he had whittled out of a tamarisk branch. 'To quote Musa, "This is my staff, and I walk with its aid. This is my staff, and with it I tend my flock. It has many fine qualities!" In Arabic we have poems for everything. Do you know any?'

Years ago I had memorised one of the *Mu'allaqat* (the *Suspended Odes*) of Zuhayr, lines about being fed up with life and never knowing what the morrow will bring and watching the Fates kill hapless mortals the way a camel stamps in the dark. As I pondered whether it suited the occasion, Noureddine changed the subject.

'Speaking of religion, how do you divorce a woman in Russia?'

'Well, you go to the courts and—'

'God has decreed that it's enough for the man to say, "You are thrice divorced." As for the woman, she can divorce her husband only by forfeiting her property to the man. The man needs her permission to have a second wife, however. Unless, of course, she has an *'ayb* [a disgrace or defect].'

'What kind of *'ayb*?'

'There are many kinds of *'ayb*. You see, if a man isn't careful in choosing a wife, well, we have a saying, "Honour cannot be bought or replaced." Look, if a woman has been in your bed then comes to me, should I sleep with her? Think about it. Would I want to sleep with her?'

'Well—'

'She's probably got an *'ayb*. What would I want with her after she's been with you?' He bounced along, now alternately poking the earth and prodding the mule with his staff. 'I don't want to marry a woman unless I know her honour's intact. She could have an *'ayb*, or she could make a belly with you and then come blame me for it. Make sense?'

'Yes.'

'You see, for us, it's honour above all. The value of a girl is in her honour. She's worthless without it.'

'But in the cities there are so many prostitutes.' In fact, there is no neutral word in Arabic for a person who sells sex, so I said *qahbas*. 'Do whores ever get married? They have no honour, right?'

'Poverty is very important in such matters. Poverty can force a woman to sell her body. Even a whore deserves a chance to be married. Everyone does.'

'But who marries them if honour is most important?'

'Why, a man who's also worthless might marry her. It happens. Everyone should marry. A man for his health and sanity *has* to marry. But if he remains single, he should fast two or three days a week and at all costs avoid eating peanuts and almonds, which could light his fire. The Qur'an says—'

Ali cut in. 'Noureddine, I've got a riddle.'

'Oh! Tell it! Tell it!'

'If you feed it, it hungers; if you give it drink, it dies.'

'I know the answer! Fire! Fire!'

'Right you are.'

We neared the village and saw Berber men in heavy
striped djellabas and skullcaps sitting on rocks by a *piste*
leading up toward the houses. They greeted us, and we
stopped to chat. One shouted to me, 'Come, let us show
you how to pray!' Another: 'Embrace Islam! If you speak
Arabic you must embrace Islam!'

They meant to express goodwill toward me by urging
me to convert. I smiled and tried to think of a way to
answer without causing offence. Noureddine came over
and stood next to me. 'I'm going to teach him all about
Islam.'

Ali said, 'God will send him faith when He chooses.'

'God willing!' all said. That put an end to the conversation, and we moved on. It was a tactful way to evade the
question, and I would remember it.

When Noureddine fell behind, Ali said quietly, 'He
makes you uncomfortable by talking about religion,
doesn't he? He's very stubborn. Once he starts he'll never
stop. I know him.'

Ali had never once brought up religion with me,
though he believed in God. For us both, faith was a personal matter, and that we accepted it as such made it
possible for us to become good friends. Noureddine,
however, took seriously the Qur'anic injunction to spread
the word, and I wondered how I was going to feel about
him if he really did begin to preach to me about Islam. I
had spent enough time pondering religion to know that I
did not believe, though I had no objection to those who
did.

We huffed our way up the *piste* into Insay, where dirt
lanes ran into mazes of mud houses, hoping to find a
shop selling cigarettes. From behind barred, glassless

windows in the towers above us, girls giggled as we passed. A few shouted '*Bonjour!*' and peered down at us. Ali replied with enquiries about cigarettes, and learned that the cigarette vendor, along with almost every other male in Insay, had gone to market in Agdz, a day's hike to the south. Today was souk day there, and everything here was closed. This news depressed him.

We followed the *piste* higher and higher up barren escarpments, returning to the valley floor only toward the end of the day, where we found that we had to ford the knee-deep Drâa several times, our feet achieving only tenuous purchase on the mossy rock bottom.

We camped that evening at the edge of the wadi opposite Jbel Kissane, a long, convoluted lump of rock jutting above distant palms on the valley's eastern side. After dark, I filled a pail with cold river water and retreated to a secluded tamarisk, where I perched my mirror on a branch and shaved by flashlight, and then bathed. Soon, clouds rolled over the stars, cloaking the valley in black, and rain threatened. The distant roar of winds over the mountains reached us, and gave the night a menacing feel.

After a dinner of couscous we stretched out on the sand by the fire. I felt clean and thoroughly revived after my bath. Noureddine expressed admiration for my 'hardiness'. He could never bathe, he said, in such 'cold' (it was about twelve degrees) without getting sick. He would stay dirty until we reached his house in Ouriz tomorrow.

I took out my shortwave radio and turned it on, lighting upon a BBC Arabic Service report about Tunisia. Thunder rumbled. Since we were in the riverbed, which could flood in a storm, I asked Ali if we should move.

'One must never trust the wadi,' he said, looking at the sky. 'That's what the Ruhhal say. I think—'

'Tunisia,' said Noureddine. 'Hm. How many people are in Tunisia?'

Ali and I glanced at each other, and then at him. 'What?' we said simultaneously.

'You heard me. How many people are there in Tunisia? What's the population?'

'I think about eight million,' I said.

'No, there are *six* million people in Tunisia. Not eight.'

'Okay. Okay.'

The report moved on to events in Pakistan. I wanted to listen and turned up the volume, forgetting about rain and floods. The news concerned General Musharraf, the return of democracy and—

'How many people are there in Pakistan?'

'Noureddine! What does that have to do with anything? I'm trying to listen to—'

'Can't answer the question, I take it. There are eighty-five million. How many people does Israel have?'

'Why do you keep asking this question?'

'You should have the facts in your brain before you listen to the news or you won't be able to understand it. If you don't know how many people are in a country what use is the news?'

'At this rate I'll never hear the news.'

'I'm not making up these facts. They're true facts. I read them in a book.'

'I don't doubt you did. But—'

Much talk followed in which Noureddine displayed his erudition – he cited the populations of several Islamic countries – and I gave up trying to listen to the radio.

Once we had determined that he knew more statistics than Ali or I, we changed topics. Noureddine was especially interested in Cold War politics and the doctrine of Mutually Assured Destruction. I could see he took his studies seriously, and had few opportunities to exhibit his knowledge. But he was longwinded about it, and never allowed us to get a word in. In the midst of Noureddine's ramblings, Ali slipped into his tent. I found myself yawning uncontrollably, aching from the hike, and said I needed some shut-eye, but Noureddine rattled on. I finally just got up, said goodnight, and climbed into my tent.

I fell asleep to distant claps of thunder and the whoosh of great winds over high peaks. But at two in the morning I started awake. Noureddine was chanting the Qur'an.

Ouriz

BY DAWN THE storm clouds had vanished. The sun seeped through my tent door and warmed me after I had passed another night shivering and half-awake in my deficient bag, listening to Noureddine chant the Qur'an. I started dozing off in the growing warmth, but soon I heard Ali and Noureddine arguing on the other side of the tent wall.

'Enough talk. Load that mule,' Ali said. His voice carried the urgency of a nicotine addict who hadn't smoked in two days; Noureddine's nattering was the only thing between him and a pack of Marlboros. I heard the mule being saddled, and then a steady chugging torrent of urine – the mule's – pounding the baked earth.

Noureddine stuck his head in my tent door. 'Good morning!'

'Good morning.'

'I'd like to invite you to be a guest at my house in Ouriz. I have something to show you.'

'Thanks very much. What is it?'

'It'll take us a while to see, this thing I have to show you, so we'll have to spend the night there. I'm very excited because I've never showed anyone this thing, that is, this thing that I'm going to show you. Please, honour me with your presence.'

'Okay, but what is it?'

He walked back to the mule and went on loading.

I climbed out of my tent and tossed my gear into the saddlebag. Ali looked haggard, with cloudy eyes and a matted firwal. I drank some tea and ate some bread, and we set out for Ouriz.

A few hours after decamping we came within sight of Agdz, which stood on high ground above oasis palms. Agdz's cement centre promised cigarettes, but since our destination was Ouriz we would not be going there. Or so I thought.

'You know, I can't wait till Ouriz to buy my cigarettes,' said Ali with jailbreak urgency, glancing toward Agdz. 'I think I'll have to leave you both and head to Agdz. I'll meet you at Noureddine's.'

He peeled off and made for the palms, taking long strides. Noureddine, the mule and I marched on, following the winding course of the shallow river, absorbing the sun. More than ever before, I took pleasure in the heat, which soaked into my aching body as might vapours from a medicinal spring.

Nearing Ouriz, we began to see the first signs of the Drâa's casbah civilisation. At a bend in the river just beneath Jbel Kissane rose the crooked clay portals and staggered watchtowers of the Berber qsar of Taliouine. Here and there by the qsar's walls, bricks of adobe the size and shape of cinderblocks, freshly hacked out of the riverbank, were drying in the sun. Saddled on shaggy loads of straw, teenage boys rode donkeys, whipping them along with little switches. Women, scarved and in pleated sirwals, with their blue and red djellabas hitched up around their waists, squatted and scrubbed caftans in the Drâa's green waters, or slapped robes over stones to beat out the soap. They smiled and averted their eyes as we approached. Perspiring men in sweat-stained skull-caps hoed plots of alfalfa and wheat divided by fences of thatched palm fronds.

As we passed the qsar, a half-dozen barefoot little boys stampeded out of the portals and ran toward us, laughing and shouting, '*Bonjour!*' and 'Nasrani! Nasrani!' We waved hello, and veered off the bank of the Drâa to find a trail leading to Ouriz. But we discovered stones had been laid to direct the river when it was in spate; these made for walls we could not climb over with the mule. We kept on, searching for a path through them.

Noureddine was fretting as we walked along the walls. 'Look, here we've got to work together, you, me and the mule – pardon me. The mule – pardon me – may need our help. You see, mules – pardon me – have a tough time where the path is chopped up like it is here. Normally, a mule, pardon me—'

'Why do you keep saying *hashek* [pardon me]?'

'Why? Well' – here we began climbing a path that zig-zagged up the shoulder-high embankment – 'a mule – pardon me – well it's not so polite to talk about them. So we must ask forgiveness. You see mules – pardon me – well they . . .'

He could not bring himself to finish explaining. Later

Ali filled me in. 'A mule might eat human excrement, so we consider it an unclean animal. No camel would stoop that low. We're a bit embarrassed when we have to talk about mules and even donkeys to people we respect, so we say *hashek*.'

Noureddine stopped talking and prodded the mule up the path, but at the first bend there was a hole a couple of feet wide. The mule hesitated, but took a step. There followed a panicky neigh and a crashing of pots, a kicking of hooves, the thud of hooves on earth, the sparking of hooves against stone. The beast had stumbled, and he was struggling under the load, which had now shifted. His tongue lolled out, he slavered green spittle, his eyes bugged. As he struggled to rise, he kicked madly, raising a cloud of dust and sending his rear hooves out with lethal speed.

I jumped back. Noureddine, evading the flashing hooves by inches, leapt to the mule's side. 'Your knife! Please, quickly! Your knife!'

I gave it to him. He slashed through the nylon ropes and the load fell off; pots, pans and tents bounced down the path past me. The mule was free and jumped to his feet, unharmed. He trotted off a few steps and stood at ease, and then lowered his head to munch on some alfalfa, looking rather blasé.

Noureddine went over and stroked his mangy head; the mule nuzzled him and chewed. I began reloading the saddlebags as he knotted back together the cut lengths of rope.

'A mule – pardon me – is a man's best friend. But he's not so smart, so he scares easily and stumbles. After all, his father was an ass. Pardon me.'

Ouriz is an Arab village of blocky, straw-roofed mud houses and sandy roads set amid Berber qsars. Noureddine told me that its Awlad Yahya inhabitants raised goats, sheep and cattle, and farmed the oasis. Talk of tribes, Awlad Yahya or otherwise, would have sounded anachronistic in urban Morocco, where tribal identity has gone the way of sabres and caliphs, but among the Ruhhal (including recently settled Ruhhal, such as the Awlad Yahya), belief in a single eponymous progenitor affords people an identity based on ancestry. Tribal pedigree is no abstract issue for Ruhhal. Roaming over vast territory and owning no land, nomads have little besides ancestry with which they might identify themselves and by which they might distinguish friend from foe. In the days of raiding, members of a tribe were bound to come to one another's aid in a domain where no one could live alone, and where every stranger was a potential enemy.

The tribal system has historically been democratic. Members of a tribe elect leaders called, variously, *sheikhs* (venerable elders), *amirs* (commanders) or *qa'ids* (leaders), whom they invest with authority to rule, and from whom they withdraw investiture if that authority is abused. Unfortunately, fractiousness has always characterised the tribal system (sub-tribes and clans abound); and in Morocco sultans, kings and colonisers have always sought to manipulate rivalries among clans to strengthen their own position and gain access to their lands. In the Drâa, however, no one succeeded for long – until the French pacified the region by force in the 1930s.

As we hiked out of the oasis and into Ouriz, I asked Noureddine how the Arab Awlad Yahya felt living among Berbers.

'Islam unites us, no matter whether we're Arab or Berber, no matter what tribe we are. "There is no difference between you, except in piety," says the Qur'an. In God's eye, we're all just sons of Adam.'

We reached his house, the adobe walls of which extended for almost an entire block. Its green steel door was open at the top to let in air, with filigreed bars. From within the house there came a mooing of cattle and a cackling of chickens. Noureddine knocked.

'*Shkoon?* [Who's there?]' a girl's voice asked.

'*Qreeb.* [I'm right here.]'

A minute or two passed as female members of the family relocated to private quarters. There must have been many of them, for a clatter of sandal-shod footsteps filtered through the filigree. A ten-year-old girl with long chestnut hair tied in a ponytail finally opened the door and let us in. We unloaded, and put our gear inside the entranceway. Noureddine left the mule tied to a pole outside.

Noureddine's house was huge – one of the largest in Ouriz. It consisted of fourteen or fifteen high-ceilinged adobe rooms built around two cement courtyards. Out back there was a yard divided into pens holding two cows, a tethered donkey, a half-dozen sheep and goats, and a squawking covey of chickens and roosters. In one corner of the yard stood a beaten-up brown Mercedes of the cheap kind used as taxis all over Morocco. Noureddine told me that he had tried driving a cab but had given up after finding Ouriz was not ready for such luxuries.

'You have everything here, don't you?' I asked.

'God provides. Praise be to God! We have to be ready

for anything, even war. God favours the servant who prepares for everything.'

He told me about his family. He was one of eighteen children. Since his father's death not long ago he had been responsible for feeding the entire household, which included, in addition to the brothers and sisters still living with him, his wife and son, his mother, and various cousins, aunts and uncles. This seemed like an astonishing burden to me. With so much to worry about, his invincible cheer was heroic.

He led me into a room at the far side of the men's courtyard, where Ali was waiting for us, his fouqiya pockets bulging with Marlboros, his face radiating serenity. Translucent windows opening on the courtyard let in cold bluish light. (As with most Moroccan houses, for privacy's sake no windows looked on to the street.) Hand-woven Berber carpets of red and brown wool covered the concrete floor; wires ran along the base of clay walls, carrying current to a television and a boom box that were draped with shawls to protect them from dust. There were no chairs or sofas; one took off one's shoes at the door and sat on the floor, leaning back on embroidered puffy cushions strewn here and there. I collapsed onto a cushion and felt fatigue wash over me. Ali had brought meat for kebabs, which soon he began grilling in the courtyard over charcoal.

While Noureddine was out of the room Ali came in and leaned over to me, fingering a cigarette. 'Listen, there's something you should know. You shouldn't tell people you're headed to Tan-Tan. Just say you're going to Zagora.'

'Why?'

'Because I'm still trying to arrange permission for you to travel from Mhamid west. That's the border with Algeria, and it's very sensitive. People here talk. If they hear you're going to Tan-Tan, it could be reported to the government, and they could take you for a spy.' This was a disturbing reminder of risks to come.

After we had all feasted on kebabs, Ali arose and said goodbye. He would return to Zagora, where we would meet in eleven days for the Feast of the Sacrifice, which he invited me to spend at his house.

The girl with the ponytail entered the room, her eyes lowered, carrying a stainless-steel tea service covered with a cloth. Noureddine took the tray and, sitting cross-legged, began the ritual boiling, pouring and repouring of the tea from kettle to glass and back again, tossing in chunks of sugar and copious, aromatic sheaves of mint. He tested it and then served me my first glass. It was refreshing, if thick with sugar, and we both savoured it. Noureddine disliked Ruhhal tea as much as I did.

Al Jazeera, the Arab satellite news station from Qatar, was on. We were sitting under a straw roof in a mud house, but Al Jazeera showed us soap and deodorant commercials in which Arab housewives dressed in Western clothes, spoke classical Arabic and fretted over dishpan hands and embarrassing odours. Here at Noureddine's there was nothing Western: the smell of livestock permeated the room, and there were many flies. Toddlers ran about the courtyard in tiny djellabas and skullcaps. A couple of girls ten or eleven years old would peek around the door at me and whisper about the Nasrani. With their café au lait skin, dark shiny hair and warm opal eyes, they would one day become beautiful women – just as veils fell over their faces.

After we finished our third cup of tea, Noureddine stood up. 'Are you ready for my surprise?'

I said I was. He led me outside. We walked up an alley to the edge of Ouriz. From a sheath beneath his belt he drew a foot-long butcher's knife and used it to point toward what looked like a wart atop a saddle-shaped mountain that began just behind the village. Above the wart gnats swirled. Vultures.

'That's Jbel al-Nasara' – Christians' Mountain – 'and we're going to hike to the top of it.'

'What are those vultures doing up there?'

'You'll see!' He said something about Jews and thrust his weapon back into its sheath. 'Come on!'

'What did you say?'

'Just come on!' He bounded ahead up the slope.

I pondered his dagger, the carrion-eating birds and what could have happened to Jews up there. I also considered the ache in my legs and the mountain itself, which was steep and covered in slag. I hesitated: I didn't feel like climbing it. But Noureddine had so many mouths to feed and so much responsibility to bear that it seemed ungracious of me to refuse him, so I started walking.

Thirty minutes later, as I sweated, stumbled and cursed my way up heaps of shifting slag, all notions of charity vanished. Hawks harried us, dive-bombing us and screaming as if we were encroaching on their nests (which we might have been). Every muscle that had been aching tolerably from three days of hiking now burned with pain; my every other step missed its mark; I slid and skidded from rock to rock, sweating, winded and growing dizzy. Noureddine skipped his way heavenward with obscene ease, brandishing his dagger and chanting from the Qur'an. The pimple atop the saddle had vanished; above me crags swirled, the sun spun.

After three hours of climbing I stood out of breath and rubber-legged atop the mountain, balancing in the gusty azure. Surrounding me was Noureddine's surprise: stone alleys, houses, cellars and squares – all built of the same slag we had just clambered over, all crumbling or collapsed. Far below, casbahs hunkered under the ochrous ridges of Saghro, connected by oases looping their way south.

Noureddine was grinning. 'What a brilliant tribe it took to build this!'

'Tribe?'

'The French, the French tribe, of course! Who else? What a brilliant tribe they were to build this!'

'*What* is this?'

He gave me a startled look. 'Why, ruins. What does it look like? Don't you understand?'

'I'm not sure I do.'

'These are the ruins of a French fortress. The French feared getting diseases from us. They made us their colony, but they didn't like living with us, so they moved up here. Just imagine how they could get all these rocks up here!'

'Well, they must have used forced labour.'

'Oh yes, they were imperialists, you're right, but *smart* imperialists. They were smart and that's why they could colonise us. What *brains* the French tribe has! Look at the result of their brains! An entire town on top of this mountain. Not only were they safe from diseases, but who could attack them up here?'

'The hike alone would kill the enemy.'

'You're right.'

Noureddine gave me a tour, hopping from rock to rock. I climbed around gingerly, fearing a misstep could send me tumbling three thousand feet down the mountain. There were alleys and tiny squares, small roofless rooms Noureddine called living quarters, and a flat empty spot toward the southern end he referred to as the shooting range. That the ruins had one day been a fortress was beyond doubt, though I had never read of it in any guidebook or history text. The outer walls, he said, were once of adobe.

'No shell can penetrate adobe,' he said. 'That tribe thought of everything! Knowledge and knowledge alone allowed them to build this. Look at how the streets are laid out so straight. Pure *knowledge*!'

Knowledge – *'ilm* – ignited a passion in him. He relished repeating the word, whose Arabic root letters conjured up other illustrious nouns – scholar, wise man, luminary, even the world itself. I began to see something beyond quirkiness in his fascination with statistics, in his love of riddles. The same appreciation and thirst for knowledge, no matter what its source, had helped the tribes of Arabia build an empire that lasted centuries, and a civilisation that survives still.

He went on. 'The French brought the Jews up here to live with them. You see, our Jews didn't work the land. They had factories and traded – that is, they used their *brains*, like the French. They had soft tongues' – here he stuck out his tongue and stroked it with his grimy forefinger – 'but the mind of a devil' – here he pointed to his temple. 'They were so intelligent you could never let down your guard or they'd outfox you.'

'How do you know all this?' There were few Jews left in Morocco, and none, as far as I knew, in the Drâa.

'The elders told me. The Jews and the French knew the value of knowledge. I respect them for that.'

'How many years of school did you finish, Noureddine?'

'Oh, I made it through elementary school, but I got kicked out at sixteen. Our government doesn't want us to study; it needs only dumb people. It has no need for people with brains; there are too many Moroccans as it is, and smart people are difficult. At the time I didn't understand all that, so I fell into their trap. But the year after that I *did* understand. Then I was seized by a desire to learn all I could, a desire to cram my head full of facts.'

'You went back to school?'

'That's not possible here, once you're out. So I left home for Zagora and Taroudant, where I attended *madrassas* [schools attached to mosques]. To learn you *must* travel. You can't sit at home counting flies. "Seek knowledge, even in China," the Prophet said. Above all, to learn you have to study the Qur'an. It took me three years to memorise it.'

'You know the entire Qur'an by heart?'

'Yes. If you don't know the Qur'an, you don't know anything. Then I got another book and learned where all the continents are and exactly – *exactly* – how many people every country has. Knowledge must be *exact*. To talk about a country you have to know the basics before you get into other things. You should know, for instance, *exactly* how hot or cold it gets there. I'm not talking about things women say, I'm talking about facts. To learn facts I made research the basis of my life, and I study ruins whenever I find them. That's why I agreed to guide you. I wanted to find out what a Nasrani is like, what a Nasrani thinks, what facts the Nasrani can tell me. I'm doing research, you see, even as we stand here.'

I looked into his eager brown eyes. Since we had met he had shown none of the Socratic humility one would associate with a quest for enlightenment, but what he said stirred me, and I felt a surge of admiration for him. He was cheerful and flourishing as an autodidact under a domestic burden that would have broken me.

'Sometimes', he said, steadying himself in the erratic wind, 'I act like my head is empty, so people will stuff it full of facts. My aim is knowledge. There's nothing higher on God's earth than knowledge. In ruins like these there is truth.'

The sun was now falling, its softened rays gilding the grand casbah of Tamnougalt, our next destination, to the south. We climbed carefully out of the ruins and started back down the mountain to Ouriz.

THE CASBAH OF TAMNOUGALT

JUST AFTER SUNRISE the next day, as we were driving the mule out of Ouriz, I discovered I had forgotten my toothbrush, and ran back to Noureddine's house to get it. I knocked on the door.

A young woman's voice rang out. '*Shkoon?*'

'*Qreeb.*'

The door opened. Dawn light fell on cerulean eyes flecked with bronze and set in a milky-white oval face, on mahogany-brown hair spilling over a djellaba of midnight blue. A tiny white hand held the door latch; miniature plastic sandals shod petite sculptured feet.

The woman, whom I took to be Noureddine's wife (following Islamic custom he had not introduced her to me, so I wasn't sure), smiled at me.

'Yes?'

'I – I'm sorry, I forgot my toothbrush,' I said, surprised, dumbstruck even, by her beauty.

Still smiling, she moved aside that I might enter; I

thanked her, took a step, and tripped over the transom. Barely avoiding a pratfall, I ducked into the bathroom, grabbed the toothbrush, and stumbled back out into the street, apologising to her, and jogged back to catch up with Noureddine and the mule.

The encounter unsettled me. Where no woman goes unveiled in public, even the sight of a bare female face stirs the blood. It was easy to see why Moroccans referred to an unveiled woman as *'aryana* – naked – for she is exposed to the eyes of men, who, deprived of the sight of women outside their family, could not but sin with her in their thoughts. Such thoughts could lead young men away from God; Islam therefore enjoined women to cover up.

Saying nothing about the meeting, I rejoined Noureddine, and we continued on our way, winding down through Ouriz and entering the oasis.

Palm fronds agitated by the breeze spattered sun in a shifting mosaic of light and dark on plots planted with carrots and onions, garlic and beets, wheat and barley. Yard-wide irrigation ditches known as *saqias* criss-crossed the plots, but Noureddine knew the paths around them. From here to Mhamid, the *saqias* irrigated rows of pumpkins, melons and peas, and orchards of orange, pear, apple and fig trees. Once we were deep inside the oasis, only almond trees, covered in snowy blossoms that buzzed with bees, reminded us of the dry climate. One need not have read a stack of Arabian travelogues to entertain the thought that this was some sort of Eden, for the people of the Drâa themselves refer to the oases as the *jinan* – the plural of *janna*, which translates as Paradise as well as garden.

Of the species of trees in the Drâa, it is the date palm – of which the Drâa is said to contain at least two million specimens – that makes the oases arable, even inhabitable. The shade of the palms cuts down evaporation and reduces by half the amount of water crops need to survive. The people of the Drâa use every part of the palm: they eat its dates (a large tree produces more than two hundred pounds a year); they use its wood to build their homes; they work its fibre into rope, its fronds into roofing and fencing. In recent decades the palm has suffered from a blight called bayoud, which now afflicts a tenth of the trees; here and there we saw a stricken palm, deathly brown and desiccated. Farther down the valley, we would see entire groves that had been killed by the disease.

We walked now at a leisurely pace, luxuriating in the shade and the vistas, shouting greetings to the ploughmen labouring in their plots. Noureddine recited the Qur'an, rattling off sura after sura into the glades. His command of the verse seemed impeccable.

In a bower between *saqias* he slowed his pace and halted his recitation. Something was troubling him.

'What religion are you?'

'Christian.'

I said '*Masihi*' to be exact – a follower of the *Masih*, or Messiah. He knew that I was a Nasrani, but through overuse 'Nazarene' has degenerated into an all-encompassing label for non-Muslim white people. I didn't believe in anything, really, but I had learned that in Muslim countries it was incendiary to say so. To acknowledge agnosticism provoked lectures; to profess atheism put one in league with Satan. The Arabic words for 'atheist' carry the hellfire echoes of infidel and apostate.

'What kind of Christian?'

'There are both Catholics and Protestants in my family.'

'That's not what I asked. What religion do *you* believe in?'

'Well, I've read the Bible and parts of the Qur'an. My parents—'

'You shouldn't believe in a religion just because your parents believe in it. You should believe because you've questioned and done research, and that research can only lead you to one answer: Islam.' His voice was rising. '*You* should know this, since you read Arabic. There's no excuse for your not studying the Qur'an.'

'Well, I—'

'Islam embraces all the celestial religions. We believe in all your prophets, all those of the Jews and Christians, who are People of the Book. Jesus was a prophet, a messenger of God, and I believe in him. But he wasn't the Son of God, he was just a man; his message was incomplete and the sons of Adam didn't heed it anyway. And think: why would God need to have a son? It makes no sense. The Sura of Miriam says, "It is not for God to take a son unto Him. Glory be to Him! When he decrees a thing, He but says to it, 'Be,' and it is." The Prophet Muhammad (God bless him and grant him salvation!) was the Seal of the Prophets.' He paused. 'God is as close as the vein in your neck, and he knows your heart. There is no god but God, and Muhammad is His prophet. This is the most basic knowledge, the simplest of facts. To know anything at all you have to know this first. Or, to put it another way, if you don't know this, you don't know anything.' He took a deep breath and exclaimed, '*La ilaha illa Allah!* [There is no god but God!]'

I didn't know what to say, so I kept silent. But I thought about his words. Five times a day, from every minaret in Morocco and all across the Muslim world, muezzins announce in the call to prayer, 'I bear witness that there is no god but God and Muhammad is the prophet of God.' In seventh-century Arabia this declaration heralded a revolution and a new age, denying the existence of the many gods popularly worshipped at the time and recognising the One God, Allah. These words make up the *Shahada* (Testimony), which all Muslims must utter at least once in their lives with comprehension and conviction, or they are not really Muslims.

Resounding in the call to prayer, these words retain their immediacy still. How many thousands of times had I heard the *Shahada* echoing over Marrakesh and into my house, waking me in my sleep, interrupting my dinner or bringing to a halt whatever conversation I was having, reminding me and everyone else that we, according to Islam, answered to something beyond ourselves and our own desires? Only on hearing these words have I come close to faith. They brought God, as Noureddine (and the Qur'an) said, as close 'as the vein in your neck'.

When I came out of my reverie Noureddine's sermon had moved on to the Day of Judgement: '"when the sun shall be folded up and the stars shall fall, and the mountains shall be set in motion . . . and the seas shall *boil!*" Remember' – he tapped his neck again – '"as close as the vein in your neck!"' He shook his finger at me. '"Thy soul suffices thee this day as a reckoner against thee!"'

Preaching much animated him, and he was nearly skip-
ping along, using his staff to jab the mule ahead with
greater and greater vigour. He might have gone on for
hours if we hadn't spotted, through a break in the palms,
the gates of the casbah of Tamnougalt. An adobe fortress
of many towers and several storeys, the casbah appeared
at once to be both a vision of battlements from ancient
Arabia and a freshly baked palace of gingerbread. The
Drâa ran sparkling and jade green beneath it; behind it
were the distant, iron-red ridges and flinty arêtes of Jbel
'Asal.

We made our way out of the oasis and into the maze of
lanes surrounding the casbah, raising dust as we moved
down streets deserted because of the midday siesta. At
the end of an alley we espied the citadel's wooden main
door. We knocked and knocked. There was in response
only a cooing of doves, a plaintive braying of donkeys.

The door finally opened to reveal a paunchy fellow of
thirty or so with a sharp nose and curly black hair, wearing a flowing white headdress. '*As-salam 'alaykum!*' he
said.

'*Wa 'alaykum as-salam!* [And may upon you be the
Peace!]' I replied.

Noureddine gave a lengthier, more overtly pious
response. '*Wa 'alaykum as-salam wa rahmat Allahi ta'ala
wa barakatuh!* [And may upon you be the Peace and the
mercy of God the exalted and His blessing!]'

As the mule stomped his hooves, uneasy under his
load, the man introduced himself as Omar, scion of the
qa'id of Tamnougalt. He offered us rooms for the night
in the casbah, and we accepted.

For three centuries the Berber qa'ids of Tamnougalt

ruled a twenty-mile-long stretch of territory from Agdz in the north to Timiderte in the south. The French allowed the qa'ids to remain on their thrones as local administrators, thereby giving colonial rule a Moroccan face. Only in 1952 was the last qa'id deposed. When the kingdom of Morocco was established in 1956, the sultan moved the seat of local administration up the valley to Agdz.

After plying us with tea and biscuits, and finding a berth for the mule and rooms for Noureddine and me, Omar and his brother Abdelmelik showed us around their casbah. Three hundred relatives of the qa'id, and the qa'id himself, once dwelt here. Chamber opened on to dim vaulted chamber, winding passageways with stone staircases led from floor to adobe floor; lintels dyed with indigo, henna and saffron patterns held up ceilings of mud and palm fronds that were reinforced by palm crossbeams; between courtyards ran dark tunnels; there were corbelled arches and machicolations of palm wood; there were secret rooms, granaries and wells, both in use and decrepit. It was hot outside but cool inside the casbah. Omar said that in the storage rooms the temperature never changes owing to the adroit use of shade in the design of the structure; yet a patch of sky and a draught of fresh air were never more than a step or two away from the darkest room. The only touch of modernity was the lighting: stanchions that once supported torches now held electric bulbs. On every corner of the vast fortress guard towers stood. The most important ones faced south toward the desert, the direction from which nomad raiders once threatened.

At one set of inner portals Abdelmelik let me pass but

shut the door softly on Noureddine. He then led me through more doors and down a hallway.

'These are our private quarters,' he told me. 'Since our women are here we have to keep Muslims out.'

'Why only Muslims and not me?'

'You're used to seeing unveiled women. Muslims are not.'

Around another courtyard we found women busy baking, washing clothes, making tea; there was much chatter and laughter. They did not acknowledge me, and I avoided looking at them.

'We're now forty-five people here in the casbah,' said Abdelmelik. 'We get no support from the state – those days are over – but we have our fields in the oasis and we get by. We marry only women who will wear the veil and maintain our traditions. We have no need here of women who have modern ideas or want to be European.'

We wandered through a portal and on to the street, where we were joined by another young man from Tamnougalt, who introduced himself as Ahmed. Dark-skinned, thin and tall, with discerning eyes, Ahmed looked to be a Haratin Berber. He walked with us into the mellah, or Jewish quarter of the casbah. The five hundred Jewish families who once lived here had left after the wars between Israel and the Arabs. The mellah was in ruins, all rubble-strewn streets and boarded-up windows, collapsing walls and caved-in roofs, though in places Stars of David survived, carved into the clay above doorways. Berber families had moved into some of the less dilapidated houses.

We stopped and contemplated the ruins. Tamnougalt had supported one of the largest Jewish communities in

the Drâa, and at times. Jews persecuted in northern
Morocco fled here to seek refuge. Their presence may
possibly date to a thousand years BC, but the ancestry
of the Drâa Jews, like the ancestry of the Jews in the
rest of Morocco, remains a mystery: either they were
Berberised Jews or Judaicised Berbers. In any case, they
were among the most ancient inhabitants of the land.
By all accounts they created intellectual centres rivalled
in North Africa only by the cities of Fez and Qairawan.
They enjoyed good relations with the sultans of the
north, and even took part in the Arab conquest of Iberia.
Islam ordained that Jews, as People of the Book, be
treated with tolerance, and the sultans permitted them to
be administered by their own sheikhs. Enjoying the
sultan's protection, the Jews chose to live separately from
Muslims in the mellahs, which, however, as time passed,
grew increasingly cramped and filthy. Although Jews
became diplomats, doctors, teachers and wealthy traders,
they had to pay a special poll tax (as did Christians);
they were prohibited from riding horses or carrying
weapons; and when they passed mosques they had to
remove their shoes. When Europeans began penetrating
Morocco in the nineteenth century, Jews in coastal
towns, with their knowledge of languages, often acted as
consuls and intermediaries. Association with foreign
powers came to have negative connotations, and many
Jews were tarred as foreign agents.

Still, had it not been for the creation of the state of
Israel in 1948, the mellahs in the Drâa (and elsewhere in
Morocco) would probably be teeming with life today. In
1948 there were 600,000 Jews in Morocco (out of a population of six million). By 1967 this number had fallen to

200,000. By 1973, before the last exodus, there were 20,000. This exile to Israel (and Europe and the United States) was voluntary. Many Muslim Moroccans regarded it as treason: they could not understand why the relatively prosperous Jews, who had always been loyal to the king, would resent their second-rate status and emigrate.

My guides didn't understand it either. The departure of the Jews was a great loss for Morocco, they said, and none professed to know of any discrimination to which they had been subjected. 'Tamnougalt was thriving until the 1970s,' Ahmed said, 'when the last Jews left. After that the droughts began coming more and more, and people began leaving to work in the north.'

After we had returned to the dark and cool of the casbah, Omar and Abdelmelik drifted away to take care of family matters; Noureddine left to find oats for the mule. Ahmed and I settled into divans in a vaulted chamber, and a servant brought us mint tea. Ahmed followed world events more closely than I would ever have expected for an inhabitant of such an isolated demesne, and we began talking politics – something we would not have done in the days of King Hassan II (who died in 1999), when remarks other than 'God grant the King victory!' might have been regarded as subversive. In a conversational mix of classical Arabic and dialect, Ahmed told me his views on a variety of subjects. The new king, Mohammed VI, inspired cautious enthusiasm. 'Changes are being talked about – a constitutional monarchy, for instance – but until they are put in law we will have to wait and see . . . Your President Bush doesn't have the, shall we say, *level* to be president, he was only the governor of a state, and a backward state at that . . .

Putin is a KGB man. What ideas could he have for reforming Russia? Russia's days are over as a super-power, and it is natural that the United States is working to finish it off . . . Arafat represents only a corrupt elite; he is one of the wealthiest Arabs and uses his position to gain more wealth . . . OPEC is run by American oil companies behind the scenes, and they are profiting by the rise in oil prices . . . France is an effete country that makes loud noises but has no power any more . . . Three continents are vying for influence in the Arab world: America, Europe and Asia . . . Qaddafi is finished as a leader in the Arab world, no one believes in him . . . Saddam is strong and popular with Arabs but has no thoughts in his head . . . The days when rulers could fool their peoples ended with the coming of the Internet and satellite television.'

Satellite television, in particular Al Jazeera, had armed Ahmed with knowledge that would have been hard to come by here ten years ago, when media in Morocco were all state-controlled. But as we talked I felt something akin to foreboding. What would he do with his knowledge here, where the authorities demanded little more from him than submission? He and other young people, the more worldly and more educated they became, could only grow frustrated with their lack of voice in government. The partial liberalisation of the kind Mohammed VI was introducing could well raise democratic expectations that no monarchy could fulfil and survive.

Noureddine returned. Finding me talking with a Muslim, he must have concluded that Islam was the sub-ject and my conversion the imperative (though Ahmed had never mentioned religion). He launched into a sermon on the book in which my deeds would be written, the tabs God was keeping on my heart, and the joy my embracing Islam would give him. Ahmed understood that our conversation was over and, showing no interest in Noureddine's proselytising, left us. I was sorry for that, and found myself resenting Noureddine as an intruder. Or, I should say, I found myself resenting Noureddine's zeal.

There might have been more to Ahmed's departure than a lack of interest in sermons. Ahmed watched Al Jazeera and questioned; Noureddine read the Qur'an and accepted it as literal truth. If the two young men were to engage in politics, they would be irreconcilable enemies; they would continue the conflict between the secular modernisers and the Islamists that has rent the Muslim world since the end of colonial days. In Morocco the overwhelming power of the king (based as much on palace security services as on the royalist sentiments of the uneducated masses) has for the most part kept the conflict from exploding; it has kept people like Ahmed from asking too many questions too loudly.

It was late. Still invigorated by my talk with Ahmed, I said goodnight to Noureddine and went up to my room, using a flashlight to navigate the tunnels and clay corridors, scattering bats out of palm lintels, leaving footprints in the dusty earthen floor.

Upstairs in my room I laid out my sleeping bag on the divan. The moonlight was flooding through my window, flooding over Jbel Kissane, flooding on to the oasis below. The palms, stirred by a breeze, rippled in the silver light as might waves on a gently surging sea. A donkey brayed from somewhere in the mellah, sheep bleated in their pens, the Drâa trickled beneath the casbah walls. Once this casbah had been the abode of a qa'id in the Land of Dissidence, and I imagined the severed heads of enemy troops adorning stakes near the gates; now it was peaceful, inhabited by nobles who threatened interlopers like me only with a surfeit of tea and hospitality. In the dark I imagined more: I saw lengthy caravans moving through the oasis; I saw their Ruhhal leaders, exhausted from the desert crossing, riding emaciated camels down the narrow lanes; I saw shackled slaves dragging their feet, prodded along by sabre-wielding guards. Despotism, drought and disease, plagues of locusts and bouts of war had in the past been the lot of the Drâa's people, who had accepted their suffering as the will of God. If they began to think otherwise and ask questions, what would happen?

I fell asleep, listening to the sheep.

AIT HAMOU SAID AND THE BERBER MARKET OF TIGHOUMMAR

'CAN'T YOU SEE the justice of Islam?' Noureddine asked. He jabbed the mule along with his prod. 'Islam is justice. Islam commands us to respect our parents. Islam forbids us to steal and murder. Is that not just?'

'Of course it is,' I said, 'but so do Christianity and Judaism.'

'Yes, but Islam is the *perfection* of those religions. Islam orders us to chop off the hand of the thief, stone the adulterer, and whip – but only whip, not stone – the unmarried fornicator. A fornicator who's a bachelor doesn't deserve stoning because he hasn't committed the same crime, which is obvious. You see, Islam distinguishes different *degrees* of crime. No other religion does.'

'Noureddine, I'm not arguing with you.'

We were on our way again, heading south, following a rugged *piste* along the base of Jbel Kissane, beneath slopes that were a vertiginous tumble of dun-coloured slag and burnt-sienna schist, spied over every hundred yards or so by caves near the peaks. The valley was broadening. Watchtowers loomed above the distant Berber casbah of Ait Hamou Said, our next destination.

'Islam—'

'Can't we talk about something else?'

'Islam completes Christianity. That should be obvious. Why would God have sent the Prophet Muhammad (God bless him and grant him salvation!) if Jesus had succeeded in his mission? Why? Tell me why?'

'I don't know why, but, Noureddine, I get your point. You've been talking for three hours now about—'

'Why? I'll tell you why. Because Islam completes Jesus' mission – and our lives, that's why. It has prayers for us to say on every occasion. Praise be to God, He has met every need of man. Praise be to God, and may He be exalted! There is no strength or power except in God! Don't you see the truth of Islam? Don't you?'

I could stand the sermon no more and quickened my pace, leaving Noureddine and his mule behind. All morning I had been listening to him preach and had tried to answer his questions. Over and over in different ways I had tried, and failed, to staunch this spew of holy verbiage. Noureddine was convinced that my objections stemmed from adherence to the wrong faith, when I had no faith at all and objected to nothing he was saying; I only objected that he was saying it so interminably, and at such high volume. But his upbringing taught him that the world was divided into spheres of competing faiths, which excluded the possibility that religion might not matter to some people. If I said, and I had said, that I respected Islam and Muslims, then why didn't I want to convert? If I said, and I had said (and it was not true, but it seemed like a tactful way of putting an end to his harangue), that I could not become Muslim without upsetting my parents or my wife, he told me to embrace Islam and convert my parents and my wife. Otherwise, the price was the Eternal Blaze, the 'burning winds and boiling waters' of Gehenna. Explaining how I had come to hold my secular world view, or that my world view was not unique but shared by hundreds of millions of people brought up in secular Western societies, might elicit a tirade that could last until the Day of Judgement, so there was nothing left for me to do but run.

Having jogged ahead, I settled back into a steady gait a hundred yards up the *piste* from him. He did not take offence: I glanced back and saw him smiling and waving his finger at me in mock reproach.

On a stony, sun-drenched plateau dominated by a spreading acacia, above undulating fields of alfalfa and blossoming almond trees, with the ruins of an unnamed fortress just to the north, and the cave-dotted ridges of Jbel Kissane to the east, I stopped to pass the siesta hours. Noureddine soon came cantering up.

When he opened his mouth and his tongue began to stir between his gapped uppers, I raised my forefinger. 'Silence! I need silence to think over what you've been telling me!'

He nodded and began unloading the mule, taking care to make as little noise as possible.

I threw a mattress down on the stones beneath the acacia and reclined. Noureddine turned the mule loose to graze, and then pulled out of the saddlebag a black plastic bag filled with beef he had bought in Tamnougalt. After starting a fire, he chopped the beef into chunks, which he marinated and covered with a spice mix. He then speared the chunks on skewers and set them to roast above the embers. A rich odour of burning flesh pervaded the air and set my mouth watering. Above us a high-tufted Houbara bustard landed on a crag and strutted about; near by, a magpie had taken up watch, perhaps lured by the scent of meat.

The brochettes did not disappoint. Seated in the warm sun, we used shards of bread to slip the meat from the skewers into our mouths, where it melted, spicy and tangy with vinegar. After the brochettes, Noureddine produced dessert: oranges and tangerines fresh from Tamnougalt's orchards. The seedless fruit cleansed our palates. Our stomachs filled, we lay back to rest until three, as was our habit. I closed my eyes. Noureddine's homilies notwithstanding, I wished to be nowhere else on earth. The untainted food, the fresh air, the warm sun, the peace of this Saharan valley produced a sense of wholeness that allowed me sound, dreamless sleep.

At three we packed up and set out for the hour-long hike to Ait Hamou Said. Noureddine was excited about showing me the casbah there ('There is truth in ruins, and this casbah is really ruined'); he had a friend in the village who would give us a tour and explain its history.

Set on an eminence above the palms, the casbah of Ait Hamou Said, from the outside, appeared to be well preserved, its mud towers and battlements in good repair. Its inhabitants had abandoned it in the 1970s and built a village outside its walls. I knew nothing more about its history, and was eager to learn. But Noureddine's friend turned out to be a glum Berber youth who led us up a path toward the door, swivelling his forefinger around in his nose and displaying no particular interest in or knowledge of the casbah.

As we entered the portals of the casbah, a stench assailed my nostrils and I almost retched. My companions walked on, reminiscing about relatives seen at recent religious feasts.

The youth halted. 'This is the mosque,' he said to me, taking his finger out of his nose and making a broad gesture toward a dark, malodorous room.

The stench, I now saw, came from dried human waste scattered over the floor. Amid the piles, fat black beetles scuttled to and fro, pushing balls of scatological booty. The youth gestured to the left. 'And this is the reception room.' More excrement squirmed with beetles. 'Come, let us climb to the second storey.'

'Wait,' I cried out weakly, covering my mouth with my hand. My interest in the casbah's history diminished sharply, replaced by disgust with the filth. 'Wait!'

They trudged on, chatting, and I followed. A dark staircase wound up to the next floor. At a turning our guide frightened a bevy of bats out of the rafters; they came fluttering willy-nilly down the staircase toward me, startling me and almost causing me to lose my footing. Noureddine and his friend crunched their way on to the second floor through dried crusty hanks of turd, squashing beetles with every step.

'This', said the youth, 'is the observation deck.'

The youth knew no more about the casbah than what various rooms were for. Noureddine embarked on a historical discourse composed of the self-evident and the commonplace ('This is an old casbah . . . The family who lived here was very powerful . . . Now the casbah is deserted'). He neglected to mention what was even more obvious – that we were standing in crap.

I cut him off. 'Noureddine, look down.'

He looked down and shifted his weight with a crunch from foot to foot. 'Oh.'

'What do you mean, "Oh!" What are we doing here standing in shit?'

'Is something bothering you?'

'Let's get out of here!'

He frowned quizzically. 'But you haven't seen the rest of—'

'Look what you're standing in! Aren't you disgusted?'

His eyes widened. 'You're right! These people don't understand the value of ruins! They have no idea of the truth in ruins!'

I turned to our guide. 'Why in God's name do people come here to relieve themselves? I mean, to get here they have to hike halfway across the village! Isn't there a more convenient place?'

'They don't live here any more, so they don't care.'

'But why pick this casbah for a toilet?'

He shrugged.

'It's simply that these people are ignorant and don't know that ruins tell stories,' said Noureddine. 'They should go to the bathroom somewhere else.'

I could stand the stench no longer. I stepped carefully back into the staircase, scattering beetles, and felt my way down the walls until I got to the door and fresh air.

It was time to find a campsite, so I started walking back toward the oasis. Noureddine, exiting the portals with his friend, called out after me. 'Please, wait. Let's not camp in the oasis.' He was loitering resolutely close to the casbah door.

'You're not thinking of spending the night in this casbah?'

'No. No, not really.'

'Then let's head for the oasis.' I walked a few steps and looked back: he was rooted to the spot. 'What's wrong?'

'It's the palms. They suck up the oxygen and leave karboo, so it's hard to breathe in the oasis.'

'You just had no problem inhaling that stench, and now you're telling me you don't want to breathe the air in the oasis?'

'Oh, but this isn't something I heard from a woman; I read it in a book. About the karboo. It's dangerous to sleep among the trees.'

At my insistence, and despite Noureddine's misgivings, we camped deep in the oasis, far from the casbah. We said little to each other that evening, and we turned in early. I found myself regretting that I had raced out of the casbah and had shown such obvious disgust with the filth. Noureddine and his friend did not see the filth because they were accustomed to it. Public places in Morocco got little of the care homes did, and they were frequently foul. Realising this did not make the stench any more agreeable to me, though.

No matter how many years I had spent in Morocco, there were things to which I could never adjust, filth and proselytising among them. As a guest in the country, I had abstained from voicing my opinions about religion, but now I thought again why should I keep silent when so many Moroccans (and adherents of Islam in other

Muslim countries in which I had sojourned) mercilessly and obtrusively critiqued my faith and predicted my damnation? Well-intentioned or not, such presumptive preaching was, finally, as irritating as it was alienating. In their eyes the world was still divided along medieval lines into *Dar al-Islam* (the Abode of Islam) and *Dar al-Harb* (the Abode of War, or the lands in which Muslims were to battle the infidels). To Noureddine, my stubborn lack of interest in religion was a wall to be breached. He possessed the ultimate Truth, and I must be conquered and surrender to it.

As I slipped into sleep, I found myself dreading the coming days, which were sure to contain their share of sermons: since leaving Tizgui, I had hardly eaten a meal or walked a mile without enduring relentless exhortations to accept Islam. There was no way to resolve the issue of religion; the subject was best avoided. This I vowed to do.

Next day we picked up the oasis trail south, passing through Berber villages and qsars, heading for the Tuesday morning souk at Tighoummar. I walked ahead of Noureddine now, giving him little chance to talk of religion. On the second day we left the Berber villages behind and laboured up the Saghro massif, hiking through barrens of dun rock punctuated by dust devils that spun and wandered through the emptiness as though lost. The sun was setting when finally we saw Tighoummar, situated beneath a high serrated ridge.

Noureddine agreed to brave the karboo and camp in the oasis so that early the next morning I could visit the souk. We needed meat, oranges, vegetables and Cokes, but I had reasons other than buying provisions for going to the market: it was a social event, a chance for villagers to pass on news, and I was longing to meet new people.

The sound of hooves beating the dust began before dawn. Just after sunrise I set out for the market, falling in with the procession of donkey-borne Berbers in pointy-hooded djellabas as they climbed an ashen trail up the rise toward the town. The Feast of the Sacrifice was drawing near, so traffic was heavy.

Built half on the slopes of Jbel Saghro, Tighoummar consisted of a low ruined adobe section – the old town – and a cement-and-adobe new town above it. The market was held in the new town, alongside the Drâa road, between two facing rows of *qaysariyas* – a word with a Roman derivation that can mean anything from empire to Caesarean section to bazaar, but here signified rows of concrete stalls painted in red-brown hues to match the adobe buildings nearby.

Clad in orange turbans and robes of fine brown wool, wearing silver daggers on orange sashes, Berber sheikhs haggled over piles of peppers. Berber commoners in djellabas of coarse wool surveyed mounds of salt and sacks of spices. Hanks of beef hung amid thick clouds of flies; butchers swung cleavers and hacked apart ribs and rumps; beheaded chickens spouting blood from their necks hopped and flapped amid nervous sheep tied fore-leg to foreleg; boys with knives led to their death rabbits on leashes, goats on ropes. In quieter corners village heal-ers knelt over spreads of roots, powders, pastes and ointments that made up the Berber medicine chest. The souk resounded with the doleful ballads of the Egyptian songstress Oum Kalthoum or the manic beat of Berber mountain music, or both at once, depending on the prox-

imity of the boom boxes broadcasting them. A heady
reek of manure, dust, blood and urine pervaded the
mountain air. There was much greeting, embracing, jab-
bering and calling upon God to witness the accuracy of
scales, the health of livestock on sale. There were few
women; in Morocco the men attend the markets.
Throughout the bazaar surged the energy and excitement
of the coming Islamic feast. Among this crowd I felt, if
in no way spurned, alone and invisible, an alien inter-
loper.

I did not dwell on this. I bought two kilograms of beef
plus the vegetables that Noureddine had requested, and
drank a Coke and ate a packet of Tango cookies, appreci-
ating the break these sweets offered me from our
expedition diet. The vegetables were still encrusted in
loam; the beef from a cow slaughtered in the village; the
fruit picked from surrounding orchards. Cooking in the
Moroccan countryside is simple and hearty, all cucumber
and tomato salads, meat and vegetable stews and couscous prepared in earthenware pots, rice and beef grilled
over coals, kefta balls and chicken. At times harira, or
bean soup, is served, and for a feast an entire sheep may
be slaughtered and roasted. On such food we, and the
people of the Drâa, thrived.

Back at camp Noureddine and I ate and rested, saying
little, a residue of tension still between us. The next
morning we set out for our first Arab village which was
just ahead. There I hoped to find respite from alienation;
I was supposed to put up at the house of a Muslim saint
I knew, and spend time with his hard-drinking son.

MARABOUT AND SON

WITH A CIGARETTE wobbling between his lips and shedding sparks on to my sweater, Mahmud, the saint's son, shook my hand as we stood in the sepulchral entrance hall to his house. He mixed his Arabic with snippets of American slang heavy with a Macon-County drawl.

'*How's it hangin', duuude!* I'm so happy to see you! Oh, I feel I'm alive again! The past is not dead! I'm so so happy! It's not *all fuckéd up!*'

He was so happy he almost had tears in his eyes. I had tears in my eyes – from the acid cloud of Marquise Blend smoke collecting around my head.

I had first met Mahmud in 1996 through an American friend from the Peace Corps who had lived in Mahmud's village and gone by the name of Fuad. Mahmud, Fuad told me, as we waited by the road, was a philosophising cab-driver eager to learn all he could about the outside world from foreigners. Fuad could never speak of him without smiling bemusedly and shaking his head. When hearing of Mahmud, other Peace Corps volunteers shrugged with similarly sympathetic befuddlement and said things like, 'He's one of a kind!' Some sort of quirky afflatus had touched him and, it seemed, destined him to be more than a taxi-driver living hand to mouth in a mud village. The consensus was that Mahmud was a curious and unique spirit in a land where unquestioning submission to the traditions of Islamic society was the norm.

Punctuality was not among his virtues. Two hours late, Mahmud came careening down the road in his silt-brown station-wagon taxi with such velocity, and braked in such a reckless squall of dust and flying gravel that he nearly ran Fuad and me over. Then he shook my hand at length and sprinkled me with Marquise ash, telling me that any friend of Fuad's was a friend – no, kith and kin – of his, and that he was placing his house, taxi, goats and brothers at my disposal for the duration of my stay. We spent the next few days together, driving up and down the Drâa, with him telling me his version of the valley's history. (Like Noureddine, he at times was less than exact.) But I was impressed by what he said to me after we had passed an afternoon with the village poet: 'What a man! When a man leaves behind a poem or a story or a book, it is as though he lives on after death. I must leave something behind for posterity!'

Mahmud's concern with legacy made sense, for he was the son of a sharif (descendant of the Prophet Muhammad) who, though illiterate, sported a royal pedigree extending back to the ninth century, to the Idrisid Dynasty that had ruled Morocco from Fez. And his father was not only a sharif, but the Muslim equivalent of a saint, a marabout, according to North African Sufi traditions that credited certain sharifs with semi-divine power known as *baraka*. A dose of *baraka* passed on through the blessed fingertips of the marabout could allegedly heal the sick, bring good luck or ward off misfortune. Even a marabout's tomb conferred *baraka* on those who visited it

Baraka is said to pass from father to son, but establishing saintly status requires some sort of proof, for not all the sons of marabouts carry *baraka* in equal doses. Mahmud's father, who is pale, allegedly acquired his status in a trial by fire. At a wedding villagers began taunting his father (who was dark-skinned), saying that his infant son was not his, for how could a dark man produce light-skinned progeny? To resolve the matter, the marabout's father placed him in a bread oven, declaring, 'If he is not my son, let him burn!' and slammed the door. Fifteen minutes later, when the villagers opened the oven door, they found the infant unharmed and shivering. This they interpreted as a sign of *baraka* and God's favour. In other words, he had the power, and he afterwards supposedly demonstrated it by healing the sick and bringing good fortune upon those he blessed.

Now, standing in Mahmud's entranceway, I patted out the glowing embers on my sweater and told him I was also very happy to see him. Noureddine greeted him respectfully, but with a palpable scepticism, declining his offer of a bed. He would stay with relatives in the village, for whose house he departed after we unloaded. Mahmud led me down the hall to the cavernous main room and ordered couscous be prepared with the beef I had brought as a gift.

We sat on the floor. On the high adobe walls were tacked yellowed poster-portraits of Hassan II and Mohammed VI. A decrepit television flickered with snowy images of the latter. Next to the television, portals led to a tiled court-yard, around which were scattered manifold rooms, each with filigreed glassless windows. In the far back cows mooed and sheep bleated. Sprawling on carpets next to us were a dozen or so children; some, Mahmud said, were the sons and daughters of absent brothers and sisters, some were his own. None, he told me, attended school. His aged mother set her sad, cloudy eyes on me, and addressed me with a keening voice, her tongue running over stubbed teeth, asking how Fuad was, and when, with God's per-mission, he might be coming to see them.

The marabout returned from his daily constitutional. Ancient, snaggle-toothed and hook-nosed, clad in plush white robes and a high white turban, his eyes half-occluded by drooping skin, he had not changed since I had last seen him.

'Welcome, friend of Fuad!' he shouted to me, his voice hoarse from decades of pronouncing *baraka*-inspired incantations. 'How excellent it is to behold a friend of Fuad! Ah, Fuad!' Raising his hands, he uttered a brief panegyric on Fuad.

'Fuad! Fuad!' chorused the family. Fuad's very name energised them. For his generosity, his unflappable cheer and his willingness to tackle any problem the villagers brought him, he was much beloved in the village.

With the aid of several children, the marabout slipped off his white, pointy-toed slippers, set his cane against the wall, and took a seat cross-legged on the floor. I made elaborate enquiries about his health, and learned that God had blessed him and he was strong, though in his eighties.

I asked Mahmud where his wife was. Fatigue dulled his hitherto lively eyes. 'Oh, my wife. I have married again. I now have two wives.' He glanced across the room at a muscular young woman wearing a scarf tied fiendishly tight around her brow. 'But let's talk of happy things.' His gaze wandered again and words came to his lips as if conjured by a hypnotist. 'Madeleine Alll-brright.'

'Madeleine Albright . . . makes you happy?'

The muscular woman laid a bowl of dates in front of me and a chant arose from the children: '*Kul! Kul!* [Eat!]'

Mahmud handed me a date. '*Kul!* Bill *Cleen-toon.*'

I bit into the date. 'What about Clinton?'

'*Kul!*' he said, his brow now wrinkling gravely. '*Ghair kul!* [Just eat!]'

The dates were sweet and meaty, but, as I chewed, a cloud of fat black flies descended on them. I then noticed that flies were everywhere: they covered the children's faces, poked around their mouths and eyes, drank their drool, and sipped at the mucus dripping copiously from their noses. Flies swarmed on every inch of exposed skin on all present, and I had to wave my hands every few seconds to keep them off my face; the others paid them little attention. Out in the valley so far I had seen few flies, but where animals and people shared dwellings they were inevitable. I suffered troubling presentiments of the stomach problems and diarrhoea they could cause.

Bashar, one of the teenagers, grabbed a palm-frond

switch and waved it around my face, like an Orthodox
priest blessing me with his thurible. 'We must fight flies!
They carry germs!' His words died amid the rising angry
buzz.

Mahmud waved away some flies and handed me
another date. 'She's got ants in her pants and wants to
dance!' he murmured in English, and then returned to
Arabic. 'You're here to learn about the Drâa, and the
Drâa is my life . . . *Coe-leen Pow-well*. Allow me to show
you the Drâa.'

'I'll be grateful.'

He leaned back against the wall and rubbed his eyes
again. The women retreated to the back of the house to
cook dinner; the rest of the family fell silent, and all eyes
turned to the television. No one among them was literate;
the classical Arabic in which the announcers spoke was
nearly incomprehensible to them. The snowy images of
the king and the news broadcast that followed presented,
for them, an entertaining collage of images, nothing
more.

A couple of hours later the woman I took to be one of
Mahmud's wives brought out two crudely glazed terrines
(one for the men, with whom I sat, and another for the
women, who were huddling separately in the far corner of
the room), in which piles of vegetables and chunks of
striated beef topped pyramids of steaming, saffron-hued
couscous. Bashar went person to person, proferring the
maghsal (a steel bowl covered with a perforated lid) and a
tea kettle of warm water. We extended our hands over the
maghsal for the washing ritual. Mahmud and the marabout
rinsed their mouths into the *maghsal* with much lusty
spitting and slurping. After that, we turned to the food.

'*Bismillah*,' pronounced the marabout.

Using their right hands, they scooped up handfuls of couscous and bounced it on their palms until it coalesced into balls, which they popped into their mouths. I ate with a spoon, having never mastered the manual technique. I occasionally swept the flies off my meat when no one was looking.

But Bashar saw me waving. 'We once had a Nasrani staying with us, a fat Nasrani named Jason. Jason hated flies, too.'

Popping a potato into his mouth, Mahmud remembered Jason. 'Yes, he would point to our couscous and say – here he slowed his voice to a robotic monotone – "I won't eat that. It has many germs."'

'Many germs' had become a catchphrase of hilarity – the family burst into guffaws. 'It has many germs! It has many germs!'

'By God he was a dolt,' said Mahmud. 'He had long green boogers coming out of his nose, and the flies ate his boogers.'

The American slang elicited another bout of raucous laughter, delivered through mouthfuls of masticated semolina. Flies crawled over the couscous in the bowl. I stared at the green chunky vegetables.

The marabout hawked up phlegm and spat over his shoulder. '"Many germs!" By God!' Oil ran from his chin, and flies clustered there, forming a buzzing black beard.

Eventually only the meat remained. The marabout grabbed it and pulled it apart into chunks, which he distributed to all. Grease glazed everyone's hands, and flies were thick on our slippery fingers.

After dinner Mahmud and I stepped out into the chill air of the March night and set out for the Téléboutique so that I could call my wife in Moscow. As we walked down the street we collected a procession of neighbours, who shook my hand at length and announced, 'How wonderful was Fuad! . . . Fuad built our well! . . . Fuad gave us water! . . . Fuad gave us hope!' Everyone had a story to tell me about Fuad – how Fuad had drunk tea at one's house; taught another's children English; made bounteous still another's harvest with his wise counsel on seeds and soils. He was generous, very generous, with the poor, good people of the village. They came close to ascribing him with the power to make the rain fall: 'The years he lived here rain came in abundance,' one man said. 'Then he left, and we have had only drought.'

After I made my phone call Mahmud and I continued our stroll. He told me about his life since we had last seen each other, in 1996, still peppering his Arabic with American slang and the names of US public figures. This linguistic mishmash was Fuad's most enduring legacy to him, the product of hundreds of hours of offhand tutorials. Relevance did not matter; the snippets of English were incantations Mahmud uttered to conjure up another world, a world without the poverty and drudgery he knew every day.

He sighed. 'I've married again, as I've told you. Women are devils. *How's it hanging, duuude?* They aren't devils in America, I think. But here they are. It's civil war, having two wives. I have to sleep with one, then the other, always switching off. It's exhausting. But it's not only that. If I bring one a bolt of cloth . . . *nice ass* . . .

then I have to bring the other a bolt of cloth or she gets jealous. It's *all fuckéd up*.'

'But you were always complaining you had no money when you had just one wife. Why did you marry again?'

He shrugged. 'Madeleine Albrright. What was I supposed to do? I wanted the other woman, too. God has made man to want many women. *Hey, Baby . . . Coo-lin Powwel*.' He rubbed his eyes. 'I had to buy the new wife a separate house. They couldn't get along . . . Oh, the money! And my taxi is getting sicker by the day. I drive and drive, and still the money isn't enough, and the wives complain. Women are devils, by God. *Get off my case . . .*'

We reached his house. Once inside, Mahmud stacked rocks in front of the door as a makeshift burglar alarm. At midnight he and the rest of the family wished me goodnight and abandoned the main room. The hike across the oasis had been exhausting and I was beat. I rolled out my sleeping bag next to the wall and positioned a cushion under my head. Minutes later, my eyelids grew heavy and drooped shut.

Soon after, a woman's shrill voice woke me up.

'You drunk! You spend our food money on booze!'

'Leave me alone, demoness!'

'You look at other girls in the street! You son of a dog!'

'Satan has afflicted me with you!'

'You deserve hell, donkey, for what you do to me!'

'You should know a lot about hell, demoness!'

A baby began crying, sheep started bleating, a cow mooed long in distress.

'You woke up the baby, donkey!'

'She-devil!'

'I'm leaving you!'

The door from the courtyard swung open and banged against the wall, chips of adobe sprinkled over my sleeping bag, moonlight filtered into the dark. Plastic sandals clattered over the cement floor past my head. There was a sound of bouncing rocks: the fleeing she-devil was tossing aside the rocks in front of the door and rattling the lock, trying to get out. But the door would not open. Glowing cigarette embers then appeared in the courtyard door and danced like a firefly across the room. Ashes fluttered down to my face. There were sobs and the retort of rocks hitting the wall, cries of 'Let me go, donkey!' intermingled with Mahmud's entreaties of 'Please, I'm sorry!' Then more sobs and finally a clattering of sandals in my direction and a repeat bobbing of embers. On their way back to their room they slammed the door to the courtyard.

I tried to get back to sleep, but a half-hour later the racket arose once more, and again sandals clattered past, more embers bobbed, more rocks hit the wall. At regular intervals throughout the night the drama renewed itself. Only as dawn light seeped into the courtyard did the arguing cease, and I dozed off.

But not for long. Through my slumber I heard a throat clearing. Then: 'Allah, Allah.' I slit my eyes and perceived the marabout staring down at me from the doorway. Leaning wearily on his cane, he hobbled over to the wall and sat down next to my head. He massaged his face, covering his eyes.

'Allah, Allah. God bless you, friend of Fuad! Are you asleep?' He peeked between his fingers and then cleared his throat more loudly. 'GOD BLESS YOU, FRIEND OF FUAD! ARE YOU ASLEEP?'

I sat up, bleary-eyed.

'Oh, you're awake. Good morning. Allah, Allah! I have a daughter studying in Zagora. She has no food to eat and no clothes to wear. She's got no money, you see. God grant you mercy. God grant you strength. Give me six hundred dirhams.' He stuck out his hand.

I was taken aback. I had brought them meat as a gift and was buying their groceries; in addition, I planned to leave them a two hundred-dirham (about twenty-dollar) token of my gratitude, as I had done on my previous visit. (In a country where fifty dollars a month was a salary, twenty amounted to more than a token.) But the six hundred dirhams he was asking for was a lot, especially since I had only a limited amount of cash with me on this part of the trip, and there was no bank until Zagora.

'She needs money,' he said, massaging his cheeks. 'She is hungry.'

I pulled out my wallet and handed him two hundred dirhams. 'I'm sorry, but this is the best I can do right now.'

'God bless your parents, friend of Fuad! God grant you strength and success!' He snatched the bills and held them up to the light. 'God bless . . . Wait, this is only two hundred.'

I explained my situation. He looked at the bills for some time, glanced back at me, and then held the bills up to the light once more. Finally he folded them and slipped them into his robe's pocket, and brought his two hands together, opening them in a gesture of blessing. 'May God shower you with His bounty, friend of Fuad. May God grant you mercy and long life and peace.' He got up and hobbled out.

I lay back and closed my eyes.

The mother came in. 'Allah, Allah,' she said in her keening voice. She sat down where the marabout had just been. 'The battery in Mahmud's taxi is *'ayana* [sick]. By God, he needs a new battery. It will cost eight hundred dirhams. If the battery dies, he won't be able to ride his taxi and we have so many children to feed and they will go hungry . . .'

I told her that I had just given the marabout money for the daughter, and that I could afford no more. She, too, began massaging her eyes. The daughter in Zagora was old enough to fend for herself, but the children were many and right here, and the hunger would be great.

This put me in a difficult position. 'I'll see what I can do,' I said, calculating my likely upcoming expenses in my head.

She arose and made for the courtyard, saying, on her way out, 'God bless your parents, friend of Fuad!'

Bashar came in next. 'Allah, Allah.'

'You, too? For God's sake, Bashar! It's not even six in the morning!'

'Me too what? I'm exhausted from all that racket Mahmud and his wife made. Allah! Allah! She is a demoness! Who could have slept?'

The marabout appeared again in the courtyard doors. He hobbled past me and slapped a prayer rug down on the floor, throwing up a cloud of dust. Facing east, he knelt and began reciting his dawn prayers, hawking up phlegm between suras and spitting on the floor, alternately prostrating himself and spitting, reciting the Qur'an and spitting.

Only later in the morning did Mahmud emerge from his room, looking worn out and sour.

'It's these wives. Devils, I tell you . . . civil war . . . *Albright* . . . devils.'

He waved dismissively at his own words and rummaged through clutter in the corner, looking for his cigarettes. He asked me to accompany him to the souk in Agdz with his father. The Feast of the Sacrifice was only five days away, and provisions had to be bought for the many relatives who would be coming from the north to visit. I said I'd be happy to go.

He seated the marabout in the front of his taxi which had deteriorated, a glance told me, into a shell of a shell of the taxi it was in 1996. I got in the back, carefully closing the door so as not to break it off, and trying not to look too closely at the dilapidation.

'Oh,' Mahmud said to me. 'Get out, please. *Nonsense, baby*. I'm sorry. You've got to push. The battery is sick. *All fuckéd up*, you see.'

Five or six boys of assorted ages gathered at the rear of the taxi, vying to help me, and Mahmud turned the key. The engine cranked and coughed. We pushed, and the taxi lurched ahead. I jumped in as it inched forward, and we trundled down the alley toward the road.

The cab rattled with tiny plastic banners on chains bearing quotes from the Qur'an about God granting mercy to travellers. We would need this mercy. The vehicle that should have been scrapped five years ago was now a rolling catastrophe of ripped rubber and dented steel. Screwdrivers and coat-hangers protruded from locks. Levers on the door did nothing when turned, except for the one beneath my window: I pushed it and my window slid with a crash into the door crevice. A mess of wires protruded from where the radio should have been. The sun roof, a sheet of cracked glass, cast spidery shadows over us.

We headed north on the Drâa road. It soon transpired that we were not just driving to Agdz; we were open for business. Here and there villagers minced out to the road, waving and hailing, and Mahmud halted for them to board, urging them to get in before the motor died. We picked up veiled young women with tattooed foreheads, old men with henna-splattered hands, freshly bathed boys in pressed djellabas and immaculate white skullcaps, a paunchy malodorous fellow with an inch-long fingernail on his fat pinky. They all greeted the marabout warmly. A few kissed his hands, told him their afflictions, received his blessings, and listened as he called upon God to alleviate their distress. Once we reached their destinations they shouted, '*Wquf! Wquf hinaya!* [Stop! Stop here!]', passed Mahmud five or ten dirhams, crawled over the knees of the others, and broke free of the taxi. From the road they made their way toward distant qsars and casbahs beneath the slopes of Saghro.

This would be the last souk day in Agdz before the Feast of the Sacrifice. Held in an empty lot outside the town, the Agdz souk far exceeded the market of Tighoummar in dust and frantic commerce. Thousands of Berbers had come down from the hills to buy everything from turnips to sheep to shoes. The sun was getting stronger and umbrellas were out. Everyone present was shouting at full volume, for all the stands had tape-recorders blasting Moroccan songs, jangling tunes with ululation and spitfire clapping. Porters warning '*Balek! Balek!* [Watch out!]' stumbled along under sacks of

vegetables or wheeled carts carrying panicked sheep and
jostling goats. At every turn we were bumped, elbowed
and shoved. But the marabout, crying, 'Allah! Allah!'
waved his cane and cleared the way. The faithful greeted
him profusely; many of them stooped to kiss his hands
and grab some *baraka*.

We climbed a dusty low hillock in the middle of the
market. Suddenly, the marabout raised his arms. This
was a signal. All around us merchants switched off tape-
recorders.

The marabout declaimed in a stentorian voice: 'God
grant our King Mohammed VI *victory*! May His Majesty
long reign over the Arabs! May he *rule* in peace and health
and prosperity! May God grant our *king* long life and
power and abundant *strength*! In the name of all the *awliya'*
[the Favourites of God, marabouts long deceased] I call
upon God to grant Mohammed VI everlasting *triumph*!
May God grant our king . . .'

During his oration I glanced around. Shoppers had
opened their hands as if in prayer; a few had dropped to
their knees and lowered their heads. I felt pressured to
make some display of reverence, but I resisted. Mahmud
showed no sign of piety; on the contrary, he had lit up a
Marquise and was affecting hauteur, leaning on a beet
merchant's umbrella and posing like a swarthy James
Dean. Or like the son of a powerful man.

Watching the marabout preach and the crowd venerate
him, I sensed a historical truth – and a living deceit. The
Alaouite sultans who had vanquished the Berbers of the
Ait 'Atta tribe ruling the Drâa in 1640 ('after many battles
so terrible that they would have greyed the hairs of an
infant at the breast,' in the words of one chronicler)

would come to rely on the marabouts to hallow their image and legitimise their rule in the Land of Dissidence. Moreover, the raids of Arab Ruhhal prompted the oasis-dwellers of the Drâa to seek leadership and protection from the marabouts, who obliged them – and ended up dominating the valley. Later, the faith-based passivity the marabouts espoused ill equipped Moroccans to resist colonisation by the French, with whom the marabouts would collaborate during the decades of the protectorate.

Marabouts enjoyed popularity because the mystical Sufi doctrines they taught were more attractive to the masses than the sterner Islam practised by traditional Muslims. But the kissing of his hands, the kneeling, the awe shown by the people around me for this illiterate mortal was un-Islamic, for in Islam no person should purport to act as an intermediary between other men and God. Even worse, the marabout took donations from the people: food, clothing, cash and junkets. The marabout's *baraka*, in short, was the family's livelihood.

It was not for me to object to this, and I kept my musings to myself. But surely marabouts were now as ever little better than shills for the regime, encouraging people to submit – once to the French, now to the king.

'God! Homeland! King!' the marabout shouted, and concluded by calling on God to grant Morocco victory. In what he did not say.

He lowered his arms and people raced to kiss his fingers. The tape-recorders resumed their cacophony. Dragging our sacks of vegetables, we made our way back to the taxi and left for the village.

The next morning Mahmud returned from the house of his second wife, his face drawn with fatigue. 'It's these damn cigarettes,' he said to me, puffing smoke. 'They cost so much. So damn much.'

'Why don't you stop smoking?'

'Stress. There's always a wife or one of these kids of mine asking for money. Food and clothes and all that. I'm not made for this kind of life. I'd just like to relax and have a beer and think about my legacy.' He took a drag on his Marquise and hacked a few times; his lungs rattled hard and deep. 'Look, would you like to go see the *zawiya* [shrine] of al-Qadiriya in Timisla? It's very historical, and I can tell you all about it. A sharif called Moulay Rachid runs it. I can't promise you will meet the moulay but we can try.' A moulay, or lord, is a sharif who is said to wield marabout-like powers. The *zawiya* of al-Qadiriya, Mahmud added, included a mosque, a *madrassa*, a prayer hall and a reception room.

After our trip to the market the matter of holy men had been vexing me, but I did want to see the *zawiya*, which had historically been one of the most powerful and important shrines of the Drâa. The *zawiya* was said to be guarded by 'Abid (literally 'slaves'), and this intrigued me. During the protectorate the French ordered the manumission of the 'Abid, but many, I heard, had remained with their former masters, living as they always had, working for food and shelter, afraid of freedom. If this was true, I wanted to see it.

Outside, a weak sun filtered through cracks between dark clouds; the wind drove ragged banks of rust-coloured dust across the valley. We got into Mahmud's cab, and after the push-and-shove launching ritual were on our way. We lurched off down the road a few kilometres and turned left on to a *piste* leading to the village of Timisla.

On the way, I told Mahmud what I had heard about the 'Abid, and asked if they were still really slaves. My question greatly excited him, for history was still his passion. 'All you have heard is true, by God! Moulay Rachid has thirty slaves who guard the *zawiya*. They're fiercely loyal to him. If he commands them to kill the American, they will draw their swords and do him in. Cut and slash! Whoosh! Heads flying! Their job is very important. You see, people come from all over Morocco to give money to the *zawiya*. It's a refuge, and the 'Abid guard it. Say, for instance, you murdered someone. A murderer can't be touched within its walls. In times of war it's a sacred place and can't be invaded. The moulay reconciles warring parties, he heals the ill. Oh, I hope you can meet him! He has the *baraka*! The 'Abid are so fierce! The *zawiya* is so rich!'

'What warring parties are there now for him to reconcile?'

'I can't speak for someone with such powers. I'll let him tell you everything.'

We rattled down the *piste* into Timisla, cutting our way through clouds of dust rolling off the slopes above. Timisla appeared poorer than most Drâa villages; its inhabitants were black people who wore the rags and downtrodden looks one might expect to see on slaves. We drove past them up to the *zawiya*, which stood on a rocky promontory just north of the village. The *zawiya* looked like any other mosque, with its dome topped by a brass crescent moon and star, except that it was surrounded by a high wall. At the gate stood a tall, aged black man – an 'Abid, I presumed – in a royal-blue djellaba and a white turban.

We got out and walked up to him.

'*As-salam 'alaykum*. I would like to meet Moulay Rachid.'

He gave me a cold stare.

'I am a friend of Fuad.'

At this he raised his eyebrows slightly, and then motioned us to follow him. He led us through a white-washed tiled courtyard dominated by a withered, lopsided acacia and a disused fountain. Above the court-yard stood the adobe tower where the moulay lived. Passing through an arched door, we entered a side room furnished with round-the-walls divans and a colour tele-vision.

'Wait,' he said, and walked out.

'The moulay will tell you everything!' said Mahmud.

We sat down and commenced waiting.

'Mahmud,' I asked, 'you're from marabout blood. Do you want to carry on your father's tradition?'

'Oh, I can't be like him. I drink and smoke, so I don't have the *baraka*. You've got to be pure to have the *baraka*.'

The 'Abid came in again and served us tea. He then switched on the television, took off his slippers, and reclined on the divan. Another fellow, the moulay's driver, wandered in and sat with us. Satellite television was on. A bearded imam in a black hood was giving the *khutba* (Friday sermon) to hundreds of kneeling Muslims in a mosque somewhere in the Middle East. He called on all the faithful to fight Zionism, to fight the imperialists behind it, and to say no to those who said yes to a nego-tiated settlement between the Israelis and Palestinians, for God was with the Arabs and they would triumph!

One must meet force with force, he thundered. A hundred million Muslims must rise and fight the Israelis, and fight the enemies of Islam in Palestine, in Chechnya and in Kashmir!

He delivered his *khutba* in classical Arabic. Mahmud, the 'Abid, and the moulay's driver were probably all illiterate (Mahmud certainly was), and would be unable to understand it fully. But the imam was quoting the Qur'an; they recognised the suras as the Word of God, and that was enough to command their fervent support. They livened up and leaned forward. 'By the will of God!' they shouted, affirming the calls to battle. 'May God's will be done! There is no strength or power except in God!'

When the sermon ended the scene switched to Mecca, where thousands of haj pilgrims were slowly circumambulating the Black Stone of the Ka'ba, wearing the *ihram* – the white robe of humility. Those seated around me switched quickly from battle cries to the recitation, in low, pious tones, of the Fatiha, the opening sura of the Qur'an. When a commercial came on the 'Abid changed the channel and a Libyan station flashed images of men in turbans doing a sword dance. Another switch landed us back at Al Jazeera, where computer graphics showed the station's golden logo dipping into turquoise water and shooting out again. The graphics coalesced into *al-akhbar* – the news. At this my companions lost interest.

Where was Moulay Rachid? It was now almost eleven.

'No doubt he is doing holy things,' said Mahmud. 'By God, he has *baraka*.'

A half-hour later Moulay Rachid walked in. He was in his thirties and well shaven. His perfumed plumpness

and intelligent, almost epicene face showed good genes
and money. But he did not look holy.

'You're the American who wants to see me?'

'Yes,' I said, rising to shake his hand. I understood
right away that questions about vicious slaves and healing
powers were going to sound nonsensical.

'What about?'

'Well, first, I'd like to pass along greetings from Fuad.'
I hoped that Fuad's name would work its magic. But he
stared impassively at me and said, 'Oh. And how is
Fuad?'

We sat down and I passed on Fuad's latest news, which
he received indifferently. Then I asked him to tell me the
history of the *zawiya*. He glanced at his watch and stifled
a yawn. 'We're originally from Iraq . . . I don't really
know when my ancestors came here. It was a long time
ago, all that.' The measured cadences of his classical
Arabic bespoke a sound education.

'What about the *zawiya*'s powers?' I asked. Mahmud
sat up straight.

'Powers? We're a *zawiya* in name only. Once we were
like the government, but now of course we have the king
in Rabat.'

'He has healing powers,' said Mahmud.

'Do you?' I asked.

'Some people think so. Some people give us money
and come for our festival.'

'He is a Favourite of God,' said Mahmud. 'He has
much *baraka*. Really. You should see what his *baraka* can
do.'

Moulay Rachid's face betrayed no pride, no affirmation or denial. It did show ennui. I could imagine this

fellow, who might have been a year or two younger than I, studying at a university in the States, drinking beer in a campus pub, and being just one of the gang, set apart from his American friends by only his 'exotic' heritage, but trying to fit in. His wealth would have helped him fit in: his teeth were white, his hands soft and clean, his hair glossy and coifed. Mahmud and the others had black teeth, callused palms, wiry hair and sinewy builds. Their poverty had marked them, and wherever they went in Europe or the States they would be marked men, aliens.

But what of the moulay's 'powers'? Would they ever be put to the test in today's world? If the moulay – or a minister in Rabat or any other wealthy Moroccan – were to discover a tumour or suffer a stroke, would he rely on *baraka* for a cure, or would he visit the oncology or cardiology ward at the finest European clinic available? The police would arrest murderers, if they sought refuge in the *zawiya*; and 'warring parties', if the conflict in the Western Sahara were any indicator, turned to neighbouring countries or to the United States for arms and supplies. Al-Qadiriya, just as the moulay said, was a *zawiya* in name only. Having lost its authority to the state, it had outlived its purpose.

Sitting with him, I was overcome by a sense of futility and falsity. The *zawiya* was empty. The sword dance on television was a relic of the past. The imam's call to battle with the Israelis and the 'imperialists' – the same call that Arab demagogues have been repeating for five decades now – was equally outdated, and doomed to evoke cries of support from the faithful, but no action, for the most powerful Arab states all cooperated with the West. The Arabs had fallen into eclipse centuries ago, and, still looking to the past for solutions, had not managed to pull themselves out.

Mahmud stirred on his divan. 'But it's not just the *zawiya* that has powers, it's the marabouts.'

'Are the marabouts really so powerful?' I asked the moulay.

'The marabouts are one hundred per cent above other people,' Mahmud said. 'One *hundred* per cent.'

'Are they?' I asked the moulay again.

'Some think so.' He looked at his watch.

'No, really, they are,' Mahmud said. 'What a marabout says will be. God will make what a marabout says come true. Really.'

'Some believe this,' said the moulay. He rose, excused himself, and left the room. He did not return. Our meeting was over.

Mahmud fell back on his cushions.

I got up. 'Let's go.'

He sat for a moment staring at the carpet, crestfallen.

'Thanks for showing me the *zawiya*. I learned a lot, really.'

On the way out to the taxi he looked even glummer.

'Don't be upset, Mahmud. I found all that very interesting.'

He still wouldn't look at me.

'Really.'

The moulay's driver bummed a ride off us back to the main road. On the way, Mahmud began repeating that the 'Abid were indeed loyal slaves, and would indeed have run me through with their swords had their master ordered it.

The driver laughed. 'What are you saying? We have

human rights and courts of law in this country! The
guards would be thrown in jail if they hurt anyone!'

We bumped back down the *piste* toward the road.

'*Ants in her pants . . . outrageous . . . boogers*,' Mahmud
said pensively as he drove down the Drâa road, after the
chauffeur had got out. 'I've been wanting to introduce
you to the son of the last Qa'id al-'Arabi, Hamid bin al-
'Arabi, since you arrived, but I've been too upset. It's
the damn kids, you know, always hungry, always wearing
out their sandals. You don't have so many kids in
America.'

'How many kids do you have?'

'Eight or nine, I think.'

'You think?'

'Well, I've got a few more wives, divorced, in other
towns, and some of the kids are . . . *outrageous, baby* . . .
are with them. The thing is, here I'm the only one in the
house working, and the donations my father gets aren't
enough for us to live on. *All fuckéd up*, you would say.'

The family of Qa'id al-'Arabi had once ruled much of
the Drâa. From whichever side you approached it, the
qa'id's three hundred-year-old house recalled a sultan's
palace. Covering the area of a city block in the village of
Oulad Atmane, the structure descended in staggered
levels from the top of the hill to the road; a tower stood at
each corner; and crenellations ran along the multilevelled
roofs. It was astonishing to recall that all this was built of
clay and could melt away in a heavy rain.

As we drove up to the house Mahmud accelerated and
honked the horn. He made a sharp left and we shot up on
to a vacant lot beside the house and stopped; on such an
incline there would be no need to push-start the car.

We knocked. The door swung open, aided by the wind. Mahmud called out, '*Kain shi wahid?* [Is anyone home?]' but there was no response, so we walked in. Shafts of dark and light fell from windows high on the walls, giving the entrance room the gloomy aspect of a dungeon. We stumbled along, heading for beams of light coming from the stairwells, and climbed from floor to floor, scattering bats, birds and flies, listening to the wind wander through the chambers. There were no people about. Where was Hamid bin al-'Arabi?

On the uppermost level sand blew through glassless windows, and out of the dark a stooped and hobbling figure emerged wearing a dusty brown djellaba and an even dustier, once-white turban.

'Hamid bin al-'Arabi! *As-salam 'alaykum!*' cried Mahmud. Salams were uttered by all. Mahmud kissed his hand, and the old qa'id set his drooping eyes on me. he had many moles, and his skin was encrusted with dust.

'Welcome. Please, be seated!'

We sat on the floor, on a balcony where a carpet was spread. A glum teenage boy joined us, sitting cross-legged on the carpet; the qa'id introduced him as his son, and then walked out to make tea. Apparently still used to holding court or receiving supplicants, Hamid had found nothing unusual in two people having admitted themselves to his home. Nevertheless, I felt like an intruder and whispered this to Mahmud.

'No reason to worry. He wants the company. Just leave him a few dirhams when we go.'

Hamid hobbled back in, holding a tea service that rattled with the tremble in his hands, and sat down opposite us. The wind gusted outside and dust blew all over us. I realised that we weren't on a balcony at all: a wall had caved in, leaving the room half open to the sky.

Mahmud told me of the power the qa'id possessed, how far his domain had once extended. But the old man didn't want to hear this.

'We lost our power when the French came. The fortune my father left, well, my brother sold it all for drink when I was ill. So we have nothing now. Our 'Abid fled when the droughts started, and my relatives sold their lands and left for the cities of the north.' We sipped tea. 'We came ages ago from Palestine and Yemen, by way of Mauritania, and settled here to rule. That was long, long ago. Now we have nothing. And this son of mine, he has diabetes and can't work. Allah, Allah, I am tired.'

The wind kicked up more dust, and we shaded our eyes. After we finished the customary three glasses of tea, I slipped Hamid a few bills, thanking him for his time, and apologised for disturbing him. We left him sitting with his son, trembling in the blowing dust. The meeting completed the impression of ruin and irrelevance into which the notables of the Drâa had slipped.

Mahmud and I sat in silence as we drove back to his village. I was too upset to speak. It was not really the visit to the qa'id that had upset me; rather, I dreaded arriving at Mahmud's house. We would find the television on, the toddlers screaming and snot-nosed, the women squabbling, the teenage boys not in school but kicking the soccer ball in the alley, and the marabout praying and spitting, all under a dense haze of flies. Mahmud would argue with wife number one, and then head down the alley to bicker with wife number two. He might later visit a bar in Ouarzazate, where he would drink half his monthly earnings in one evening ('I can drink twelve beers at one sitting,' he had boasted to me).

He was not in control of his life, and it was coming apart. Thinking of his frequent and absent-minded utterances of English words and American names, I even began to question his sanity. Each passing year was adding to his burden, dampening his spirit. He had married again, spoiling his relationship with his first wife. Too many children had been born into his household, and he couldn't earn enough to feed them all. The stress had pushed him to drink, which only increased his penury. His family needed the donations villagers made to his father in return for *baraka*, but the marabout was ageing, and his death would spell even further hardship. On his death I could envision the family breaking up: the teens would head north, first to the tin-shack slums of Casablanca, where they would search for work and find nothing, and then across the Strait of Gibraltar to Europe. There they would join the crowds of immigrant labourers living clandestine lives, looking for jobs and evading the police. Maybe Mahmud would join them.

At first I blamed him for his own decline – after all, he had married again, sired more children, and he drank and smoked of his own free will – but I was at least partly wrong. His misery stemmed from an ignorance encouraged by the Moroccan system of government. As Noureddine had concluded, the authorities had no need of educated citizens; indeed, Moroccans were not citizens at all (in the Enlightenment sense of the word), but *subjects* of the king, and the king demanded of them *submission*, little more. To induce submission, the Moroccan government did little to eliminate illiteracy, poverty and ignorance. Seen on the national level, all this might be cause for tongue-clicking and conferences on development and foreign aid; in the person of Mahmud it was grievous to witness, painful to bear.

I could do or say nothing that would help, except leave him some money. To assuage my conscience more than anything, I decided to do this.

As we drove into the village a dust storm blew through the valley, bending the palms and browning out the sky, filling the air with dirge-like gales.

MOONLIGHT AND FEVER

IN 1996, THE last time I said goodbye to Mahmud, I had stopped in his village on my way back north after my disastrous Saharan sandstorm escapade with the Peugeot. Standing by my damaged vehicle outside his house, I told him that my radiator was leaking and asked if he could recommend a mechanic.

'Why go to a mechanic when there's pepper?'

'Pepper?'

He ordered a cup of pepper to be brought from the kitchen, opened the hood of my car, unscrewed the radiator cap, and poured in the spice.

'There! By God, now you can drive all the way to America in this car!'

I drove fifteen hours to Rabat and the radiator never leaked. At that time Mahmud seemed to me a spirited man who hoped to make something of himself. Feeling pity mixed with pain, I perceived him differently now.

Noureddine, shaved and dressed in a fresh white

shirt, arrived at Mahmud's with the mule, and we began loading up. A dust storm still howled through the valley, obscuring the mountains in brown haze and turning the palms into ghosts of thrashing green. As tense as things had been between Noureddine and me during our last days together, I felt relieved to see him now. Mahmud stared at us, sucking on his cigarette, saying nothing.

After he had yanked the last ropes taut and squeezed a final hoarse gasp out of the mule, Noureddine ordered Bashar to hold the reins and asked me to come inside Mahmud's house. The marabout was rolling up his prayer rug and the floor beside it was speckled with sputum. I remembered my last departure, and how he had commanded Fuad and me to sit in front of him as he called upon God to grant us safe passage. We had both kissed his proffered hands afterwards – I now felt disgust at having done so. I had not believed in his powers, of course, but I went along with the tradition out of respect. But *what* deserved respect?

I suddenly resented Noureddine: surely he would kiss the hands, and expect me to do the same.

'Sit!' the marabout commanded us, himself settling on to some cushions.

I hesitated, but Noureddine took a seat in front of him and nodded to me to do so too, so I did. The marabout opened his hands in a supplicatory gesture and looked heavenward. Noureddine did the same.

The marabout addressed me. '*Allah yiftah 'alayk* . . . In the name of God and Sidi Nasir and all the *awliya'*! There is no power and no strength except in God! May God grant you reception wherever you go! May God ease your passage and smooth your path! May God grant you health and success in your journey! *Amin!*'

He repeated the invocation for Noureddine. After a moment of silence, he extended his hands and closed his eyes. Noureddine and I stood up, leaving his hands outstretched. The marabout opened his eyes and looked at us with something between shock and surprise. I thanked him for his hospitality, but he made no reply. He lowered his hands.

'Please give him a little *bàraka*,' Noureddine whispered, using the word in its monetary sense. I handed the marabout a hundred dirhams. He slipped them into his djellaba and turned away.

We walked out to the alley to where Mahmud was sulking. I gave him some dirhams, which he pocketed without a word. We shook hands and he disappeared into his house. Noureddine prodded the mule and we set out into the gritty wind.

The sandstorm died that evening. Three hours later, under a darkening but cloudless sky of violet inlaid with a pearly crescent moon, Noureddine and I set up camp beneath the ramparts of the ruined casbah of Tinsouline, in the Tinsouline Oasis. I felt ill, and remembered the dates, the flies. Our campsite, however, was pleasant, secluded by a tall but crumbling clay wall.

After we had finished erecting the tents, we sat down and Noureddine kindled a fire to make tea.

'I didn't want to kiss the marabout's hand,' I said.

'And you shouldn't have.' He looked up from the tinder as it glowed and caught fire. 'Marabouts are . . . it's *shirk* to believe in them, *shirk*.' The one unpardonable sin in Islam is *shirk*, or polytheism, associating another being with God. 'In Islam no man may raise himself above another man, no man may claim to be closer to God than another man – that's *shirk*. God is most high, higher than any man. Even imams are not closer to God than others – they're not like your priests. An imam is just a man.'

'But you accepted the marabout's blessing. You even asked me to sit for it.'

'I did that out of respect for his age and because you'd been his guest. But I did not kiss his hand. That I would never do. Belief in marabouts is heresy. What gives him the right to bless anyone? Nothing. You and I and he are all made by the same God on high. God doesn't need a marabout to perform His work. Those who give the marabout money for *baraka* are deluded, they are ignorant.' He began slicing cucumbers for a salad. 'You see, as I told you, our government wants people ignorant, it needs people to believe in marabouts because the marabouts tell them to believe in the king, who is supposed to be Commander of the Faithful. But I tell you, no one in Morocco or in any other Arab country has the right to say he's closer to God or higher than any other man. The Commander of the Faithful is God Himself. We're all equal before God, *all* of us.'

Without knowing so, Noureddine was explaining tenets of a Muslim sect that first troubled the Alaouite Dynasty in 1811. Then, King Saud of the Arabian Peninsula called upon leaders around the Arab world to adopt Wahhabism, the austere brand of Islam gaining adherents among his Bedouin tribes. The precursor of modern-day Islamic fundamentalism, Wahhabism held, among other things, that veneration of sharifs and marabouts was *shirk*, that the Sufis were heretics and that the Qur'an must be understood as the literal truth. Wahhabism came to dominate Saudi Arabia, but it did not take hold in Morocco. Nevertheless, its puritanical principles eventually reappeared in other Moroccan fundamentalist movements, first in the Western Sahara during the French era, and then, following independence, among students and the urban unemployed. Although Moroccan fundamentalists have eschewed violence, the ongoing conflict between fundamentalists and the government in neighbouring Algeria provides the king in Rabat with ample reason for concern. Today, fundamentalism is regarded as the main threat to his rule. For most of its practitioners, however, fundamentalist Islam promises an antidote to corruption, poverty and despair; it is an affirmation of Muslim identity untainted by Western influence.

Noureddine may have been a fundamentalist but he was not a fanatic. He wanted a just and true life, and he practised Islam to achieve this end. His thoughts, at least as expressed to me, went no farther than that; they did not include overthrowing the government or calling for holy war against infidels. But fundamentalist doctrines, whether Christian or Islamic, *could* lead to exactly such extremes. Perhaps only fear of the government kept him and others like him moderate.

Faith ordered his life. He worked hard to provide for his family, and he did not complain. He observed Islamic prohibitions and did not drink, smoke or gamble. He was respected in his village. He spoke his mind – something rare in Morocco. Most important, he sought the truth, which he saw as something to be arrived at through study, and for him this meant studying the Qur'an. If I did not necessarily agree with his methods, I concurred in his goal. Moreover, as a guide he was complaisant, reliable and honest. If he could weary me with his endless religious exhortations, he had my well-being at heart. This I would accept from now on.

Beneath the casbah and the drooping palms and the moon there was a soothing silence, a pervasive peace. We chatted by the fire, the tension between us having given way to a shared repugnance for marabouts, *shirk* and phoney *baraka*. We dined on a salad of cucumbers and tomatoes, spiced with red pepper Noureddine had bought in Mahmud's village, and then said goodnight.

As I crawled into my tent, I felt weak and feverish. An hour after dark a wind picked up, bringing not dust but fresh, cool air; it soon threatened to blow away the roof of my tent, so I took the roof off, which left me free to watch the moon and the stars through the gauze of the tent's inner wall. The wind cooled my burning forehead.

Soon after, Noureddine began his nighttime prayers. Here in the moonlight, half delirious and listening to him chant the Qur'an, I remembered other places where I had heard the same suras. They had rung out over the red clay warrens of Kano, across the Sahara in Nigeria. They had drifted through the lonely rock villages of the Pomaks in the Rhodope Mountains of Thrace, in northern Greece; they had floated over the lunar steppes of Turkish Anatolia, in Erzurum and Sivas. They had sounded in the Silk Road city of Kashgar in Xinjiang, and echoed from the sandstone walls of the Red Fort in

Old Delhi. In all these places and more Muslims prayed, repeating the same verses in the same language; in every Muslim land an identical call to prayer issued from minarets five times a day. Shiite and Sunni sectarian differences aside, uniformity of faith, tongue, ritual and litany created the *Umma* – the Islamic nation, a community of believers who are all equal before God, if divided by national borders. With the *Umma* behind him, Noureddine believed he could face any tragedy, bear any burden. When one of his sons died recently, he told me, he did not cry, but accepted the death as the will of God. 'God gave my son to me, and God took him away. We say there are "some children that belong to God, and to God they return". Praise be to God!'

I once wished for a feeling of community so strong, a faith so comforting. But, for me, religion was elective, and I managed to get along without it. For Noureddine, Islam, like the sky, overarched the earth on which he stood, and he could not imagine the world without it.

To my surprise, however, he ceased preaching to me after we left Mahmud's. Perhaps he understood it was no use, or maybe he felt my distaste for marabouts owed itself to his teaching and was victory enough. I would like to think that he, for the first time, accepted me for who I was.

The next day, as we trekked toward the black iron anvil of Jbel Zagora, with Zagora town spreading beneath it, the oasis broadened into a sea of palms, and Jbel Kissane wound away to the east. The soil turned from fertile loam to dry gravel; in the evening the shaving cream dried on my face before I could apply the razor. The Sahara. Humidity hovered in the teens; although we walked hard in the sun, I did not sweat, and my lips grew chapped. I made myself drink water throughout the day, though I wasn't thirsty; walking in the desert, one can sweat four gallons a day without realising it. The sweat evaporates too quickly to be noticed.

'This is no longer my land,' said Noureddine as we entered Zagora, tired by the heat and sun, 'and the mule, pardon me, doesn't feel at home here. This is the desert, the land of the camel and the Ruhhal.'

BLOOD IN ZAGORA

'My son, I see in a dream
That I shall sacrifice thee; consider
     what thinkest thou?' . . .
'My father, do as thou art
bidden; thou shalt find me, God willing,
     one of the steadfast.'

The Qur'an, Sura of the Rangers

A GRAVEL STREET in Zagora, sun-drenched and rutted. The reek of sewage and exhaust fumes sours the sultry air; the rattle of carts and the braying of donkeys resound from dirt valleys. A weatherbeaten sign depicts a camel and a nomad in a faded indigo turban, above which is the legend 'Timbuktu – 52 Days'. Beyond the sign stretch cement *qaysariyas* painted reddish pink to resemble adobe; in front of the shops are cafés with Coca-Cola logos hand-painted in Arabic. There are youths loitering by the cafés, pimpled and gangly in indigo-coloured nylon robes, their curly hair stuffed under indigo-coloured nylon turbans. Digging match-sticks into the plaque mottling their teeth, they scan the street and wait.

At the corner appears a young blond tourist in shorts

and Tevas sandals, with permed hair and a blond soul
patch on his chin. Two of the youths, their robes trailing,
step away from the café and lope out along beside him,
one on each side. The tourist quickens his step, but one of
the youths grabs his left arm.

'Halloo! *Oostralee? Français? 'méricain? Ça va?*' When
the French elicits no response he mixes in the English he
knows. 'I am *homme bleu*. You spend night in my *tente?*'

The other youth shouts to his rival, '*Din ummuk!* [God
curse your mother's religion!]' and grabs the European's
right arm. 'Not to listen!' he tells him. 'This boy thief,
voleur, big thief. *I* am real *homme bleu* from desert, *vrai-
ment*. This boy city boy. See photos?' He whips out a
plastic-sheeted album of yellowed pictures showing
dunes, camels, Bedouin tents.

The first youth shoves the album aside. '*Sir tqawwid
inta!* [Fuck off, you!] This boy *con*. He been in police
station for *narcotiques*. Me, *I* child of sands *enfant de sable*
like in Ben Jalloun book.'

'No I not *con*. This boy *zamal* [fag]. He lie, he a
pédéraste going fucky-fuck with men for money. I have
camel outside town. I make you good price, only for you
this price only today. How much you pay to see *tente* and
camel and—'

'*Tbun ummuk!* [Your mother's cunt!]'

'*Tbun ummuk, inta!*'

The youths fall to scuffling, the album tumbles into the
dust, toes flex and sandal straps strain, store-bought
djellabas rend to reveal jeans and T-shirts. The tourist
hurries on. But at the next corner: '*Ça va? Oostralee?
Français? 'méricain?*'

In Zagora, a drab, mostly French-built administrative

centre, there are no 'Blue Men', as Tuaregs are widely known, owing to the indigo dye with which they colour their robes and which rubs off on their skin. (The Tuaregs are nomadic Berbers dwelling mostly in the Sahel.) But there is little work in town, so a great many youths pose as Tuaregs to entice Nasranis out to Ruhhal tents on the edge of town, where they ply them with tea, offer them hashish and extract from them exorbitant sums for rides on tick-covered camels. Other *guides* shove their prey into shops off the main road and pressure them into buying shoddy carpets or synthetic nomad attire.

The Nasrani feels beleaguered, harassed and threatened by the onslaught of *faux guides* in Zagora (and other Moroccan towns). Most of all he feels exploited, both as a source of income and as a target for the release of undeserved and at times fierce hostility. But the Nasrani might be relieved to learn that, in the not so distant past, his lot would have been far worse. For hundreds of years before the French and Spanish took over in 1912, Morocco kept itself closed to Europe, fearing 'infidel contamination'. Moroccan pirates frequently attacked European ships, seizing their goods and taking their crews into captivity. This was as much a form of *jihad* against unbelievers as it was business for state coffers: the sultan took most of the loot and often ransomed captives back to their governments.

But victims and aggressors switched roles in modern times. By the nineteenth century Europeans – the British, French, Portuguese and Spanish – were penetrating Morocco, exploiting it economically, preparing it for colonisation. They flooded the country with their goods, putting local artisans out of business, creating demand for products (beds, matches, metal tools) that only Europe produced at the time. They granted sultans loans they couldn't repay and pressured them into making concessions that included protected status for resident Europeans and monopolies over Moroccan trade. They encouraged Europeans to move to the country in large numbers. To live separately from Moroccans, Europeans built entire *ville nouvelle* districts in cities, but they also settled in the countryside, much to the shock of religiously conservative locals, most of whom had never seen a Christian before. Outside the *villes nouvelles*, Morocco at this time was much as it had been in the Middle Ages, a land of clans and tribes, marabouts and sharifs, where city gates closed at dusk, and where there were no roads, hospitals or telegraph lines.

The sultans began visiting Europe and grew aware of the need for modernisation. The Europeans were eager to help out, with the result that Morocco ceded them control of its finances, customs and police, and became dependent on European grain imports. Humiliations and absurdities mounted. At the insistence of European counsellors, Sultan Moulay Abdul Aziz issued new silver rials, but most of these were smuggled abroad by European merchants. The sultan abolished tax exemptions for marabouts, but squandered meagre state revenues on automobiles for himself (the country had no highways), crowns (sultans wore no crowns), wild animals for his private zoo, theatrical costumes and assorted other fatuities, including a bicycle which he and his wives spent days riding around his courtyard.

With each passing year of European 'assistance', the

Moroccan people grew poorer and more desperate. Eventually the sultan's own troops and various tribes from the interior revolted against him and slaughtered European settlers. In 1912 France and Spain, outraged, insisted that the sultan sign the Treaty of Fez, which turned Morocco into a 'protectorate', the stated aims of which were modernising the country and preserving its traditions. To promote these fictions, the sultan was retained as a figurehead. Most of the country, including the Drâa Valley, went to the French; the Spanish got the Western Sahara and two exclaves on the northern coast.

European settlers prospered to the Moroccans' detriment. In time their number would jump fourfold to 325,000, and, as before, they received the highest-paying jobs and the best agricultural land; their children studied in schools while those of the Moroccans did not. After thirty-eight years of 'protection' only 15 per cent of Moroccans had received any education at all.

The French, like the Saadi and Alaouite sultans, understood that there were really two Moroccos: the region of fecund plains, abundant mineral deposits and temperate coasts (*Maroc utile*, they called it); and the mountains and desert, lands of tribal warfare and hunger that historically belonged to *bilad al-siba*. It was in *Maroc utile* that French interest and influence were strongest and hostility to foreigners remains the most palpable. For a long time the Ruhhal and villagers of the Land of Dissidence experienced less French interference and consequently emerged from the colonial era more welcoming toward outsiders. Zagora, deep in *bilad al-siba*, is an exception, owing to its size, its French past and the relatively large (for the Drâa) number of tourists who visit it.

I thus had little desire to stay long. Once I'd attended the Feast of the Sacrifice and outfitted myself, I would return to the desert.

After arriving in Zagora Noureddine and I pushed our way through the *faux guides* of the centre to the Ksar Tinsouline hotel. There, we exchanged addresses and promised to write, both feeling pleased to have spent time with the other, both taking satisfaction in having completed a difficult trip.

We said a warm but unsentimental goodbye. Noureddine smiled and shook my hand.

'If God wills,' he said, 'we will meet again.'

'If God wills. Go in safety!'

'May God keep you safe!'

We embraced, and he left me to find oats for his mule and start the return trip to Ouriz.

I ensconced myself in a suite that gave on to a disused pool and an overgrown garden of date palms and orchids. It was a ramshackle room, all in all, but its heavy maroon curtains shut out the sun, the air-conditioner bathed me in cold air, and the king-size bed was soft. After a few days' rest, my feet healed (they had grown bloodied and blistered from two weeks of hiking) and my fever fell. I was ready for the feast, and I was pleased that I would be spending it with Ali's family.

The Feast of the Sacrifice commemorates the willingness of Abraham (Ibrahim in Arabic) to submit to God's will and, on His command, kill his only son Isaac. Symbolising the 'submission' that is Islam's essence, the Feast of the Sacrifice is the most important holiday of the Muslim year. Throughout every neighbourhood in Morocco (and all across the Muslim world) sheep were growing nervous, knives were being sharpened, families were drawing together.

On the day of the feast, across from the Ksar Tinsouline, hundreds of men in white hooded djellabas and a few veiled women poured out of a mosque after the noon prayers and *khutba* that marked the commencement of the festivities. A motorcade of half a dozen polished black Mercedes limousines pulled out of the parking lot, carrying the provincial governor and his aides, who had attended the *khutba*, back to his palace. Ali's brother Mbarek arrived to take me to their home; he told me that Ali had been delayed in Mhamid and would miss the first meal of the feast.

Mbarek wore a baby-blue djellaba that accentuated his pallor and gave him a look befitting the state functionary that he was. We walked down the potholed lanes from the hotel listening to sheep bleating in neighbourhood court-yards. In doorways little boys were brandishing long, shiny knives and laughing and horsing around; at corner spigots women were rinsing spits and washing pots. Near Ali's house one boy pointed a knife at me and shouted, 'What's that Nasrani doing here?'

Ali lived in a yellow concrete row house. That most people living in his neighbourhood (and the rest of Zagora) were former nomads, or the children of nomads, showed in the garbage they carelessly piled up in gutters or in the corners of alleys. An almost Bauhaus starkness characterised block after block of this neighbourhood; nothing was personal, everything recalled the hurried efforts of government architects who had to build a great deal of housing quickly.

Inside Ali's house I still felt half outside, for Saharan

sun poured into the central courtyard, around which yellow-painted rooms were situated. The house was filled with children's shouts and women's shrill laughter.

I greeted Ali's father, a jug-eared elder with a white goatee and the wiry build of a Ruhhal. He was sharpening a foot-long knife on a stone, and cautiously testing its blade on his forefinger. He knew of my plans to descend the Drâa to the Atlantic. 'It was once beautiful to roam the desert – there were sheep and goats and grass. But now, now with the drought . . . Allah, Allah. I don't know what you'll find.' He made one last test of his blade and nodded to Mbarek.

It was time. Mbarek led me back outside, where an anxious crowd of relatives had gathered. Sun bleached the dusty lane. Drums were beating in far-off courtyards; children up and down the alley pounded sticks on plastic buckets; there were ululations and the cries of babies. One of Ali's uncles – muscular, middle-aged Abdullah, who was barefoot and dressed in a pleated white sirwal – now held the knife the elder had sharpened. He looked my way and shouted, '*Yallah!* Bring him on! Bring him on!'

Behind me feet scuffed the gravel, hooves scattered stones, teenagers cheered. Two youths were dragging a hundred-pound, black-and-white sheep by the horns and tail out of the house. It blinked madly, its pink tongue flailed sideways from its tiny mouth, its bleating alternated with pants and gasps.

In one deft move, Abdullah and Mbarek snatched the sheep's hooves out from under him and his back thudded on to the earth. Raising his knife, Abdullah intoned, '*Bismillaharrahmanarrahim!* [In the name of God the

Merciful, the Compassionate!]', pulled back the head to
expose the throat, and then plunged the knife into the
oesophagus, sawed through the trachea and into the cord-
like jugulars. Blood pumped in hot, vivid parabolas,
painting the walls, staining the white dust. The sheep
choked and kicked and gasped. Abdullah and Mbarek
jumped away from the bucking hooves and spurting
blood. Children were laughing and drums were beating;
the women ululated joyfully. The sheep's head now
flopped back on its slashed neck, but its chest was still
rising and falling, blood was still gurgling in its throat,
splattering on the sand. More than anything, the animal
appeared to be choking to death.

The red parabolas diminished and died. Abdullah
tapped the sheep's leg with his blade and the kicking
resumed; spasms wrenched the body; there followed
more choking and blood-bubbles from the throat and a
quivering of the legs. The sun fell on the blood pooling in
the gravel. Up and down the street blood now poured
from the gutters of houses where sheep were being
slaughtered on rooftops. Blood ran in the sewers.

Minutes later another tap of Abdullah's blade confirmed death. He and Mbarek grabbed the hind legs and
pulled them together, wrapped a wire around them, and
hoisted the carcass up on a rod protruding from the concrete wall. Working from the hind legs down to the head,
Abdullah cut into the hide and pulled back the skin,
showing its milky-hued insides; he stripped the skin from
the fatty, butter-yellow flesh; the hide finally bunched up
around the head, as a shirt might catch at the collar. He
drove his knife perpendicularly into the neck and made a
slit down to the belly; Mbarek dowsed the incision with a

bucket of water. Out tumbled the bloated stomach, still attached to the abdomen by lumpy translucent intestines. Abdullah then extracted yard after yard of small intestine. Then, having made a cut where the large intestine began, he poured a kettle of water into the anus and blew into the cut in the large intestine; turds shot out at the rear. That done, he picked up the squishy red-blue lungs and blew into them through the trachea: they inflated in tandem, turning bright pink. He rinsed the innards with a kettle of water and handed them to Mbarek, who packed them into buckets. The two men then lifted the carcass off the rod and took it inside, where they strung it up again and began slicing apart the meat.

Within a half-hour mutton was grilling over coals alongside organs wrapped in fat and skewered on spits. More relatives were arriving, touring the room, shaking hands, pronouncing the ritualised greetings of the feast, and then sitting down on carpets strewn over the cement floor. The women of the house, swathed in the batik, blue, green and yellow milhafas (wraps) of the female 'Arib, waved their henna-patterned hands as they chatted, rotated brochettes over coals, poured glasses of bitter Ruhhal tea and gossiped. Young girls baked circular loaves of bread in the clay oven. The men, Abdullah among them, were now resting, seated on the floor around the walls, their legs drawn up to their chests. But no one was truly at ease: the lusty odour of burning flesh and roasting innards made us glance time and again at the grills.

Abdullah, his hands wet from his post-sacrificial ablutions, looked at me. 'You're going down the Drâa? You're lucky. I remember the grassy slopes and mountains, the easy days of wandering during my Ruhhal life, before I joined the army. I remember . . .'

The first brochettes of meat and liver came off the coals, and saliva squirted in our cheeks.

TO THE QSAR OF NESRATE

IT IS DOUBTLESS no coincidence that the Arabic word for beauty, *jamal* (pronounced with a long second 'a'), shares triconsonantal roots (j–m–l) with the word for camel, *jamal* (pronounced with a short second 'a'), for in the mind of the Ruhhal beauty and the camel are wed. To Ruhhal, camels are the belles of the desert, and their elegantly lashed, mucus-sodden eyes and pouting blubbery lips inspire whispered compliments and poetic accolades. Yet they are more than just pretty faces. In liberating the denizens of Arabia and North Africa from life in oasis towns and making inhabitable the great sand seas surrounding them, camels are nothing less than the progenitors of Ruhhal identity.

Native to the Arabian Peninsula and introduced into North Africa with the Arab invasion that also brought Islam, the single-humped *Camelus dromedarius* can go without drinking for five days in summer and two weeks in winter; in one session at the well it can drink more than twenty gallons. In duress, Ruhhal can shove a stick down its throat and drink the vomited water. Using a sharpened straw, they can sip blood from its jugular; they can wash their hair in its urine. Camels also provide milk, meat, fur, medicine and hide for tents; the combustible nuggets of their bouncy dung serve as fuel. The camel is the Ruhhal's Wal-Mart.

But camels are more than all this. They are gifted, Ruhhal say, with prodigious memories; they must be persuaded to obey and never beaten; they must be allowed to end their lives, which can last thirty years, in dignified retirement. Camels are the currency in which Ruhhal store and compute their wealth, and by which they gauge their social status. Hitti says the Arabic language contains approximately a thousand words describing camels in their various breeds and states of maturity; I counted only ten words in use in the Drâa. Still, among the Ruhhal with whom I travelled, one could no sooner refer to a *ba'ir* (adolescent) as a fully grown *jamal* than one would call snow rain because both are made of water.

On a red, dusty lot beneath Jbel Zagora, Ali introduced me to the pair of camels and their masters who would accompany me fifty miles south to the dunes of 'Irq al-Yahudi. Chief guide Hassan was lanky and greying, chocolate-skinned and stoop-shouldered, with a crotchety air and a smoker's cough. He wore the long white fouqiya and black firwal of the 'Arib; he spoke the Hassaniya Arabic of the Saharawis (the Ruhhal tribes of the Western Sahara, of which the 'Arib are one). When Ali told me that Hassan would be with me not only to 'Irq al-Yahudi but all the way to the Atlantic, I regarded him with some concern: his cough and age hardly boded

well for the traversal of 425 miles of desert, but he was an
'Arib and had grown up on the sands; he had Ali's trust,
and that was good enough for me. (Or so I told myself. In
any case, he had a week in which to prove himself before
we passed the point of no return at 'Irq al-Yahudi.) His
camel, 'Azzi, was a cuddly stallion of impeccable manners; if I stood next to him, he nuzzled me, smearing me
with his gluey snot and bilious spittle. This was not particularly pleasant, but it could be worse: a cantankerous
camel could vomit cud in his master's face, inflict a filthy
bite, or deliver a stamping kick powerful enough to crush
a leg or smash a skull.

The other Ruhhal was a Berber by the name of Zayid.
He wore a tattered taupe djellaba and kept his face veiled
in a sky-blue firwal, which suggested a puzzling modesty; he rarely spoke, and when he did he stuttered, in
marked contrast to most Ruhhal. His camel, an ash-grey
adolescent called Mas'ud, was his alter ego, roaring, hiss-
ing and disobeying commands, bellowing with petulant
rage if we even looked at him.

Mas'ud's ill manners vexed Hassan. 'Clearly you don't
know how to handle your camel,' Hassan told Zayid.
'What sort of Ruhhal are you? No camel of *mine* would
behave that way.'

'He's just a teenager.'

'Teenagers need discipline.'

For Hassan, as for most Ruhhal, a camel's manners
indicated the character of its master. A peevish animal
suggested a weak-willed master and evoked disdain.
Hassan would eventually express his disdain for Zayid by
refusing to use his proper name. At various times during
the trip, in Hassan's parlance, Zayid would become

Ziyad, Zidan, Lahcen, Hussein or Ihsan. Or even '*hadak*' (that one) and, more tellingly, 'that Berber'. As time passed, I came to understand that more than Mas'ud's behaviour was bothering Hassan. Zayid was one of the few remaining Berber Ruhhal in the Drâa, and historically, despite the egalitarian tenets of Islam, there had been bad blood and rivalry between the Arabs and the Berbers.

The Arab–Berber conflict began with the Arab invasion of North Africa in the seventh century. The Berbers embraced Islam, but, as a result of exploitative Arab tax policies, discrimination and slaving raids, they soon raised revolts in the name of their new religion's egalitarian ideals. In the eleventh century the nomadic Sanhaja Berbers of the Western Sahara overthrew the Arab Idrisids and established the pious Almoravid state, the first of three Berber dynasties to rule Morocco. The Berber dynasties, dominated by tribal warlords, could not unite the country or control its rural regions, which remained *bilad al-siba*. In the fifteenth century the Portuguese took advantage of Morocco's disunity and began occupying cities along the Atlantic and Mediterranean coasts. Soon they tried to penetrate the interior. It was left to the Arab Saadis (who claimed to be sharifs – a matter still disputed) of the Drâa to unite Moroccans under the banner of Islam and expel the infidels. Eventually the Saadis would give way to the Alaouite Arabs, sharifs from Tafilalt Oasis, who presided over the colonisation of the country, but emerged as Morocco's rulers when independence came in 1956. During the protectorate era the French exploited the animosity between the two ethnic groups. They enlisted many of the Berbers in their service, turning them into the guardians of their rule. These Berbers fought for France and subdued the Drâa.

Hassan and Zayid returned to loading the camels. On to each animal's back they first tossed a doormat-sized rug that served as a saddle blanket and protected the camels' skin from abrasion. On top of this they placed a mount made of two short wooden planks wrapped in cloth and joined by metal arches; over the mount they draped a pair of twenty-gallon saddlebags connected by leather straps. In their saddlebags the camels would carry two plastic crates of vegetables (carrots, green peppers, tomatoes, cucumbers and onions); one sack each of rice and semolina; several foot-long cones of sugar, to be broken apart with rocks at teatime; small boxes of Chinese tea called Extra Gunpowder; our tiny, blackened Ruhhal teapot and six sticky translucent glasses; an assortment of ancient pots, pans and cutlery; and a battered blue Buta gas tank. On top of all this were lashed our two tents, our personal effects in knapsacks, a pile of striped wool Berber blankets and three foam mattresses. Jerry cans of water were hung in balanced pairs from the sides. They corseted the beast in his load with nylon ropes running around the stomach and over the hump, under the neck and beneath the tail. Anyone wanting to ride the camel would have to sit atop this bulging mass, ahead of the hump and between the saddlebags.

Properly loading a camel involves more than ensuring that things are packed so as not to fall off. Loading is a feat of engineering based on concern for the camel's health and mood; an unbalanced burden can strain his muscles and make him irritable, disobedient or even

lame, and nothing – *nothing* – is more important to the
Ruhhal than the welfare and good humour of their
camels. Hence Hassan and Zayid bickered at length over
which pot, box or tent went in which bag or sack. If this
carrot or that tea kettle were tossed in the wrong sack,
they contended, the animal would falter, the load come
undone, and all would be lost.

After the loading was finished Ali (who would walk
with us this day) and I set out ahead, letting Hassan and
Zayid and their camels take their time behind us. It was a
cool morning; the sun was bright but did not burn; and it
was pleasant to walk and talk under the palms. I told Ali
about my distressing stay at Mahmud's. He was not
surprised.

'The sharifs have lost their privileges in the last ten
years. Before, they didn't even have to pay taxes, and
everyone respected them. Now they're like everybody
else, and they're unhappy about it. But as for the television being always on, the children, the flies, the illiteracy –
that's African life, that's life in our villages and towns. I
could never live long in a town. I always find I need the
peace of the desert, however harsh the land is. And the
people of the desert are calm. The Ruhhal know peace.'

Behind us Mas'ud bellowed and bucked.

'Could you *please* keep your camel quiet?' shouted
Hassan.

Zayid stuttered a response and petted his camel's brow,
murmuring soft words. Mas'ud calmed down.

After lunch beneath a feathery-boughed tamarisk and
a nap in its shade Ali and I allowed Hassan and Zayid to
move on toward the village of Tamegroute, where were
to spend the night, while we took a detour to the qsar of

Timtig. Timtig was divided into sharif and Haratin sections. The minority (Arab) sharifs own the surrounding land and employ the majority (Berber) Haratin as sharecroppers – an arrangement that, I heard, had produced an atmosphere of bitterness and racism. Only religious celebrations were said to unite the two groups.

We found Timtig a tranquil if unremarkable place – a settlement of square adobe houses and wide dirt lanes like so many qsars. When we arrived, most of the Haratin were out working in the oasis fields nearby.

We stopped at a kiosk in a sharif neighbourhood and ordered Cokes. The proprietor, a man in his thirties, brought out stools for us, and sat down to join us. He had a long, horsey face and buck teeth that parted his lips and gave him a constant smirk. It seemed odd to start a conversation by asking someone if he was related to the Prophet, but that's what I did.

'Yes, I'm a sharif,' he said. 'I don't want to leave here, but we sharifs have begun moving out of Timtig and going elsewhere to work.'

'What work do sharifs do?'

'Why, teaching. Teaching is our mission. We're descendants of the Prophet, after all. We have to spread our knowledge of Islam.'

I thought of the marabout – sharifian lineage did not guarantee knowledge. I asked about the origins of Timtig.

'This was originally a Portuguese village. The Portuguese tribe founded it.'

I glanced at Ali, who suggested that Berbers might have been here before the 'Portuguese tribe', since Timtig was clearly a Berber name.

'No, you're wrong,' the proprietor said, his lips spreading to reveal the great length and carious splotches of his teeth. 'The Portuguese came here and built Timtig. Then came the Ruhhal, then the Saadis. The Saadis expelled the Portuguese from Morocco. Then . . .'

He went on at length. His last assertion was the only nugget of truth in a blundering lecture, which lasted an hour and described battles between hordes of cave-dwelling Portuguese barbarians and noble sharifs. (I was never able to account for the origin or the pervasiveness of this myth about the Portuguese.) To illustrate his points, he scratched (wildly inaccurate) ethnic maps of Morocco in the dust. Ali sat back and desisted from making further corrections. Fatigue showed in his face; his education isolated him from his unlettered countrymen. No wonder he preferred the desert to the towns.

After Timtig, Ali left us to head back to Zagora. The three of us walked on, and soon found ourselves entering a wedge of hamada (flat, stony desert) where Jbel Tadrart joined Jbel Bani, and above which stood a rectangular minaret – that of the *zawiya* of Tamegroute. To avoid attracting thieves or bothersome children, we wanted to camp out of sight of Tamegroute village, yet be close enough that a walk there in the morning would take no more than a half-hour. This plan looked tough to arrange given the terrain. But the hamada turned out to be dimpled with depressions and studded with acacias that could conceal a tent, and we found a place to pass the night in privacy.

We unloaded there and set up camp. Zayid hobbled the front legs of the camels with lengths of rope to prevent them wandering far while grazing during the night. But then he began muttering, 'Allah, Allah,' through his firwal, and rummaging in the pockets of his robes.

'What's wrong?' Hassan asked.

'I forgot my chewing t-t-tobacco in Zagora. I . . . I . . . *Allah!*' He turned and started walking toward Tamegroute.

'He's not on our level,' said Hassan, watching him go. 'In Mhamid you'll meet Mbari, who'll be with us from 'Irq al-Yahudi till the Atlantic. Mbari is an 'Arib. But this, this *Berber* . . .'

An hour later Zayid returned with a plastic sachet of tobacco and a bulging right cheek. But only a few minutes passed before more firwal-muffled 'Allah, Allahs' issued from his lips.

'Now what?' asked Hassan.

Zayid masticated and spat tobacco flux on to the sand. 'Allah, Allah! I put my c-c-coins in this bag after buying my tobacco, but it has a hole in it.' He made mincing, timid steps to and fro. 'I've lost twenty dirhams. Allah, Allah!' He spat again. 'I've got to g-g-go retrace my steps.'

He stepped out on to the hamada and followed his footprints back toward Tamegroute. Two hundred yards and half an hour later, he raised his arms toward heaven. 'Praise be to G-G-God!' He stooped and collected something off the sand.

Hassan shook his head and stirred the couscous boiling on the Buta burner.

After dinner we sat around the fire, watching shooting stars, listening to jackals yelp beneath the darkening masses of Bani and Tadrart. Zayid pulled down his firwal and asked Hassan something in Shilha.

'I'm not going to speak Shilha with you,' Hassan answered. 'You have no manners to speak Shilha in front of Si [Mister] Jelal, who can't understand.'

Zayid pulled his firwal back up over his nose. I began pitying him, so I decided to make conversation.

'Where are you from, Zayid?'

'Tagounite. Usually I roam with my g-g-goats and camels as far as Foum Zguid, but the d-d-drought killed all the grass last year. This has been a bad year, too.' His voice quavered. 'I've had to buy them feed from the m-m-market, which is costing me too much m-m-money.'

I took a good look at him. His firwal was unravelling at the edges, his djellaba was in tatters. On a cord around his neck hung the binocular case of the Ruhhal, but it had deteriorated into a pouch of worm-eaten leather, and its buckle was broken. Instead of the usual tyre-rubber sandals of the Ruhhal, he wore stained, laceless sneakers. His socks, which had pictures of Bugs Bunny emblazoned on the calves, had disintegrated at the soles and covered only the tops of his feet. Even by Moroccan standards, he was a poor man. I tried talking to him some more, but he grew so nervous answering me that I gave up. I switched my attention to Hassan and asked him to tell me about himself.

'I'm a military man. I grew up on the sands and roamed between here and Tan-Tan, but then I joined the army and fought in the Western Sahara. Ten years I spent in the army. I quit a few years ago. Now and then I guide tourists around Mhamid on short trips, or I do the odd bit of camel-grazing and goat-herding, things of that nature. Above all I respect truth and hard work. I'm very *nishan* [straight, honest]. I don't like people who bend right and left, whose words don't match their deeds. *Nishan*, that's me, by God.'

There was something didactic in his tone that set me on edge, and his profession of honesty naturally made me suspect the opposite. But it was too early in the trip to draw conclusions.

Falling stars were streaking over the moonlight hamada when the last call to prayer rang out, signalling that it was time to turn in. The call came from the *zawiya* of Tamegroute, which had once been one of the most important centres of Islamic learning in North Africa. After my disappointing experience at al-Qadiriya I felt no desire to talk to Tamegroute's moulay, but it was still a much-frequented centre of healing, so I would not miss visiting it the next day.

'See that palm tree by the gate?' Rachid asked me. 'It's four hundred and fifty years old. From Iraq. My family brought it here when they set up the *zawiya*. We're sharifs.'

Dressed in spotless white robes, Rachid, a caretaker of the Tamegroute *zawiya*, moved with the sort of grace I had imagined a sharif should possess. The *zawiya* his family had founded was said to date from the eleventh century, not the sixteenth, but he told me what he knew: what the elders had told him. In the centre of the *zawiya*'s walled courtyard stood olive and tamarisk trees; a green-tiled mosque occupied the eastern grounds. Beyond the mosque was a *madrassa* and a library that once contained forty thousand volumes, but most of them had been transferred to the National Library in Rabat. The Sufi brotherhood that ran the *zawiya* no longer operates, and the *zawiya*'s political power had waned long ago.

On the concrete sidewalk bordering the walls people were camped out in the shade, boxes and blankets spread about them. These folks had come from all over Morocco in search of cures for their afflictions. Most sat and stared straight ahead, like patients under sedation in a mental institution; others slept curled up under thick wool blankets; a few swept their spots on the pavement or fiddled with their belongings. As long as they lived here, they were fed and sheltered, and their children could attend the *madrassa*. Rachid said I could not talk to them, but he would tell me what he knew of them.

'Each visitor has his own story about how he became sick,' Rachid said, 'but we analyse them all. For the most part, we determine jinn' – spirits – belief in which is widespread all over rural Morocco – 'to be the cause of illness. Jinn have taken them over. It's very serious. Many of these people are so possessed that they can't even pray.'

'What do you do for them?'

'We cure by the will of God.'

'Which means?'

'If God wills it, they'll get cured. Some stay until death. We've had twenty-five people die right here.'

This seemed an odd boast from the caretaker of a healing establishment.

'A lot die during prayer; they prostrate themselves and don't get up. They never even know they've died, and sometimes it takes a while for us to notice, too. Just like Musa [Moses].'

'Musa?'

'You know, Musa: the king who ruled by his staff. He died sitting down, but no one knew till the worms had eaten him from the inside out. One day he just crumbled to dust and his staff fell over.'

'I wasn't aware he died like that. Neither the Bible nor the Qur'an says anything of the sort.'

'That's how he died.'

Next to us was a heavy woman with three noisy children. She rattled her pots and pans; she had cordoned off her space with sheets of cardboard.

Rachid looked at her. 'Take this one. She tried to do magic on her husband, to turn him into her donkey.'

'Her donkey?'

'Her donkey. She tried to make him her "Yes-Madame!-Right-away-Madame!" donkey who would do whatever she said. This is a common problem all over Morocco – women getting into magic they don't understand, and then ruining their husbands with it. Well, that magic turned right around on her and made her crazy. So she had to come here. You've got to be extremely careful to use magic properly, or it can make you fly right off this earth! I've seen it with my own eyes.'

Rachid's matter-of-fact talk of magic was nothing unusual in Morocco, where folk beliefs still coexisted with faith in Islam. I did not dispute it or show surprise.

A middle-aged woman was crossing the courtyard, noisily dragging a bucket on a rope to the well. 'And what's wrong with her?' I asked.

'Her husband divorced her, so she came here with her daughters. He regretted the divorce and came to take her back, but the jinn wouldn't let her leave. It's very upsetting watching the jinn work. They're ruining her life. But God will prevail. Come, let me show you our mosque.'

I rose and followed him, but then I remembered that it was forbidden for non-Muslims to enter mosques in Morocco. I was about to say so when a man stopped us as we neared the door.

'Where are you going?' he demanded.

'It's okay, this Arab's a Muslim,' Rachid said, pointing to me. Nothing appeared further from the truth, I could only think.

'Then let him show me his certificate.'

'That's okay, no problem,' I said, stepping back. 'I don't—'

'He left his certificate on his camel,' Rachid inter- rupted.

'I need to see a certificate. I can't let him pass.'

I apologised for the intrusion and pulled Rachid away. I had seen enough.

If I didn't believe in jinn, the *zawiya* was an asylum for tortured souls with nowhere else to go. It allowed them salubrious escape from the confines of family and com- munity when these became overly restrictive. Certainly staying in the *zawiya* beat living on the street and beg- ging, or turning to theft and prostitution, common vocations for those who have fled home in Morocco as elsewhere. And if death came to seekers of cures within the *zawiya*'s walls, it would be a dignified death under clear skies, next to a comforting mosque. The *zawiya* thus performed a function the state could not, and I was pleased to have seen it.

I thanked Rachid and, giving him a tip, said goodbye and left for our camp. It was noon, and in two hours we were to set out for Nesrate, one of the grandest qsars of the valley.

'Would you *please* shut up your camel?' Hassan shouted to Zayid, who was trying without success to couch Mas'ud. This time, like most times Zayid loaded or unloaded Mas'ud, the camel was bellowing and gurgling, baring his yellow teeth and vomiting his cud. Zayid whispered to him but otherwise did little to calm him. The camel thrashed around, and I couldn't help warning him against being bitten.

'Oh, there's no danger of that. Mas'ud has a good heart. He wouldn't ever bite me. He's the camel I let my children ride. His old owner beat him, that's all. And after all, he's just a teenager.'

Hassan rolled his eyes and turned to 'Azzi. With the gentlest tug of his rein, the animal couched – swiftly, smoothly and in silence.

We were setting up camp on the hamada across from the village of Ben Ali, near where the Drâa narrows to a flume to flow through Anagame Pass (in Jbel Bani) into the oasis of Ktawa. Irritable and worn out, we had spent the day lost in a grove of palms and gold-leafed bushes, searching in vain for a shortcut Zayid 'knew' led to the pass. The dunes made walking tough, and in places palm-frond fences built to slow the progress of advancing sands blocked our path, forcing us to backtrack and take long detours.

As the mountains faded into the dusk we finished unloading and collapsed in our tents, listening to ululations and laughter echoing across the empty hamada from Ben Ali.

Shortly after dawn the next day I suggested to Hassan that he and I take a detour into Ben Ali to buy meat. We arranged to meet Zayid in the pass itself, two hours' hike ahead.

We trudged all over Ben Ali in search of meat, but we discovered that, the feast having just ended, there was none to be bought: butchers would not slaughter animals for sale while people still had their own stocks of lamb at home. This disappointed me, but more disturbing was what I saw of Hassan's manners. When entering Moroccan villages, I had long been accustomed to following certain rituals (greetings, making enquiries about health and family members, accepting glasses of mint tea); only after the ritual ended would I mention, as if offhand, what I needed. Hassan had other ideas. He ignored the invitations villagers proffered us to drink tea ('Our mission is meat, friend, not tea!'); he dealt harshly with begging children ('Beat it, kid!') and quickly dispatched toddlers asking for *un stylo* ('Shame on you! You don't need a pen!').

After he had snapped at a villager who had invited us to his home, I had had enough.

'Hassan, take it easy. We're only in as much of a hurry as we want to be. These are friendly people here, and we—'

'I'm a military man,' he said, 'and we have one mission: meat. Not tea and not visiting. And don't you forget, that Berber Ziyad—'

'Zayid.'

'Whatever his name is, that Berber has our camels.'

We gave up looking for meat. On the way out of the village we came across a kiosk selling Cokes and Tango cookies. I bought some and treated Hassan. He lowered the firwal from his mouth, munched determinedly through two six-packs of cookies and guzzled down his Coke, squinting into the rising sun. When he finished, he tossed the wrappers into the dust, plunked the bottle on the counter, and pulled up his firwal again. We set out to find Zayid for the seven-hour trek to Nesrate.

In the days of dissidence, Arab Ruhhal settled in Nesrate and made local Haratin an offer they couldn't refuse: sharecrop on Ruhhal land or face the fury of desert raiders alone. The Haratin accepted, and the Arabs eventually became the aristocracy of the qsar, which grew and expanded to bring under its control a number of adjacent villages. In its glory Nesrate could raise an army of 1400 soldiers. A customs post manned by hundreds of troops once stood at its gates to extract duty from caravans bringing slaves and gold from Timbuktu. Nesrate was also the site of one of the few counter-attacks launched by Africans from across the Sahara in reprisal for Arab slaving expeditions: two hundred Tuaregs attempted to lay waste to the qsar in 1545.

We camped that evening beyond the palms of Nesrate's oasis, next to a mosquito-filled wadi of low bushes. Nesrate, we quickly learned, exemplified urban sprawl of the adobe hut variety: we no sooner crossed through the portals of one qsar than we were leaving it for another. All the qsars went under the umbrella name of Nesrate, but they were really separate villages with their own names.

The following morning we ended up in the qsar of Ouled Ammar, somewhere north of Nesrate proper. There, Hassan and I found, after much rambling about and knocking on doors, a butcher's shop – a clay store-front with a tile counter, over which hung hunks of beef covered in flies. The flies didn't matter to either of us: we had been meatless for several days and were desperate.

'Meat,' blurted out Hassan to the butcher, an indifferent Haratin in a bloodstained djellaba and soiled turban. 'We want meat . . . and no bones . . . take that finger off the scale . . . cut off that gristle . . . toss in a few innards there . . . give me these guts, not those . . .'

The butcher obeyed, slapping chunks of meat around, flailing at them with his cleaver, slopping guts into piles, and ignoring the swarming flies. We paid and left. With two kilos of meat in hand, we headed to downtown Ouled Ammar – a barren lot where several grand adobe homes converged by a Téléboutique and the Café Sa'ada (Happiness), a kiosk with a blue canvas awning and a few rickety plastic chairs. But this was luxury for us. We ordered Cokes and sat down in the shade.

'What rank were you in the army?'

'Corporal.'

'You liked the army, didn't you?'

'By God, I loved it. The military was for me. Order! Discipline! Spying!'

'Spying?'

'The beautiful thing about Morocco is the spying that goes on, in the army and out. If I see a stranger over there, I go and report him to the sheikh. The sheikh reports to the police chief. The police chief tells the governor. The governor tells the minister. The minister tells the king. And before you know it that stranger is seized, the trouble he's planning is thwarted.'

'What trouble?'

'Strangers here are usually from Algeria. Algeria is not like here. Algeria's a republic.'

'Which means?'

'Living in a republic people become dangerous. Algerians are no good. Our brother Arab countries – we can't trust any of them. Always plotting against us. So we need a police state to keep order. Spies and police, that's what we need.'

Next to us sat a well-coiffed young man in jeans and an Izod shirt. He heard me speaking Arabic and stood up to introduce himself. Before Hassan could tell him to bug off, I invited him to have a seat. His name was Larbi; he laid ceramic tile for a living in Casablanca and had been visiting family in Nesrate for the feast. He asked what I was doing here, and I told him.

'I think tourism is great,' he replied. 'I wish we Arabs had the same curiosity about the world as Nasranis. Look at Arabs when they get money: all they do is spend it on booze and sex. Their heads are empty, they're just animals. The Saudis, the Emiratees, they're donkeys with no culture at all. By the way, what are your traditions concerning meat?'

'Traditions?'

'I mean, do you eat it? I met a German who didn't. It's not in their tradition to eat meat.'

I explained about vegetarianism.

'Well, our Book allows us to eat meat. In America you don't have any traditions, but we have a tradition for everything. I'm not sure this is good.'

After we finished our soft drinks, Larbi walked us back to camp. 'This is a good time to be in Morocco. We have a young king who's doing a lot for the people. He's opening up programmes to fight illiteracy. I've sent my wife to one and now she can read enough at least to know what bus she's taking. Life will be getting easier for us. Mohammed VI will change things for the better.'

Would he? Hassan looked uncomfortable hearing talk of the king: politics was a taboo subject for the decades Hassan II was in power, and he had not adjusted to the more liberal policies of Mohammed VI. Near camp we parted with Larbi, and I wished him well.

When I had passed through Nesrate in 1998 I was impressed by its towering adobe palaces, by the vitality of its markets, and by the comely Berber women who, out of modesty, turned to face the wall when our small caravan passed. But the next day when Hassan and I returned for supplies I could find nothing to like about it. We wandered for hours around dusty lanes among single-storey houses that smelled of dung and cattle piss. We could not locate the palaces; Nesrate was so large and complex that even Hassan lost his way.

It was a hot morning. Soaking in sweat, our skin smeared with dust, we stopped at a flyblown storefront so that Hassan could buy batteries for his flashlight. As soon as he opened his mouth to ask for them a small turbaned Haratin man squatting on the bench next to him began howling. The other men around us laughed; the Haratin appeared to be retarded. He was waving a long barber's razor and scratching his genitals like a monkey, stamping his bare feet in the dust. Every time Hassan opened his mouth, the man would wail and stamp and brandish his razor, and the others would laugh, drowning out his request.

There was a tap on my shoulder. '*Bonjour!*'

I turned around to face a youth with rotten teeth and a head shaven except for upturned curls in the front. He was wearing jeans and a T-shirt with a rock group insignia – a *faux guide*, to be sure. I said hello and turned away.

'*Je ti dee bonjour. Ti me connee pah?*'

'Sorry, but no, I don't know you,' I answered in Arabic.

Frustrated, he turned to Hassan and asked something in Shilha. Hassan shot him a disdainful look and went on trying to place his order with the shopkeeper. Then the *guide* switched to Arabic and tugged my arm. 'Look, I'm Driss. You and Ali spent the night in my house in 1998. Don't you remember?'

I took another look. All at once I did remember him, and much else. In 1998 I was travelling in a two-camel caravan with Ali and Omar, a bow-legged and bearded old 'Arib camelherd who wore a bone-handled dagger on his belt. Driss then lived in a simple Drâa house consisting of a broad courtyard and rooms floored with packed earth. He welcomed us inside and offered us a meal.

We unloaded the camels and gathered around the tagine bowl in the courtyard, using shards of pita bread to scoop up chunks of chicken and rice. After the meal Driss's friends, all unemployed Berber youths, dropped in to visit, greeting each of us with a soft handshake followed by a customary tap on their chests. Driss himself lived off a small herd of goats and sheep that he pastured in uncultivated parts of the surrounding oasis. He was the soul of Drâa hospitality and tradition, and I remembered taking solace from this one youth who hadn't succumbed to the tempting conventions of Western dress.

But now he was a caricature of a *faux guide*. How had he changed, and why? I apologised for not acknowledging him, and shook his hand, trying to convey with a smile my regret at having treated him so abruptly.

'You've changed, Driss.'

'I sure have. I've just come from Merzouga' – dunes popular with tourists in eastern Morocco – 'where I worked at a campsite. I learned the language of the Nasranis there.'

'You mean French?'

'Of course. Now I'm opening up a campsite. I even have a toilet there. You should come visit. *It's cool, man, vreemont!*'

This transformation was pathetic, I first thought, but only poverty and despair could have made him abandon his traditions and sincerity. He had changed because, to make money, or at least to make more money than he had earned with his flocks, he *had* to change.

The retarded Haratin on the bench wailed and stomped his foot, brandishing his razor. More laughter from the shoppers. Driss and I chatted for a few minutes more. When Hassan finally got his batteries we said goodbye.

Hassan stepped over the retarded man, saying, '*Allah yishfeek!* [May God cure you!]' He turned to me. 'He's sick, that man. He's got no tongue.'

'What did Driss say to you in Shilha?'

'I don't know, but I took one look at him and decided I didn't like him. He was not a serious boy. By God, so many boys in Morocco are not serious.'

The next morning we set out under a hot sun, moving south along the hamada at the edge of the oasis. It was now so warm that I could no longer wear more than a T-shirt and light trousers, and I consigned my wool sweater to the bottom of my pack. We walked for an hour or so, but soon I began to feel a pain in the gut and the prickly onset of fever. I knew right away I was going to be extremely sick. I was having trouble keeping up with Hassan and Zayid, and I told them why.

'In al-Blida there's a hospital,' Zayid said. 'They can help you there.'

Hassan and I left Zayid under an acacia and proceeded to al-Blida, a mile or two ahead on the rock plain. At the edge of the village a small, whitewashed, concrete box of a building stood behind a fence on stony ground. The hospital.

Hassan took a look at it. 'Eye ointment!' he exclaimed with exasperation.

'What?'

'Go on in, go on in. That Ziyad!'

'Zayid?'

'Yes, Jawad, I mean Zayid.'

'My name's Jelal.'

'Right. Go on in, Jelal. That Ziyad!'

'You mean Zayid.'

'Eye ointment! *That's* what I mean. You'll see!'

Maybe this was something like 'eyewash', I thought, and teetered away toward the hospital.

At first I thought it had been abandoned. Sand blew in through the open door and had collected in tiny dunes around the cement floor of the waiting room. On the wall an illustrated Arabic-language poster adjured mothers to observe the rules of hygiene when preparing food (wash hands, wash plates with soap and hot water, wash fruits and vegetables before eating them, and so on). A young woman carried a baby out of a side office. She was startled to see me, and with alarm she pulled her black veil over her face and hurried out. Her baby had the loose skin and wan eyes that mean dehydrating diarrhoea, a common cause of infant death in Morocco (and all over the Third World).

The doctor was a clean-shaven young man in a checked shirt and jeans. Without looking up, he asked me to be seated. I started telling him my symptoms. On hearing me speak he looked up. He took out a register and interrupted me.

'Name?'

I told him.

'Nationality?'

I told him this, too.

'Place of birth?'

He noted the information, and then handed me a piece of paper with instructions in French printed on it. He counted out fat white pills from a tall jar and put them in an envelope.

'Take two of these pills a day, according to the instructions, and avoid drinking well-water.'

I looked down at the instructions. They were for birth-control pills.

'Oh, sorry,' he said, looking not sorry at all, 'I meant to give you *this* paper.'

The correct instructions described the administration of Metronidazole – a powerful anti-parasitic drug. I would have prescribed this for myself: it would cure whatever was ailing me. I paid him and left.

Hassan was waiting for me outside.

'What did you expect?' he said, when I told him about my interview. 'This kind of dispensary only gives out eye ointment. That should have been obvious. And of course it was Zidan who told us about it.'

'Zayid.'

'Right.'

It would take a while for the pills to work, so I decided we would rest for the day. On the south side of Nesrate we struck camp in a sandy idyll protected by a row of tamarisks, near a small grove of thirst-quenching yisrif, a bush with pods that squirt water when crushed, for the delectation of our camels. The jackals yelped all night, but we slept soundly.

By the morning the pills had cured me, and I was ready to move on.

ACROSS NARJAM PASS

TWO DAYS AFTER leaving Nesrate, we stood beneath the tall, white minaret of Sidi Salih, shielding our eyes from the sandy gusts of the Tilli, a northern wind, that had been battering us since our arrival the previous afternoon. Sidi Salih is a large village at the edge of the oasis where we had halted to buy cigarettes for Hassan and feed for the camels. Cigarettes we had found; now Zayid had gone to look for a fodder merchant, and Hassan and I were awaiting his return. From Sidi Salih we would cross a narrow offshoot of Jbel Bani via Tizi-Beni-Slimane (Beni Slimane Pass), our destination the dunes of 'Irq al-Yahudi, near the settlement of Mhamid. Beni Slimane would lead us into the open Sahara – a prospect that energised me when I recalled the beauty I had seen there during my last expedition, but unsettled me when I thought of the hardship I would undergo, and recalled how close I came to perishing there in 1996.

The more I got to know Hassan, the more I saw in

him the guide I would need for the difficult journey from
'Irq al-Yahudi to the Atlantic. His passion for efficiency
and his military sense of mission, if now and then vaunted
to irritating excess, set him apart from other Ruhhal and
accorded with my own approach to the expedition.
Though I made allowances for cultural differences, I had
never adopted the lackadaisical attitude toward order, time
and commitment so prevalent in Morocco, and saw no
reason to do so. If we ran into trouble in the weeks ahead,
if one of us fell ill or we lost our way, the Sahara would
show us no mercy, and Hassan's professionalism might
save us.

Zayid returned, saying that he had found no feed for
the camels. Hassan delighted in this news.

'Of course you found no feed. You can't find feed
everywhere in a village like this. I, however, know just the
merchant for good feed at low prices. Four hundred rials
is what we should pay for a sack of dates. Not a centime
more.'

'Then take us to him,' I said.

In an alley near the mosque Hassan introduced us to
his acquaintance – an unwashed teenage fodder merchant who looked as though he'd been gorging on his
wares. His sandals cut into the pale fat on his dirty feet,
his belly made a bulging tent of his yellow djellaba. He
dragged a sack of dates out of his house and listened to
Hassan's laudatory introduction – he was, Hassan said,
the right boy with the right dates, and he was fair in his
dealings.

'Six hundred rials,' the boy replied, unfazed by the
praise.

Hassan looked surprised. 'Oh, come. Please remember

I'm a friend of the family. Four hundred should be the price.'

'Six hundred rials,' he repeated, rubbing his fleshy nose.

Zayid sensed a chance to avenge himself. He scooped up a handful of dates and sniffed them. 'By G-G-God, this is garbage.' He tossed the dates back in the sack. 'These dates aren't even worth four hundred.'

'Six hundred is my price. Take it or leave it.'

Hassan invoked his friendship with the teenager's family and called God to witness that a discount was in order. The boy's face showed no emotion, and he restated his price.

Zayid chose a date, bit into its tip, winced and spat it out. 'My camel shouldn't eat such offal. He's a teenager and needs his vitamins. But we'll give you four hundred and fifty.'

The teen rubbed his nose again and it wobbled like blubber. 'Six hundred rials.'

It was no use – he wouldn't lower his price – so we dismissed the boy and walked back to the camels, which were loaded and standing restless near the mosque. They would have to make do on what they find in the desert before 'Irq al-Yahudi.

I couldn't resist ribbing Hassan. 'So that's the best boy with the lowest prices around here?'

'Oh, it's really his brother who's the best. But anyway, it's all your fault.'

'*My* fault?'

'Of course. He saw you're a Nasrani, and Nasranis are rich. He figured you'd be paying for the sack, so he wouldn't make a deal.'

He was probably right.

We drove our camels out of Sidi Salih toward Jbel Bani and the pass of Beni Slimane. The Tilli had picked up and was ransacking the palms; it shrouded the pass behind a sun-suffused veil of sand. Still, the wind was cool and blowing at our backs, so we enjoyed it. It was so loud that it hindered conversation, throwing each of us back on his own thoughts.

I recalled how we had crossed Ben Slimane three years before. We had found the slopes of the mountain grooved, as if they had been raked into rows by a giant comb.

'*Mijbids*,' Ali had said, pointing to the grooves – pathways worn by people and camels. 'For a thousand years our caravans passed along these *mijbids*, wearing down the earth, making these grooves.' The *mijbids* ran clear up to the pass. Omar, our camelherd, stooped now and then to toss aside a stone, doing his share of the millennial labour.

We reached the pass. The lowering sun flooded the *mijbids* with red and gold. Volcanic mountains peaked above hamada pale with washes of sand in some places, dark with basalt rubble in others, and girded on the west by the oasis of Mhamid. Ali gestured with his staff toward 'Irq al-Yahudi.

'There are the tents.'

'Where?'

The sun set. In the murk subsuming the hamada I could discern nothing but the contours of dunes.

We started down the mountainside, each of us guided by his own groove, each of us lost in thought and soaking up the cool of twilight. The firmament melted from azure to purple to cobalt; the earth seemed to fall from under our feet as we descended; we floated down through the dusk. The world emptied and in the void anything became possible. Ali loped ahead, trailing his firwal, a hooded silhouette under the Milky Way.

That was then. Now, shouting over the Tilli, Hassan told me that we were heading not for Beni Slimane but for Narjam Pass, to the east, a deviation made necessary by our stop in Sidi Salih.

As noon drew near the wind abated and the heat mounted. Beneath the mountain we entered salt flats, whose crumbling ground slowed our progress. This was bad enough, but then we dipped into Wadi Zarri, a valley of bushes exuding the arresting reek of carrion. I was riding 'Azzi, and thought to ask Hassan about what made the bushes stink so when from among them arose clouds of gnats, flies and mosquitoes. They swarmed over us and the camels, and moved along with us. Hassan and Zayid wrapped their firwals around their heads; I had no firwal and swatted and slashed the air and waved my straw hat, nearly tumbling off my mount. Spring in the valley, with its ripening dates, brought a plague of insects.

But the camels suffered the most. Bugs climbed inside their nostrils and sucked their blood, provoking them to a pitiable rage: they jerked their heads, snorted and stomped, and loped ahead to rub their tortured snouts on the backs of Hassan and Zayid. At times the camels rubbed with such vigour that they nearly knocked their masters to the ground. 'God guide you, 'Azzi!' Hassan would say, losing his balance as his camel slammed into his back.

The insects stayed with us even when we began ascending the trail up the empty chasms of reddish-brown rock leading to the pass. As we neared the pass, 'Azzi and Mas'ud were trailing yard-long threads of gooey spittle in the wind; their eyes were dripping tears; their nostrils were smeared with a mash of mucus and dead bugs. It was a heart-rending sight, and we had no way to relieve their suffering. Only when we began climbing the mountain trail did the insects take flight.

At the top of the pass we halted. Below us spread the Sahara, in nearer reaches a hamada of tawny sand littered with shards of black basalt and the rare acacia; farther away, lifeless dunes rippled along the horizon under a sky of burnished metallic glare. Dust devils hissed and spun through the wastes. We started down the mountainside, shielding our eyes from the grit blowing off the trail.

Once we made it down to the hamada we stopped by an acacia for our siesta. By nightfall we would reach 'Irq al-Yahudi, but now it was time to rest and eat, and enjoy the first treat of the desert: *khubz d'rimla* (bread of the sand). In the paltry shade of the tree Zayid built a fire, which he let burn down to a bed of embers. Hassan kneaded dough into a disc a foot and a half across. Zayid then used a stick to scrape aside the embers, which had heated the sand; in the sand he dug a hole with a stick, into which Hassan dropped the dough. They buried the loaf. Twenty minutes later Hassan used the stick to poke gingerly through the sand and test the dough; it had risen. They disinterred it and turned it over, and then reburied it to let it bake for another quarter-hour.

After Hassan had unearthed the loaf, he beat it with the

stick to knock off the sand. We divided it in three and devoured it. Its crust savoured of charcoal, its inside was chewy and rich. It was, I couldn't help thinking, the most delicious bread I had ever eaten.

As we ate, dust devils spun past us, and the camels strayed to graze on the branches of distant acacias, charred and skeletal-looking against the sky's glare. I found myself relishing the dry heat, the sterile land. It was not back in Zagora but at the pass above that the domain of the Ruhhal had truly begun.

MHAMID OF THE GAZELLES

SET AMID DESERT once abounding with gazelles, the village of Mhamid al-Ghizlan ('Mhamid of the Gazelles', or, less poetically, simply Mhamid) has long marked the end of Morocco and the beginning of the Saharan barrens dividing Arab North Africa from Black West Africa. From a distance Mhamid resembles a hodgepodge of crumbling earthen ramparts and tumbledown adobe towers hunkering on the horizon as if flattened by the ferocity of the Saharan sun. From within the eroding cement and clay warrens of its 'new' quarter, built in the 1970s to house Ruhhal coming off the sands, Mhamid resembles a refugee camp, with blowing trash, gangs of ragged children playing in the dirt and clouds of blue smoke drifting from cooking fires. Its old quarter stands on the western bank of the Drâa River, which is dry here, except for brief periods of flooding from the Mansour Eddehbi Dam timed to coincide with the planting season. The old quarter is a shadowy, collapsing mud fortress

that until recently was plagued by tension between its
'Arib and Haratin inhabitants. The Haratin gave the
'Arib a third of their land in return for protection from
the raids of the marauding Ait Habbash Berber nomads.
Eventually, as the danger from the Ait Habbash diminished, the Haratin came to resent the arrangement with
their 'Arib overlords. The border with Algeria is only a
few miles to the south, and in the 1970s fighting in the
Western Sahara touched the village; there is a military
post here. The Arabic spoken in Mhamid is largely
Hassaniya, the Saharawi dialect.

Under a late afternoon sky honey-gold with blowing
dust and the setting sun, Hassan, Zayid and I reached the
dunes of 'Irq al-Yahudi, where Ali's tent is located, just
outside Mhamid. Hassan I would see the next day; to
Zayid I said a brief goodbye. During our week together,
I had never managed to exchange more than a few words
with him; he was more comfortable tending camels than
talking to people. A Land Rover took me the last ten
miles into Mhamid, where I checked into the village inn,
a single-storey, walled-off assemblage of rooms clustered
around a tamarisk-shaded courtyard that was lit by lamps
dangling on cords.

My Drâa excursion of 1998 had ended at the inn, and
I had bizarre, unsettling memories of my first night
there. After checking-in to my room, I had come out to
the courtyard, where men in plush turbans and dara'a,
the abundant sky-blue leisure robes of the 'Arib, were
playing backgammon and sipping mint tea. The
innkeeper, a full-lipped youth named Ihsan, stood in a
faded indigo djellaba, his hair stuffed under a firwal
wound haphazardly around his head. The wind wobbled

the lamps and stirred the tamarisks in gusts that portended the beginning of a sandstorm.

'*Glis!*' Ihsan said. I sat.

I asked what there was to drink. He leaned over my ear
and whispered, 'We have a certain drink here made from
dates. We call it mahya, the *eau-de-vie* of the Sahara.
Would you like some?'

'I thought alcohol wasn't allowed here.'

He glanced at the other tables and again said, raising
his voice, 'I *ask* you, would you like some?' His peremp-
tory tone made me take a good look at him: he seemed
possessed of a malevolent sensuality; he could, I thought,
be a rapist or an opium addict. I was tired and did not feel
inclined to argue.

'Okay. Why not?'

'Oh, it's not so simple as that.' He straightened up and
looked down the bridge of his nose at me. 'It's not so
simple at all. In fact, it's *haram* [forbidden religiously].'

I stared at him, perplexed. He nodded to a waif, who
threw open the gates of the courtyard and took off running into the whirling sand. The night was black outside
the range of the courtyard lamps.

I became aware of a presence behind me: leaning over
my shoulder was a tall man of imperious bearing dressed
in a dara'a. He looked to be in his forties. He resembled
Qaddafi: his face was long and lined; his hair fell around
his cheeks in oily black curls.

'May I sit with you?'

I nodded yes. He seemed to have something to say – he
kept leaning toward me and pulling back – but then he sat
back in silence for a few minutes, listening to the wind.
His name, he eventually told me, was Brahim. As he

spoke, I smelled alcohol on his breath and noticed his eyes were blurry red.

There was an urgent pounding on the gate. Ihsan answered and conferred with three youths standing outside, and then came over to me and whispered in my ear, 'Your *khamr* is here.'

The backgammon players looked up from their game and dropped their eyes on me. *Khamr* (wine) is the word used in the Qur'an for alcohol; it conjured up sin and damnation, and was as *haram* as *haram* could be. Since it was illegal for Moroccans to drink alcohol, it was probably also illegal to bring it on to the grounds of the inn, but for me, a Nasrani guest, it would be permitted, if on the sly.

I went over to the youths to pay. They grabbed my arms, pulled me outside into the blowing sand and led me around the edge of the wall, near where a boy sat on his haunches, shading his eyes. He rose and came toward me. I caught glimpses of the yellowed whites of his eyes, a stubbled chin. From his robes he drew a two-litre plastic Coke bottle sloshing with clear liquid.

'Your mahya!'

I opened the bottle and sniffed. It smelled sweet but potent. I paid him what he asked for – about ten dollars – and returned to the courtyard. Brahim straightened at my table, and the other men looked up from their backgammon again.

I offered Brahim some mahya.

'No, I couldn't, I really couldn't. I drank in the morning, as you might have noticed. Whiskey it was, but, well, okay, why not? . . . Okay, pour me a glass, please.'

The mahya was not nearly as strong as its scent

promised, but it relaxed me. Brahim sipped it, and it loosened his tongue. He mixed French and Arabic. He had passed seventeen years working in northern Europe, where he had enjoyed many women ('*le contact était facile*') and had read the classics of French literature. He had recently returned to Mhamid to watch over his father's business, but, after spending so much time in Europe, what was he to do in a village of Ruhhal? He had no one with whom to share his thoughts about literature here. He sipped his mahya. '*En attendant Godot!*' was how he described his life. '*Hélas!*'

I looked at him and pondered the deprivations of Mhamid, and tried to imagine how I would survive them if I knew I could not escape. Brahim kept talking. He wanted to make a trip to the Middle East by camel to explore his tribe's heritage – the sort of adventure only Westerners would consider undertaking. That he was eager to take such risks for reasons so intangible marked him as a poet and set him apart from Ruhhal, who never travelled unless they had to.

The wind picked up, chiming through the needles of the tamarisks, jostling the hanging lamps. We finished the mahya. Brahim leaned toward me and ears perked up at other tables. His voice turned gravelly. 'You want . . . *wakha* . . . a girl, a . . . a true daughter of the Sahara?'

Ihsan turned and stared at me. The backgammon players froze. A hoarse voice cried out from among them, '*Pour faire le soixante-neuf!*'

'What do you say?' Brahim said. '*C'est bon, le soixante-neuf! Wakha?*'

Would the *soixante-neuf* – sixty-nine – be good? I had visions of a dishevelled hag crawling with lice, of soiled robes opening to reveal a body covered with scabs and cankers; I saw a bony infant squirming in the corner of a grotto-like room; I thought of the gambling tents and whores and free-flowing wine of pre-Islamic Arabia.

Though only Brahim and I had had anything to drink, the presence of *khamr* in the courtyard had unleashed the spirit of licence, a spirit of sin and lust most powerful among the deprived. Deprived these men no doubt were, living in remote Mhamid, where Islamic custom forbade the mixing of the sexes outside marriage and the family. I was being called upon to take the lead in exorcising the spirit. If I agreed to see the 'daughter of the Sahara', they would no doubt follow me back to her room and spy on us.

Brahim looked at me, and then cast a shifty glance to the men at the other table.

'Thank you,' I said, 'but no.'

'But she is fresh from the sands, young, and, oh!, *le soixante-neuf*!'

'Thanks, but I'm tired from the desert.'

The players glared at me. Brahim slumped back in his seat. The wind picked up and hurtled sand through the open gates, and Ihsan rushed to close them. One of the backgammon players – a young man with kohl smeared on his eyelids and the plump cheeks of a debauchee – began leering at me, slitting his eyes and taking long drags on his cigarette.

Brahim leaned forward. 'That man loves . . . he loves . . . men . . . just a little.'

The man blew me a kiss. There was no point in continuing this conversation. It was late and I was looking forward to sleeping in a bed for the first time in weeks. I

About to set out for Tizgui Falls: the author and Ali Daimin.

The village of Insay.

The Berber qsar of Taliouine, near Ouriz.

A farmer tills his plot in an oasis in the Upper Drâa.

Jbel Kissane from the Drâa oasis.

Children in a village of
the Upper Drâa.

The casbah of Ait Hammou Said.

In Zagora, preparing to set out for the desert in 1998: Omar,
the author and Ali Daimin (left to right).

The Drâa in spate near Zagora.

A street in the qsar of Nesrate.

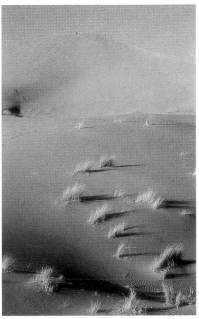

A dune at Shgaga.

Hassan, Ali and Mbari, with our camels just prior to departure
from 'Irq al-Yahudi, near Mhamid, 2001.

A Berber encampment at Oum Laâlague.

Na'im, Mabruk and Hanan (left to right).

Hassan and Mbari cleaning our slaughtered goat beneath an acacia outside Sidi Abd al-Nabi.

Hassan and Mbari skinning the goat.

Crossing Lake Iriki.

A sandstorm tears through the oasis outside Mghimima.

The Drâa emptying into the Atlantic.

excused myself and said goodnight to Brahim. I walked back to my room, with the chime of wind in the tamarisks reminding me of my solitude, of how, after all, I was a stranger here, a Nasrani, and always would be.

All the same, Brahim had struck me as intelligent – too intelligent and well read to be satisfied with life in Mhamid, and his talk of travelling had distinguished him as someone I felt I should at least visit again. I regretted that our evening had gone as it had, and did not hold his drunkenness against him. In this desert village who wouldn't look for escape?

Now I would spend five days resting in Mhamid, and working out final plans for my expedition to the Atlantic. Ali would arrive the next day, so after taking a room at the inn I went out to look for Brahim. The inn owners told me his address: he lived in a single-room house near the wadi.

His door was open, so after knocking I walked in. A fluorescent bulb cast violet light over a bare concrete room; sand covered the floor in patches. There were a few bookshelves and a couple of divans. Brahim, reclining on the divan, appeared to have changed little; he was still craggy-faced and imposing, with the same curls and dara'a robes, but before I walked in he had been hitting the mahya, judging by his eyes and speech. Perhaps because of the booze, he showed no surprise at my unan-nounced appearance, but arose and invited me to have a seat, as if I were a daily visitor. Would I like some mahya? I said that I would.

He walked over to the door and peered outside, and then came back and pulled a bottle out from behind the divan. He poured me a glass and topped off his own; that finished the bottle.

'Things are different now,' he said. 'Finding mahya is hard. It's the fundamentalists, you see. Morocco has gone to hell since Hassan II died. They're closing the bars in the cities to calm the fundamentalists. We shouldn't even speak about mahya any more.' Then, as if regretting having implied criticism of the new king, he added, 'But of course that's the wisest policy. To calm down the fundamentalists.'

'I thought the new king's plans for liberalisation were making people happy?'

'Oh, I mean, if you give people a little they take a lot. That's all I meant. What's happening in Algeria can happen here. Hassan II knew this, and he kept the pressure on the fundamentalists, he kept people down. This was wise. Now there's . . . appeasement . . . *C'est dangereux, hein?*'

Then the mahya took hold and disordered his speech. He wandered from topic to topic for a while, making no sense. Eventually he leaned toward me, his long curls drooping over his eyes.

'We 'Arib are really the Bani Ma'qil of Yemen, you know? We're not what you might call strict Muslims. I don't go to the mosque and pray, you know?' He pulled on his curls. 'This hair, does it remind you of anything? Well, I've never felt Muslim. The Bani Ma'qil' – here he got up and went to the door, and looked to see if anyone might be listening – 'the Bani Ma'qil were really Jews!'

A boy walked in and startled Brahim so violently that he spilled his mahya all over his dara'a.

'You should knock, stupid kid!'

The boy was unfazed. He also had thick curls and fleshy lips; perhaps he was a relative of Brahim. He whispered something, and Brahim turned to me.

'Please give the boy two hundred dirhams for mahya.'

I gave it to him, and the two walked out. I looked at the books on his shelves. I picked up Le Clézio, whom I had long wanted to read: he had spent most of his life in Mauritania, and wrote novels about nomads.

Brahim returned. 'We were the tribe that conquered this region. Everyone here worked for us. We were rulers, great desert raiders, we fought battles and ruled the sands. It's still my dream to travel by camel across North Africa, once I get my money. My dream, you see. I'll take my inheritance and make this journey, travel the way my ancestors came.'

'Once you get your money?'

'I'm having a difficulty with my estate. Moroccans are liars and cheats who only think of money. They have no culture and understand nothing. They do ill even to their own family.'

It grew late and the mahya never arrived. Before I left, Brahim handed me Le Clézio's *Désert*. 'Please read it and think of me.'

I headed back to the inn, book in hand.

'*C'était à ce moment-là que la lumière était belle sur la Saguiet el Hamra. Elle venait à la fois du ciel et de la terre, lumière d'or et du cuivre* [It was then that the light was beautiful over Saguiet el Hamra. It came both from the sky and the earth, a light of gold and of copper] . . .'

The next morning I was drifting into the first lines of *Désert*, letting the rhythms of Le Clézio's prose lull me into reverie as might the lolling gait of a camel. I was leaning back on embroidered cushions in the inn's high-ceilinged lobby; here and there squat palmwood tables supported silver tea services and stainless-steel bowls full of dates. Brahim was drinking tea beside me, now sober and calm.

A brown hand snatched the book from my grasp.

'Who gave you this?' In front of me stood Ihsan, who had only minutes before greeted me warmly.

'Brahim.'

'He has no right to give you my books. My books are more precious to me than money!' Stuffing Le Clézio in his jeans pocket (he had abandoned Ruhhal dress for Western garb), he walked over to a table of Nasrani tourists and smiled, placing his hands on the shoulders of the French woman.

'*Attention, hein!*' said her husband. The tourists laughed. Ihsan kept his hands on her shoulders and mas-saged them until she squirmed away.

Brahim leaned over to me. 'Please, be careful not to anger Ihsan. You see,' he looked both ways and whis-pered, 'he studied with the crown prince.'

'The crown prince? You mean the new king?'

'Shshsh! That's right. If Ihsan has a grievance against someone he can go straight to the top. He treats everyone here like slaves because of his connections. They fear . . . you know who.'

Ihsan was making play advances to another female tourist, and there followed another outburst of laughter from those around the table. I reflected on how if some-one had massaged his wife (if he had one), he would be honour-bound to challenge the man, and things could get bloody. Yet with Nasrani women he took liberties. They were, to him, little better than whores who went around naked. Yet the tourists failed to perceive the insult. To them it was all a joke.

Looking at Brahim, now twitching and nervous and glancing at Ihsan, I sensed that little was what it seemed here. Deceit was the norm, nothing was certain. One's fate could depend on the favour and whims of those higher up. The king is no figurehead but the absolute monarch of a country many regions of which once belonged to *bilad al-siba*. To stay in power, he had to be ruthless with his enemies, whether actual or potential.

Brahim turned to me. 'What are you doing in Moscow?'

'I'm a writer.'

'And how are the secret services in Russia?'

'I have no idea. I have nothing to do with them.'

He kept his eyes on mine. 'Oh, really? And how is it an American in Russia has nothing to do with the secret services? How is it that this American is here, on our border with Algeria?'

I yearned for the Sahara.

'There are 'Abid who've told me, "You brought us across the Sahara in chains and sold us like goats in your markets!" They're right, that's what the 'Arib did. That is history.'

Hassan and I stood in front of the ruined casbah of Ouled Mhaya, in the desert a few kilometres east of Mhamid. Dunes were encroaching upon the casbah, rising up its walls. From the sixteenth century until the French came this was a bustling slave market.

Hassan went on. 'The French wouldn't take the 'Abid into the army. The Arabs and Berbers they took, the 'Abid, no. They told the 'Abid, "You have no skill with weapons. Your place is in the oasis, farming." Many 'Abid were slaves through the days of the French, but stayed with their masters after Mohammed V freed them, having nowhere else to go. Some still call us "master" out of respect.'

The 'Abid's history goes back more than four hundred years, to the first decades of the Saadi Dynasty. In 1590, seeking gold, slaves and salt, Moroccan troops, mostly Ruhhal led by the Bani Ma'qil, but also Christian renegades who formed their own division (the Infidel Brigade), left the Drâa, crossed the Sahara and conquered Timbuktu, taking many prisoners. From there they marched their captives north to Morocco in large numbers. These Africans and those who followed them eventually became known as the 'Abid. As a result of this conquest and the wealth it brought, Saadi state coffers swelled and the Drâa knew one of its most prosperous periods.

But it would not last. In the seventeenth century, after Saadi rule ended, Morocco's tribal principalities began fighting each other, and the country slipped into anarchy. With this disorder the caravan routes fell into disuse, and their decline diminished the supply of gold to Morocco, weakening its economy. Sanhaja Berbers tried to impose their rule, but failed, lacking the sharifian status necessary to unite the tribes. Around that time Europeans began establishing trading outposts on the coast of West Africa, which presaged the rise of sea transport and the further isolation of Morocco.

In 1666 from the Tafilalt oasis to the east of the Drâa

emerged a new religious dynasty – that of the Alaouite sharifs. The Alaouites won legitimacy among Moroccans by promoting themselves as the defenders of Islam, and rose to power using an army of 'Abid. They managed to revive the caravan routes somewhat, and they annexed Mauritania and the Western Sahara. Much of the country, including the Drâa, remained *bilad al-siba*, but the Alaouites controlled the wealthiest lands, and even dissident tribal leaders recognised their religious (if not their temporal) authority. But by the eighteenth century the 'Abid were taking advantage of their masters' dependence on them, and they began dictating policies, making and breaking sultans, leading Morocco into the era of anarchy, famine and banditry that ended with colonial occupation. Descendants of the 'Abid now speak either Arabic or Berber, depending on who their former masters were.

Hassan didn't know exactly when the last slaves were auctioned off in Ouled Mhaya, but the casbah must have been abandoned decades ago, at the latest: sand had risen partly to block its entrance, and we had to crouch to enter. Inside, beetles scattered at my feet; there was a flurry of beating bat wings. We followed a hallway to the courtyard, where little was left except crossbeams affixed at eye-level.

'They chained the slaves here,' Hassan said, 'to these beams. And up there, on the first floor, the buyers would gather. They made quite a feast of it, eating and laughing and looking over the slaves. Sidi Mohammed, the marabout who ruled this casbah, always had much food and drink for his customers. If they liked a slave, they would come down here and inspect him.'

We walked toward a crumbling stairway. 'Careful,' said Hassan. 'These stairs could collapse.'

Taking timid steps, we climbed the stairs and emerged on to the first floor. We could go no farther than the stairway, for the floor a few feet away looked ready to fall in. Through the gaping holes in the walls, the glare and limitless expanses of the Sahara intruded, reminding us of what the slaves had suffered to get here. The caravans that brought them travelled all year, by day in winter, by night in summer, when they navigated by the stars. Shackled, marched barefoot over searing sands, a third or more of the slaves died en route of thirst, sunstroke or fatigue; if a caravan overshot a well, all could be lost, slaves and Ruhhal alike. The crossing from Timbuktu to the Drâa must have been as horrific as the Middle Passage, and I thought of the sufferings of the first Africans being shipped to the Americas.

After leaving the casbah we headed back toward Mhamid, stopping in a village called Znaga, where Hassan wanted to say hello to 'Abid friends. We stopped at what looked like a stone and adobe cattle pen. From the doorway he shouted, 'Is Ahmed home?'

A feeble female voice answered, '*Ma kainsh. Shkoon?* [He's out. Who's there?]'

'Hassan.'

'*Dkhul, ya Hassan!*'

We entered. The pen was a home. An old black woman sat on the earthen floor tending a Buta gas burner, making tea, covering her eyes with a threadbare veil. Her teenage daughter, gaunt, wearing mud-caked rags, lay next to her. The family shared the room, which was open on one side, with goats; there was a stench of scat. Hassan and the woman exchanged greetings, and told each other news about family members. Flies buzzed loudly around the excrement.

'Oh, oh, my eyes are hurting me, my eyes are going.' She clutched the veil to her eyes; we couldn't see them. 'It's the will of God.'

'May God cure you,' said Hassan, after enquiring when Ahmed was to return. She didn't know. We left them after another ritual exchange of farewell wishes.

'Most 'Abid are still suffering,' Hassan said as we approached the fort at the edge of Mhamid. 'It's sad, isn't it?'

Near the fort, a bald old 'Abid in rags was examining piles of human excrement on the ground and commenting on them. He wandered along and, between piles, greeted imaginary people with boisterous laughter, pantomimed handshakes and bows, and then said elaborate goodbyes.

He approached Hassan shaking his finger. '*Haram 'alayk!* [Shame on you!] Three of my daughters were just out with three of your sons. By God, that's the truth. *Haram 'alayk!*'

Hassan smiled at him, and the 'Abid walked on, talking merrily to himself.

'He's a lunatic,' Hassan said with a shrug. 'The poor 'Abid, the poor 'Abid. God has given them much to endure.'

THE DANGERS AHEAD

IN ONE OF Paul Bowles's short stories, a Moroccan Ruhhal, high on hashish in the desert, slices off a man's penis, cuts open his belly and stuffs the severed organ inside, and sodomises him. On awakening from his stupor the next morning, he slits his victim's throat with a razor. In another story Bowles introduces the Reguibat nomads, who are 'rich with loot from Río de Oro and Mauritania', and who are, according to local sayings, '"a cloud across the face of the sun . . . When the Reguibat appears the righteous man turns away."' To Reguibat territory Bowles dispatches his protagonist, a naïve foreign linguist interested in studying Arabic dialects. In the desert the linguist encounters the nomads, who set dogs on him, beat him, cut out his tongue, wrap him in a tin-can suit of mail, toss him in a sack and abscond with him across the Sahara. Now and then they let him out of his sack to dance and jingle for their amusement.

Bowles wrote mostly fiction, of course, but having

spent much of his life in Tangier and the Sahara, he knew
Morocco as well as any outsider ever could; to those who
have lived in Morocco, his fiction rings true. Unavoidably,
as I rested in Mhamid and contemplated the next leg of
my expedition, which would put me at the mercy of my
Ruhhal guides for weeks on end in parts of the Drâa I had
never seen before, events and images from his stories came
to mind, and I found myself experiencing nagging and, as
I kept telling myself, irrational fears. Could these stories
have been based on fact? I had no desire to dance and
jingle for anyone's amusement, and I wanted to complete
my journey with my tongue and other organs still
attached.

The afternoon before we were supposed to depart,
Hassan showed up at the inn with a diminutive, smiling
fellow in blue robes and a firwal. This was Mbari, my
second guide. We shook hands and walked over to a
nearby café to have a soft drink and chat. I asked him
how he happened to know the route to Tan-Tan.

'I grew up between here and Tan-Tan, roaming the
sands with camel herds. And I know the desert from here
all the way to Smara. I used to lead herds there, too.'

'Smara? That's Reguibat territory. Ever meet a
Reguibat?'

'I lived with the Reguibat. They're a manly tribe.'

'Of course, all those stories about their ferocity are
just . . . stories.'

'I wouldn't say that. We Ruhhal were warriors, after
all.'

I pondered this declaration, and remembered that
Bowles had drawn on rich historical tradition in creating
his Ruhhal villains. Since biblical days Ruhhal had been

widely known for their ferocity, martial prowess and a penchant for treachery. Even the Qur'an weighed in on the Ruhhal, calling them 'stubborn in unbelief and hypocrisy, and apter not to know the bounds of what God has sent down on His Messenger'. The desert raid, the *ghazw*, was the glory of the Ruhhal; the title of *ghazi* (one who excelled in the *ghazw*) the honorific of pre-eminent distinction.

Still, as far as I knew, their raiding days had ended with the French pacification of the region. Furthermore, I had enjoyed a friendship with Ali for the past five years and trusted him with my life; over the previous couple of weeks I had got to know Hassan well enough to trust him; and Hassan's praise for Mbari, plus Mbari's own gentle demeanour, convinced me that any concerns I had about the Reguibat and Bowles's stories were irrational, the product of nerves.

But ahead for me, starting west of the dunes of Shgaga, was unfamiliar desert and I was apprehensive, if not out-right afraid, of the land itself. From Mhamid 375 miles to the Atlantic the Drâa was said little to resemble the valley I had just descended from Tizgui. Gone would be the comforting presence of other people, the abundance of oases and farms, the shelter of casbahs and qsars. This part of the Drâa, which skirts the base of Jbel Bani and the Anti-Atlas, lies exposed to the heat and winds of the open Sahara, of which the basalt-strewn furnace of the Drâa hamada forms the nearest reaches. Mbari told me that he had only recently settled in Mhamid, and not will-ingly: the drought that had begun in 1997 had forced him and his family off the sands. That he had so recently left the desert comforted me; that drought had been the cause of his move reminded me of how lethal the desert could be, and I recalled the fifty-degree heat and searing Shirgi wind that nearly took my life in 1996.

We discussed one other unsettling matter: the war in the nearby Western Sahara. From Foum el-Hisn to the Atlantic, the Drâa runs close to the frontier with the long-embattled province. Just before I arrived in the Drâa, the leaders of the Polisario, angry over what they called Moroccan stalling tactics designed to thwart the holding of a referendum on independence stipulated by the truce of 1991, had threatened to resume hostilities. They had made similar threats in the past but had not acted on them; nevertheless, we couldn't entirely discount the possibility that rebels might be operating in the area. There was also a risk of running into landmines laid along the border. Moreover, the Moroccan military might assume an American wandering around down there was a spy or a Polisario agent. (Foreigners rarely ventured farther west than Shgaga.)

Mbari and Hassan confirmed that a restricted military zone lay between the outposts of Akka and Assa. They would try to think of a way to cross it. In other places along our route, where the Drâa was the border with Algeria, soldiers might be trigger-happy from clashes with Algerian smugglers. Ali had informed the Royal Gendarmerie in Mhamid of my trip and they had voiced no objection, but none of us knew how soldiers would react if we surprised them during a patrol. There appeared to be no way to address any of these possible dangers, except by putting my trust in Ruhhal who knew the desert, and keeping myself healthy enough to withstand the rigours of the land and climate.

Tomorrow we would set out.

'If God wills,' Hassan said, as we prepared to part for the evening, 'we'll reach the ocean after forty days.'

Forty days, Mbari echoed him – if God willed.

We said goodbye. I tried to imagine the cool Atlantic breezes on my face, and went back to the inn to rest. It was already mid-March, and the heat was building.

DRY WELLS

FROM BEYOND THE looming volcanic peaks of Beni Slimane a gritty wind howled down upon us, lashing ragged skeins of dung-powdered sand across the sun that was climbing above the knife-like ridges of Jbel Bani. Following the *piste*, the driver of our rusted green Land Rover lurched the steering wheel right, left and right again, and our vehicle crashed from dune to dune. Mbari, Hassan and I trampolined on its abraded seats, our heads banging the ceiling on the uptake, our chins nearly striking the dashboard on landing. All this and we were still in Mhamid.

Thirty minutes and ten miles later we skidded to a halt beneath the dunes of 'Irq al-Yahudi. We slowly tumbled out of the Land Rover. Mbari's face had turned the shade of camel cud; Hassan and I gripped the hood and steadied ourselves. It was only eight in the morning but the sun was already strong enough to burn. Curiously, the wind that had churned up a maelstrom of dust in Mhamid raised no sand at all here in the desert. Ali was waiting by his tent with three fresh camels and enough provisions to last us twenty days – the time it would take us, if all went well, to reach Akka, the first real settlement on our route.

'Irq al-Yahudi had changed much since I had seen it in 1998. On dunes where Ali's tent had once stood alone now some fifteen or twenty rope-and-wool tents described a sloppy arc, all facing north, the direction from which the *piste* wound down from the Drâa road. The only people in the tents were Ruhhal camel tour operators, who hoped to cash in on the tourist business Ali had started. They had grossly overestimated the demand for their services. Morocco, beset as ever by its reputation for *faux guides*, was having yet another bad year for tourism; and few Nasranis made it this far south anyway.

The wind picked up and walloped the flaps of the tents. Having wrapped their firwals tight around their heads, Hassan and Mbari began loading the saddlebags on the camels, shouting orders to one another over the wail of the wind.

Because the terrain ahead was so barren, we would have to carry many additional provisions that would greatly increase the camels' loads. Besides the gear we had brought from Zagora, we would now take extra crates of vegetables and sacks of couscous, semolina and rice, along with four bulky jerry cans of water (now only half full, since we planned to lunch by a well at Wadi Muzmu; to conserve the camels' strength, Ruhhal try to travel with a minimum of water); three five-litre plastic water gourds (one for each of us) that were filled to the top and wrapped in purple woollen sheaths that were themselves given a soaking to keep their contents cool; two battered tin troughs for watering the camels and use as impromptu ovens; plus the black plastic bucket in which I (and I alone) bathed. None of my guides so far had touched water except to drink it. This led to a less fetid state of affairs than one might imagine: low humidity in the Sahara hinders the growth of bacteria on the skin. I would purify my water from now on with silver-based French tablets called Micropur; I had become convinced that contaminated water had made me sick during the last few days of hiking from Zagora.

The camels moaned as the heavy loads were strapped into their saddlebags and piled high on their humps. But then Hassan and Mbari dragged two hundred-pound burlap sacks (tied together with ropes) out of the tent and hoisted them on to the back of the largest camel. He bared his teeth and bellowed, swinging his head around as if to get a good look at just who was to blame for his extraordinary burden.

'What are those?' I asked Ali.

'Oats. The first fifteen days or so you'll be passing through desert where the drought has killed off all the grass. You'll need the oats or the camels will starve.'

'*La qaddara Allah!* [God forbid!]' said Hassan and Mbari in unison.

Water released from the dam at Ouarzazate alleviated the worst effects of the drought as far south as Mhamid. But from here to Akka, the Drâa, Ali had heard, would be dry. Was there grass after Akka? 'If God wills,' he said.

Once the loading was finished we wasted no time. We embraced Ali and he wished us *rihla sa'ida* (bon voyage). Hassan and Mbari took the rope reins of the camels.

Without looking back, we struck out west athwart the
wind, skirting the dunes and soon embarking on to *ragg* –
flat, sandy earth. To the north ran the distant ridges of
Jbel Bani. To the south there was only a flat infinity of
ragg receding into the glare, and stretching toward
Timbuktu and the Sahel, more than a thousand miles
away. The wind harried us at first, but soon it died, and
the flies came. The sun continued its ascent in a cloudless
sky. It was nine in the morning on 19 March 2001.

Soon after we passed the last dunes of 'Irq al-Yahudi,
Hassan began taking me on a verbal tour of the valley
ahead.

'By God, you'll see many things in the weeks to come.
The golden dunes of Shgaga. Sand desert. Rock desert.
The desert lake of Iriki. Desert with forest where trees
grow as high as your head. You will see the town of
Akka!'

'Akka! Allah!' shouted Mbari.

'Akka! Yes! You'll see Ruhhal with their herds of
camels, and you'll meet our great sheikhs. You'll see
things only the Ruhhal know of. You'll see the sands
where I grew up.'

'And you'll see the sands where I grew up, too!' said
Mbari.

'You'll see the Ruhhal of Assa! And then, near the
Atlantic we'll enter a blessed land—'

'God be blessed! A paradise!' shouted Mbari.

'Near the Atlantic is a blessed land of clouds and
breezes and air with water from the ocean in it! White,
wet air, not like the air here. May the God who created
such air be praised and exalted!'

'Allah, *Allah!* Why stop at the Atlantic?' asked Mbari.

'We should then turn south toward Smara, the country of the Reguibat, the heroes of the desert! There is no god but God! *La sharika lah!* [He has no associate!] Allah! Allah!'

Yesterday's fears had left me now. I trudged along in the sun, sweating and shooing away flies, but listening to these two nomads in tyre-rubber sandals talk about patches of rock and sand they loved, I felt blessed. Blessed to be healthy and striding across this *ragg*. Blessed to have never (or rarely) compromised in my life, to have forsworn the security and amenities in the country of my birth for the hardship and rigours of the desert, blessed to have never followed convention. In this my life could hardly have differed more from the life of the Ruhhal at my side (for whom convention is a matter of survival), but I felt them to be my brothers; like me, they were of the road, alive most fully on the road. I had spent thirty-nine years on this earth. Suddenly it seemed to me that if my days were to end that moment, I would regret nothing. My ebullient self-congratulations culminated in the words Baudelaire's demon whispered in his ear: '*Celui-là seul est l'égal d'un autre, qui le prouve, et celui-là seul est digne de la liberté qui sait la conquérir.* [The only man equal to another is he who proves it, and the only man worthy of liberty is he who knows how to win it.]'

We stopped talking and savoured the wind, the sun; we foretasted the wonders to come. There was no breeze, only the drone of flies and the sound of our shoes crunching the *ragg*.

A ways on, I began to think back on my expedition in 1998. We had reached Wadi Muzmu, watered the camels at its well, and halted for lunch under an adjacent tamarisk. A herd of camels loitered near by, munching on the shrub and grass mottling the sands. My guides at the time, Omar and Mustafa, hailed two sun-blackened Ruhhal resting under the tree.

Their salutations commenced simultaneously. 'Peace be upon you! No harm to you! How are you? How are the family? How are the sons? How are the flocks doing? How are you getting along with the weather? Is everything all right with you?' Despite the verbiage no information was imparted; this was Ruhhal ritual pure and simple. The men asked us to join them in the shade, and we fed them lunch.

After the meal the sun bore down on the wadi and the conversation died. The feathery-needled boughs of the tamarisk fluted the rising wind; they sang, they chimed, they chanted, siren-like, a dirge that put my companions to sleep but unsettled me, conjuring up a time long ago when people were few on earth, hunting in scattered tribes under a red sky.

Now Hassan, Mbari and I reached Wadi Muzmu and camped for lunch under the same tamarisk, but its needles had fallen off; there were no other Ruhhal around; and no camels but our own stood in the wadi. The well had gone dry, the grasses had blown away, and a sun-bleached sterility prevailed. Our camels, freed of their burdens, stared bewildered at the dead brush and then turned and faced east, their tails wagging.

'*Ash-shidda* [The drought],' Hassan said after we had unloaded. 'Muzmu's dried up and the camels are home-sick.' He rummaged about in our scattered boxes and sacks for the vegetables with which he wanted to make salad. 'A camel knows his way home, always, no matter how far he travels, that's why they're looking east. A pregnant camel passes on her knowledge to the foal in her belly. If the mother drank at a certain well, her foal will know the way to that well, even if he's never been there.'

Mbari concurred. He and Hassan referred to our three pack animals as the *jmeelat*, the dear little camels. There was handsome, buff-coloured Mabruk (whose name meant the Blessed or Fortunate One), who had been fed by hand from an early age and was the tamest of the three, but also the most spoiled: he would at times sneak over to camp, lower his head, and with his rubbery lips abscond with a mouthful of carrots. For this he had earned the nickname Sinbay (Thief). There was grizzly-brown Hanan (Sympathy), who, tall and broad- shouldered, with drooping lips, carried the largest loads, including the sacks of oats. And there was taupe-coloured Na'im (Felicity), who, a mere *ba'ir*, comported himself like a teenager; he was always slow to rise in the morning, the first to complain in the afternoons, and the most eager to be unloaded and out grazing in the evenings. His hair was patchy around his face, which gave his chin and cheeks something of a peach-fuzz beard. The lightest and weakest of the three, Na'im was designated as the camel we would ride.

We needed water; we had not expected the well to be dry. 'No problem,' Hassan said, 'we'll find water at al-Mizwariya,' a three-hour hike west. After the salad and our third cup of tea, we lay back on the blankets and closed our eyes. I fell asleep. This time I dreamed of nothing.

That afternoon we trekked deep into the emptiness

toward a lowering lava sun. My companions were garrulous and in good cheer, more comfortable in the desert than in towns. For them the job of guiding me meant a return to what they had loved and were forced by drought to leave; for me, the desert presented challenges, and I could not feel at ease in it, at least not yet.

Around four o'clock we arrived at al-Mizwariya, a scattering of puny acacias near a square hole in the ground whose edges were braced by palm-wood logs – the well. Near by lay a cracked plastic bucket on a frayed rope, which Hassan tossed into the well. The bucket fell a long way before plunking into water, and when Hassan retrieved it, the water inside was cloudy. The well was almost dry, and it had gone salty.

We heard a timid rattle of plastic and metal. A woman was approaching, carrying on her back a loosely bound raft of plastic bottles tied together with string at the handles. She was wrapped in an all-concealing milhafa of blue and yellow batik. Only one eye was visible through the abundant loopy folds of cloth. When she drew near she turned her face aside, hiding the eye. We then noticed donkeys in the acacias around us, a camel here and there, and a patchwork tent a good mile away (where she must have been living). Some twenty yards behind her toddled a boy in a stained T-shirt, whose face, as he neared, screwed up with increasing alarm.

Still looking away from us, she stopped ten feet from the well. 'Peace be upon you!'

'And upon you be peace!' we answered.

Ten minutes of simultaneous queries about health, sons and elders followed. She never turned her uncovered eye to us, and only toward the end of the talk did she and

Mbari discover that they were cousins ('Mbari, is that you?' 'Fatima? Are you Fatima?').

We left her what water remained and moved on.

The Ruhhal often name places after the dead, investing otherwise lifeless corners of the desert with a semblance of human spirit. This had always struck me as romantic and ingenious: there was little here, but one made more of it with fantasy.

'Are we going to spend the night at Wadi Na'm [the Valley of Grazing Livestock]?' I asked Hassan as we strode toward the setting sun. I had pleasant memories of sleeping beneath the crooked acacia there, of the gentle breezes wafting down from Bani, of the flocks of goats jostling to water at its well, and had been looking forward to passing a night there. The name seemed fitting.

'No, we'll put down at Bir Tam.'

'Why not camp at Wadi Na'm?'

'What difference does it make? Wadi Na'm doesn't mean anything: it's just a name for a pile of rocks. By God, we Ruhhal see a patch of sand and we give it a name.'

I was in such a good mood that even Hassan's cynicism couldn't bring me down. In any case, though placenames meant little to Hassan, the Arabic of the Ruhhal, I was learning, had a word for every sort of barren terrain, and none were to be used carelessly. Empty land was in general referred to as *khla* – apt, since that word derives from the root for emptiness. The flat, tannish, sandy land around us now was *ragg*. Totally flat and empty country covered with sand and gravel was *mham*. However, empty *rolling* country covered with gravel and rock carried the name *hidban*, whereas dunes (without vegetation) were

known as *'uruq* (the plural of *'irq*) or *aghrad*. But should
a dune have a mottling of scrub on it, it would be called
a *nibka*, and anything supporting more than three starv-
ing acacias would acquire the (wildly misleading, to my
mind) appellation of *ghaba* (forest). A flat, smooth patch
of earth suitable for bringing a camel to kneel was a *mliss*,
but flat, rocky earth on which a camel could not couch
without hurting his knees was (curiously well named, to
an English-speaker's ear) *harsh*.

'*This* is the life of the Ruhhal,' said Hassan, looking at
the limpid evening sky above Bir Tam. 'The fire, the tea
in the kettle, the *duwaz* [stew] in the pot, the clean air.
There's nothing better.'

'By God, you speak the truth,' said Mbari softly.

We were camped in a crescent of dune, the only raised
earth on *ragg* that, save for the towering stone wall of Jbel
Bani five miles to the north, extended to every horizon.
Lying around the fire, we luxuriated in the smoky blue
cool of dusk. The fire was burning low, its embers carried
dancing away by the breeze; the grazing camels were far-
away shadows standing against the ashen afterglow of a
sky just abandoned by the sun. Not a bird was singing, not
an insect buzzing; the measured munching of the camels
could be heard a quarter-mile away. We had just finished
our third cup of tea, which I sugared but still found foul.
We said little, absorbing the peace of the desert.

After dinner we retired. Around midnight I awoke to
the uneasy snorting of the camels, who had couched
beside my tent. I strained to listen. Far away to the north,
and then to the south, near our camp, jackals raised their
keen, crying their hunger to the empty land.

The pink flush of dawn crept over us, revealing a herd

of camels marching slowly and silently east. Tending
them were Ruhhal, distant white specks against the grey
massif of Jbel Bani. Hassan and Mbari set their eyes on
them and squinted: Ruhhal can recognise a person at a
distance at which I could barely distinguish man from
beast.

'Is that Sa'id?'

'No, by God. But it might be Jalil.'

'No, Jalil wears a wristwatch.'

It turned out that they didn't know either of them.
After breakfasting on tea and bread we decamped.

The sun mounted the sky. We pressed on through
alternating expanses of *khla* and *hidban*, with nothing
much to rest our gaze upon. Hassan talked about the
steep banks of the curving wadi ahead, banks that came
straight down out of Jbel Bani, and the tamarisks that
grew in the wadi, providing ample shade.

'It's beautiful, Wadi al-'Atash,' he said. 'You'll like
camping there tonight.'

'If it's so beautiful why did they call it that?' The name
means 'valley of thirst'.

'It's just a name. Doesn't mean a thing.'

Late in the afternoon we came to the wadi. It was just as
he had described, with marbled bluffs jutting over zigzagging eastern banks, and easy-sloping shores on the western
side; tamarisks stood here and there above soft white sand
rippled from what must have been a recent flood, embroidered in places with scarab tracks, the criss-crossing
pawprints of jackals, and the scratchy indentations of scor-
pions. A flock of birds piped along above us, heading for
summering grounds in Europe; swallows dipped and
chattered.

As we unloaded and set up camp, a donkey trotted up to us and halted, staring rudely with his mean black eyes, snorting as though we had no right to be there. There was much camel dung and goat scat about. Somewhere near by there had to be Ruhhal.

Mbari started making tea. (He and Hassan had divided up domestic duties between themselves before the trip. Mbari: 'I don't cook, I only make tea and tend camels.' Hassan: 'I don't make tea or tend camels. I only cook.') Having dropped a chunk of sugar in the mush of Extra Gunpowder bubbling in the kettle, put the top back on and nestled the kettle in the embers, he surveyed the wadi, pulling his firwal away from his mouth to talk.

'In the days of the French a family was passing through here with their herds. They had many sons and animals – by God, they were rich, that family!' He set out three glasses and commenced pouring the tea into them, and then pouring it back into the kettle, over and over. 'Some of the family camped in the wadi, over there, the others camped up on the bank.' He repoured the tea one last time and offered it to us. 'That night rain fell somewhere in the mountains. Mud and rocks and water came flooding down and swept away animals and children and men in the wadi. Just like that. Then the water disappeared. Those who were up there, way up there on the bank, they were saved. Praise be to God!'

'Praise be to God!' Hassan said, looking at the distant sanctuary. 'God is most merciful!'

'There is none more merciful than God!'

Ali had told me, 'Never trust the wadi!' Rain, if it came, would be both the curse and the blessing of this land, and drought worsened matters by killing the little

vegetation that might keep the earth stable. If a shower
hit the mountains above, the water would race over the
porcelain earth and rocks and carry away any loose soil,
becoming a torrent of mud falling into a web of gullies
that led to the wadi. Then the torrent, ever increasing,
would tumble down the wadi into the desert – picking up
a year's worth of debris, rocks, branches and animal carcasses – until, perhaps dozens or even hundreds of miles
away, the wadi flattened out and the waters dispersed
over the sand to evaporate. I had seen this sort of flood
occur regularly around Marrakesh; every year people
died in them in Morocco. The longer the drought went
on, the more dangerous a sudden rain would be.

My companions sipped their tea. I wanted to relax as
they had, but now, with this talk of floods, I found I
couldn't.

'Wait a second,' I said. 'We're camped right in the
middle of this wadi and you're telling me we could be
swept away by a wall of water in the middle of the night?'

Mbari raised his eyebrows in alarm. 'Indeed this is
dangerous. If God wills, it could happen.'

Hassan gave me an imperious look. 'God alone knows,
God alone decides. "The slave of God thinks, but God
acts," we say. Slaves of God cannot know God's plans.'

'Hassan, we don't have to predict the future. We just
have to take precautions. Could there be rain tonight?'

'God willing!' both said. 'Oh, we need rain. The
drought is killing everything. Rain is from God. Praise be
to God if it rains! Rain—'

'I know rain is needed, but listen to yourselves. It
makes no sense to camp here now if we're at risk. We
should move.'

They sipped their tea and squinted at me.

'Well, when does the rain come? Isn't this the season when it could rain?'

'God willing!' came the chorus again.

We stared at each other, all of us equally uncomprehending.

I calmed down. The drought had begun in 1997, and there was no reason to expect it to rain tonight. Unless, of course, God willed it. Then we would be swept from here to Timbuktu.

The night passed rainless. We left unharmed in the morning, and headed for the oasis of Oum Laâlague. Despite its name, I looked forward to reaching 'Mother of the Leech', where, against the lunar backdrop of the Shgaga dunes, a spring bubbles up from under a cluster of date palms and trickles off through velvety green swards kept trimmed by the nibbling teeth of Ruhhal goats, and where in 1998 I had met someone I hoped to see again: a teenager named Brahim. He was a member of the Ait Habbash, who were once famed warriors in the Drâa and longtime rivals of the 'Arib. He carried a dagger set in a tamarisk handle, but his greased-back hair, fraying windbreaker and threadbare polyester trousers called to mind more the bidonvilles of Casablanca than the hallowed days of Habbash raids.

Over tea Brahim had told me that his family used to wander from the dunes of Merzouga in the east to Tan-Tan in the west, grazing their sheep and camels, moving where the grass was, but the drought had forced them to settle in Oum Laâlague. Even by Ruhhal standards they looked poor. Their tent was a jumble of ripped and dirty plastic sheets tossed up around an acacia; their belongings were stowed on the tent's roof, among the branches, to keep them away from palm rats and goats. The father, a weary-looking man in soiled grey robes, herded a few sheep into a line and drove them toward the stream. Women puttered around the acacia hovel doing chores, their faces averted from mine; one of the younger ones of whose face I caught a glimpse had six or seven pointy black teeth, widely spaced. When I had visited the women were busy hammering the sap out of bark to make medicine; the nearest hospital was in Tagounite, four days' hike away, and home remedies were all they had.

Radio Algeria blared the news in classical Arabic from a sand-caked wireless.

'Do you understand the radio?' I asked Brahim.

He lowered his head. '*Shwiya*. *Shwiya* [A little]. But I don't need to. It's my job to stay here at camp with the women. A woman can't talk to strangers, you see. Our tradition is that a boy stays by the tents in case guests come.'

Brahim's family numbered fourteen, and a newborn wailed in the tent out of sight. They were all illiterate; the nearest school was in Mhamid, two days' walk away.

As we trekked toward Oum Laâlague, I wondered what Brahim would be doing now. He would be old enough to work, and maybe five or six new children would have been born into his family. But we found neither him nor his family when we arrived. No one at the oasis knew where they had gone, except that they had trekked north, seeking pasturage.

We didn't linger at Mother of the Leech, but pushed on after lunch toward Shgaga, whose hulking golden

dunes dominated the eastern horizon. 'Shgaga' derives
from the verb *shaqqa*, 'to split'. To my eye, the dunes of
Shgaga only separated barrens from more barrens, the
hamada of the eastern Drâa from the hamada of the west.
But the Ruhhal noticed that wadis run around the sands
and not through them. Shgaga, thus, is the Drâa's
divide – and the limit of the desert I knew.

We reached the dunes at dusk. From the top of the
first we surveyed the terrain beyond, which was as beautiful as it was lethal: rounded mounts and pyramidal
hillocks of soft sand that would make travel exhausting
for camel or man, and offered no water, shade or vegetation. Between the dunes, some of which were a hundred
feet high, ran wadis with cracked clay beds indicating
that maybe a decade ago there had been rain. Though
according to the map we should cross the dunes, we
would not do so; rather, we would skirt the sands and the
problems they would pose by heading north and west. We
camped at the base of the dunes, in a foul-smelling
orchard of torzas, trees with narrow rubbery trunks and
broad rubbery leaves, among which floppy pink flowers
were blooming. We wondered if the smell could come
from their blossoms.

That night, as Hassan finished preparing couscous, a
visitor appeared at our fire, a plump teen with darting,
curious eyes. He sat down and, following the Ruhhal tradition of hospitality, we asked him to help himself to our
food. He accepted our invitation. We ate, our faces flickering with amber in the light of the fire. He told us that
the Ruhhal around here were migrating north, to the
Sous Valley in the Atlas, to find grass for their herds.

'Arabs could learn much from the Sous Berbers,' said

Hassan. In Morocco most small businesses are owned by Sousis, who are regarded as the most talented business-men in the country. No code of political correctness governs Moroccan speech: ethnic groups, races and reli-gions are discussed frankly and with much stereotyping.

'The Sousi does well because he is always lucky,' said the boy. 'There's no luck like a Sousi's luck. You can toss a coin and a Sousi will tell you which way it will fall. It's true, I've seen it.'

'You show your ignorance talking like that,' Hassan said. 'The Sousi succeeds because of his brains. A Sousi father puts a plate of olive oil in front of his sons and invites them to dip their bread in it. He watches. To the son who dips his bread in the most he says, "You will amount to nothing!" To the one who sops up just a little, he says, "You will go far!" All the big businessmen in Germany and France are Sousis, they outsmart even the Nasranis.'

'By God, is that so?' said the boy.

'Of course. We Arabs are good only for soldiering. We aren't awake, we aren't *conscious* like the Sousis or the Jews. We lack culture, we can't think ahead. We're good only for war.'

Mbari didn't like this assessment. 'The Sousis might run things in Europe, but the root of their success is envy. The Sousi envies. He has to get what others have. They're schemers, that's all.'

'I'm not sure the Sousis run Europe,' I said.

'Nonsense!' Hassan shouted. 'After the Jews they're the smartest businessmen in the world!'

Hassan and Mbari took to arguing. 'May God guide you to the Straight Path, Hassan, you understand nothing' . . .

'I swear by the Truth of God Almighty, Mbari, you are a dolt' . . . 'You, Hassan, and I call God as my witness, have rocks in your head' . . . 'In the name of the prophets, Mbari, I tell you that you . . .'

I finished eating. Tired of their bickering and not wanting to spoil my good humour, I excused myself, said goodnight to all and retired to my tent, which I had placed atop a nearby dune to catch the first rays of the morning sun.

SONS OF DOGS

UNTIL LATE INTO the night Hassan and Mbari berated each other. Repeatedly during the trip I was to watch minor disagreements between them escalate into curses, raised fists and flailing firwals. Yet if Arabic, with its gagging and spitting consonants, seemed the perfect language in which to excoriate one's opponent, the oaths my Ruhhal uttered were never obscene, and their disagreements were usually forgotten almost as quickly as they arose.

So the next morning no grudges were held. We left the stinking grove of torzas and spent hours navigating Shgaga's northernmost reaches, winding our way between crested dunes, always trying to keep to the hard-surfaced wadis, but rarely able to do so for long. Our destination was Hasi Biyyid, a well only a mile or so from the slopes of Bani.

As we advanced the high dunes above us petered out into low sandy swells, which eventually flattened into

hamada. When we came within sight of Hasi Biyyid,
Hassan and Mbari grew excited, noting the presence there
of a dozen Ruhhal, and hoping to find among them relatives with news about the wells ahead. As we approached,
the women hailed us, but turned away, as if delivering their
greetings to Jbel Bani. The men stood tall. Some wore
daggers stuffed in sashes tied around their royal-blue
fouqiyas, and had peaked their loosely wound firwals in the
front like crowns; others were dressed in immaculate white
'abayas (the sleek Ruhhal equivalent of the djellaba) and
white turbans.

All shouted salutations: '*As-salam 'alaykum!*'

We replied, '*Wa 'alaykum as-salam wa rahmat Allahi
wa barakatuh!*'

'*Wayn sabiheen? Mnayn jayeen?* [Where have you
passed the night? From where have you come?]
Shhalkum? Shkhbarkum? [How are you? What is your
news?]'

The news, Hassan and Mbari said, was good, praise be
to God. But the following question ended the ritual
responses and courtesies.

'*Wayn mashiyeen?* [Where are you going?]'

Hassan and Mbari looked down sheepishly and said,
with sudden reticence, 'God knows. God alone knows.'

'Come on, tell us where you're going, God have mercy
on your parents!'

'God alone knows . . . God will decide.'

The men turned to me and asked the same question. I
took the cue and also said that God alone knew, though
how I happened to have ended up in the middle of the
desert with two Ruhhal and three heavily loaded camels,
yet had no idea of where I was headed, seemed less than

believable. Just knocking around in the Sahara, I gave them to think. Incredibly, they asked no more questions, and answered Hassan's queries about wells ahead.

Hassan drew water from the well and poured it into troughs for the camels, cooing, 'Oh-oh-oh! Oh-oh-oh!' the call camels associate with water. After the camels had drunk we said brief goodbyes to the Ruhhal and moved on.

When we were out of earshot Hassan explained his evasiveness. 'Let no son of Adam know where we're heading. It's never good to tell anyone your destination if they have no need to know. We can trust our camels but not the sons of Adam.'

'Who were they?'

'My cousins,' Hassan said, looking back, as if they might be following us.

A wind was rising and dust devils rolled off the dunes, heading our way. We quickened our pace toward the cluster of acacias at Wadi Biyyid, where we wanted to lunch and pass the siesta hours.

The old Ruhhal standing before us in Wadi Biyyid had a broad forehead, sunken cheeks, doleful eyes and a pointed chin – a martyr's face from a Byzantine icon. His firwal was white, his robes white, his sirwal white. His teenage son was less celestial: buck-toothed, pimpled and long-limbed, wearing a frayed brown fouqiya over a T-shirt with a Led Zeppelin logo.

Just after noon they had stepped out of a haze of blow-ing sand to appear at our camp. Hassan furtively stuffed his packet of Casa cigarettes under a blanket, and, fol-lowing custom, invited them to share our meal.

'May God bless you,' said the elder, easing himself slowly on to our blanket.

'God is most exalted!' said the teenager, standing by Hassan, his buck teeth extending over his lower lip. 'Give me one of those cigarettes! I saw you trying to hide that pack!'

Hassan frowned but obliged. Only a little stew was left but when eaten with chunks of gravy-soaked bread it counted for a lot. The old man, it turned out, was aggrieved. As he sopped up gravy he told us why.

'I lost three of my camels. They wandered off near Sidi Abd al-Nabi and Satan led them into someone's garden. The owner had them locked up.'

'Where?' I asked.

'In someone's stable, and the ingrate owner wants sixty thousand rials from me for having put them up.'

Hassan raised his chin. 'By God, the people of Sidi Abd al-Nabi are sons of dogs. They have no ancestry, they're crossbreeds.'

All agreed. The old nomad, unused to the ways of the town, would probably end up traipsing back and forth between the police in Sidi Abd al-Nabi and the stables for days, milked of his meagre funds by bureaucrats and the possessor of his camels. His dignity and antique dress might prompt someone to take pity on him, or perhaps not; what was once the finery of desert raiders was now the uniform of the illiterate and helpless. The son, as unschooled as his father, would be no help.

The son sucked on his cigarette. A gust raised sand, sending one of our empty tin pots bouncing away into the wadi. Mbari jumped up and ran after it.

I was well pleased with my Ruhhal guides, but I found

Mbari difficult to get to know. He spoke little and, like Zayid before him, spent a lot of time alone with the camels, watching them graze, gathering leaves together and feeding them by hand; he especially enjoyed stirring the oats he poured the camels at day's end into little piles for them to eat more easily. I wondered at times if Hassan, often blustering about one thing or another, perhaps intimidated him. In any case, I was relieved to see that Mbari was someone with whom I could get along. Where long expeditions and travel companions are concerned, muted demeanours are better than florid but cloying personalities. And, unlike Noureddine, Mbari and Hassan kept their views on religion to themselves.

For hours the next day, each suffering confinement in his own mobile tornado of black flies, we advanced toward Sidi Abd al-Nabi, which lay at the base of Jbel Bani, across an interminable *ragg* glittering in its farthest reaches with the mercury lakes of mirages. I clamped my straw hat to my head and thought about the sun, which, though it was only March, was growing surprisingly oppressive. We had left 'Irq al-Yahudi five days earlier, and the meat had run out two days ago. I was feeling light-headed, and attributed this to my vegetarian diet. Even though Sidi Abd al-Nabi was the abode of sons of dogs, it still might have meat, so we decided to stop there.

I was riding Na'im, the petulant teenager. Watching distant splotches of green and white gradually become an oasis village in such heat did not make for riveting entertainment, and I would have dozed off had not Na'im developed the habit of couching without warning, which each time threatened to send me tumbling head-first over his neck and on to the *ragg*.

'*Wild al-haram!* [Bastard!]' Mbari would exclaim. He would then walk around and kick Na'im in the rear, at which the beast would clumsily bound to his feet, extending his hind legs first, and then his forelegs. And we were off again, marching toward shimmering lakes we never reached.

We eventually made out palms and square stone houses. But soon from atop my camel I spotted something that made me rub my eyes: a woman dancing in blue veils!

I told Hassan and Mbari what I saw.

'By God!' they replied. 'The sun is burning your brain!'

'But that's what I see!'

Twenty minutes later the blue veils turned into a blue djellaba fluttering in the wind; its wearer appeared to be bobbing up and down on a Stairmaster. Then, suddenly – and finally – the figure in blue was a man on a bicycle, pumping his way across the *ragg* at high speed. He was heading straight for us.

'What could he want?' I asked Hassan.

'I don't know. The people of this village are scoundrels.' Hassan's firwal was scaly under the translucent fluttering wings of hundreds of flies. 'God save us from the scoundrels of Sidi Abd al-Nabi!'

The man was pedalling hard. A few minutes later he was nearly upon us. He shouted greetings, as did we. As he whizzed past, he yelled, '*Ay l-qabayil?* [What tribe are you from?]' His words trailed away with the Doppler effect. He was soon cycling into the mirages on the other horizon, and then riding a Stairmaster, and then, before disappearing in the glare, doing a veil dance.

Sidi Abd al-Nabi didn't look like a den of scoundrels. The stone houses gave it a more solid aspect than almost anything we had seen in the valley, and above the village rose a brick minaret, trimmed with white.

'I really don't know why we should stop here,' said Hassan as we entered the acacias on the *ragg* outside the village and started looking for a place to camp. 'People without ancestry can't have good meat. We should just go on. It's only a twelve-day trek to Akka.'

'Semen! A gob of semen and a clot of blood!'

The youth leaned toward me and opened his eyes – bloodshot, pupilless scleras that seemed, by the power of suggestion, no doubt, to be cavities plugged with semen and blood. He was blind. 'God made man from a gob of semen and a blood clot! It's in the Qur'an!'

Mbari and I were standing in the middle of the village. I was teetering, now nauseated, and holding on to the wall. The youth was holding on to me, pressing his gooey eyes in my face.

Another teen, this one in sunglasses and a fluorescent green-yellow T-shirt, shoved him aside. 'Shut up! Someone from the Federal States of America doesn't want to hear you talk about semen.'

The blind teen reached down and scratched in the dust, picking up a pebble between thumb and forefinger. 'The clot of blood and semen was like this, this small—'

I looked away.

'But then it became this big, big as me.'

The other teen knocked him into the wall. He fell

down, crying out as he tumbled into the dust. 'Come with me. Ignore this stupid boy. I want to show you our marabout's tomb. He's our ancestor.'

The blind teen, muttering about semen and blood, began clawing his way up my leg, trying to get back on his feet. I gave him a hand.

Mbari grew insistent. 'By God, we need to buy meat and batteries for our flashlights. And Cokes and semolina. Please help us, God have mercy on your parents! We have no time for tombs or talk.'

The teen in sunglasses, who introduced himself as Ali, apologised and led us to the village's one shop, which was closed, so he hollered for the owner, who lived next door. The owner, a sullen man in a dirty djellaba and scuffed leather slippers, took a long time rattling and banging with the lock before he opened the steel door. He had no meat, vegetables, Cokes or semolina, but his shelves held box after box of Tide detergent. In one corner there was a pile of hard candy covered in dust. I bought some. He had batteries, too, so we also took some of those.

Back on the street Ali apologised again. 'There's not much left here these days. We were once five hundred families, but now we're twenty-two. It's the drought. It's killed our agriculture. Most of the people here have left for Foum Zguid and Zagora.'

'God help you,' said Mbari. 'Do you have a butcher?'

'No. But I have a goat I'd be pleased to sell you.'

For an exorbitant price, it turned out. He wanted eight thousand rials, but the goat he showed us (Mbari insisted) was worth half that. Mbari bounced the bleating creature up and down on his knee, proving how light it was; he then squeezed its buttocks, showing how little meat it had. They haggled over the price, but it was no use. Ali would accept eight thousand rials, no less, so Mbari let the goat go.

We parted with Ali and walked back out to camp. It was noon. The scraggly branches of our acacia offered miserably porous shade, and the flies buzzed thick around us; hungry and sweating, we lay down on the hot ground and tried to sleep but couldn't. The alternative to spending the night here would be to pack up and continue. We looked west: the *ragg* spread white under the sun, finally melding with the sky in distant gaseous glare. We would stay put.

Angry about the goat, Hassan got up and paced back and forth, flies covering his firwal and the shoulders of his fouqiya.

'These people have no ancestry. They're just Ruhhal from different tribes who settled here. That marabout isn't their saint, don't let them tell you otherwise. These people are scoundrels.'

'Well, could we find a scoundrel who'd sell us a goat?' I asked. 'I think that's what's important now.'

'You mustn't eat goat. Your stomach would rebel.'

'What about buying a sheep?'

'There are no sheep around here. No grass.'

Mbari arose and gave his firwal a defiant toss over his shoulder, sending hundreds of flies into furious flight. 'By God, *I'll* get us a sheep!'

He set off for the village, the flies resettling over his firwal. The camels turned east, looking homeward, wagging their tails. Hassan stretched out on his foam mattress. I lay down again on the flat earth and put my hat over my face, and tried to sleep, feeling flies skitter over my forearms.

Six hours later the mirages had vanished and the sun was falling. Colour – if only a dunnish tan – was returning to the *ragg*; the dunes of Shgaga jutted like mounds of lustreless gold into the robin's-egg blue firmament in the east. Mbari came back with a frisky brown goat on a rope (there were indeed no sheep to be had), bought from a cousin he discovered had settled here.

Hassan bounced it up and down on his knee. '*Smeen!* [Fat!] Praise be to God!'

'Poor goat,' I said, watching him bleat and frolic, clueless as to what we had in store for him.

'God wills that we slit the throat of this goat,' Hassan said. 'God put the beasts on earth at man's disposal. It's written that we come here today and slaughter this goat. And besides, we have to eat him: we've got to be strong to cross the desert ahead.'

In the name of God, the Merciful, the Compassionate, to the sunset cry of the muezzin, Mbari raised his knife and plunged it into the goat's throat. Blood spilled on to the thirsty *ragg*. He and Hassan began slicing skin and tearing flesh, snapping bone and inflating lungs, flushing out turds and cutting apart the liver. Two hours after that, with the sun gone and the flies asleep, we grilled and ate the meat. Then, for the last time that day, as the stars glimmered in the deep black sky, the muezzin called from the minaret. Hassan and Mbari arose to pray. Tired, still not feeling entirely well, I crawled inside my tent and shut the flaps.

Light. I lurched awake, aware of clammy heat and a pain in my intestines. Though it was only a little after dawn, I was soaked in sweat; it had been hot in my tent during the night. I looked outside and the sun hurt my eyes.

Hassan was at my door. 'Si Jelal, let's go. Today we start the hard walking. It's five days to Mghimima.'

'What's in Mghimima?'

'Nothing good.'

I sat there not moving. I wanted to fall back and sleep, but it was too hot.

'Si Jelal, really, let's go. We've got a lake to cross.'

I sensed a change in the climate and decided I would have to dress differently. For the first time, I put on the sirwal I had bought in Zagora. Loose and made of turquoise cotton, they were cooler than my other pants. I also pulled out my firwal and tried to wrap it around my head, but I couldn't stand it − it suffocated me − so I took it off. My broad-rimmed straw hat would have to do. I gathered my things together and climbed out of the tent. The air was still. The sun burned low and coppery over the cracked earth.

An hour later we were trekking silently across a dead-flat expanse of crusted, salty *ragg* that began at the foot of Jbel Bani and stretched to the horizon in the south. Ahead, to the southeast, rose the brown stone escarpments and ragged buttes of the Madwar mesa, along which we would have to pass to reach Mghimima. Flies now blackened most of the camels' upper bodies, as well as our headgear and clothes; they flew round and round the camels' heads, landing on their eyelashes to sip mucus, provoking the poor animals to holler and snort and shake their heads. At times I jogged a few steps ahead to escape the swarms, but they remassed all over me minutes later.

'Lake Iriki,' said Hassan, looking at the friable earth. 'When I was a boy it was filled with water and fish, and the bird flocks were huge. There were pink and blue birds, white birds with long black legs. We ate fish from this lake.'

The dam at Ouarzazate, combined with lengthening droughts, had killed Iriki in the 1970s. By all accounts its silky blue waters brimmed with fish, its shores were garnished with roses and palms. Now it was one of the driest places on earth: not a blade of grass, not even a thorn bush, stood on it, and only watermark corrugations in the *ragg* signalled that it was once a lake. Large tracts of Iriki were *sabkhas*, salt flats – thousands of acres of arid white sterility. Across *sabkhas* we trekked, now and then shielding our eyes from salty gusts of shifting wind.

Toward noon the wind picked up and grew steady. The flies settled on our clothes and hung on tight. Feeling oddly fatigued, I let my companions take the lead. Gradually, a heat haze (*aghmam*, they called it) settled over Iriki and mingled with mirages to impart the impression that we were trekking through a dead heaven of quicksilver. I soon fell well behind.

Pain in my gut cut me in two. I doubled over, suddenly on the verge of collapse. Hassan and Mbari marched on; it had become our habit to walk without looking back, in case one of us needed privacy for the toilet or prayer, or just wanted to be alone. When I saw them wading into the silvery flats of the mirage I made myself get up and go on.

I stumbled along for the next two hours, gaining on them and falling behind. At one point grit swirled from the lakebed and splattered into my eyes; ahead, a wall of wind-driven cement-grey dust rose off Iriki. It enveloped my guides first and then me before leaving us, moving on down the valley. A Qibli (southwestern wind) was coming on, assailing us with the heat and dust of the Western Sahara from where it originated.

We veered off the lakebed and started up hills at the base of Bani, hills covered in loaf-sized chunks of broken basalt, hills that rolled on and on like the swells of a stony black sea, with waist-high acacias dotting the scarce troughs, or wadis, running from Bani down to Iriki. The wind now battered us incessantly, hot and dry, laden with salt and dust from the lake. We were soon halfway between Iriki and the cliffs of Bani, and the hills showed themselves to be a series of staggered and crooked shelves hugging the base of the mountain.

My ankles turned rubbery and I began slipping on the rocks. Five more days of hiking through this inferno was too much to contemplate; thoughts of falling ill out here frightened me into focusing on walking without tripping. Hassan and Mbari had found a *mijbid* and were following it, but they were so far ahead of me that I had no clue as to where to find the foot-wide path through the rubble.

The midday sun pressed on my shoulders and I began to lose my footing again. I dropped to my knees near a flowering acacia and retched violently once, twice. I crawled beneath the tree, trembling and feverish, but not sweating – the wind was too parching for sweat. I thought of the goat and Hassan's warning. Dozens of bees hovered in the wind and danced around the yellow blossoms above me. Watching the bees, I passed out in the light flooding through the branches.

'Si Jelal! Si Jelal!' Hassan was leaning over me, shaking my arm and shouting over the wind, his firwal muffling his words. 'What's wrong?'

For a moment I couldn't talk or remember where I was. I mumbled something, I don't remember what.

He understood what had happened. He brought me my foam mattress and a canteen of water, and laid a pack of cookies and two oranges in front of me.

'We can't stay here long: there's no water,' he shouted. 'It's only a few minutes to Wadi Sasi. But rest for now.'

He and Mbari squatted to lunch beneath an acacia a few yards away. I took a double dose of my pills and ate and drank what Hassan had brought me. I then tried to stand, but the sun was too bright, the wind too strong, my knees still wobbly. I dropped back on my mattress. Bees still hovered above me; wind bobbed the acacia's branches; and I recalled the silver sparrow and crêpe-paper butterfly mobiles of my childhood. Soon followed sleep and dark cool; finally came *I Love Lucy*'s Lucy and Ricky Ricardo and the Mertzes in Italy; and I watched Lucy stamping grapes, a bandanna tied around her head . . .

A few hours later I woke up recovered enough to travel, and we moved on. A hike of two hours across the basalt-strewn shelves brought us to Wadi Sasi and its well. A dead donkey lay near by, rotting and bloated, but the wind carried away the stench. Balancing on the brim of the well, Mbari drew water and put the bucket to his lips.

'*Hilw* [Sweet],' he said.

I filled up my canteen and dropped in the Micropur tablets. When finally I took a sip I found the water gritty; it scratched my throat going down.

That night, under a lowering sky of whirling brown dust and the pummelling assault of the Qibli, we camped just beyond the well in Wadi Sasi. I wondered why we had bothered to push on to reach Sasi: it was nothing more than an accursed depression of basalt scree and acacia thorns. Time after time I pounded my tent stakes into the earth, only to have them hit rock and bend. My mattress was now a bed of thorns; whenever I touched the ground, thorns stabbed my skin. The larger ones, an inch or two long, poked through the flip-flops I wore around camp and penetrated the tyre-rubber sandals of my companions.

I said goodnight to my companions and crawled into my tent, still weak, but the wind screaming off the desert kept me awake, so an hour later I got up and went back to see what they were doing. They had started a fire on the lee side of their tent; the wind found them anyway and scattered embers into a fireworks display that illuminated their veiled faces.

One of our camels, Hanan, had pulled a muscle in his right anterior thigh and developed a bad limp, but I was most anxious about water and told Hassan and Mbari so. We had found some at the well, but it might be the only water for days. We could last that long, but should by chance the next well be dry or brackish, we might be in trouble.

'God will provide,' Hassan said.

Mbari added, 'It was not like this before.' The last time he had passed this way was in 1997, just before the drought. 'This was green land, and there were so many Ruhhal. There was grass for the camels. By God, the world is drying up.'

'Allah, Allah,' said Hassan. 'The Day of Judgement is near.'

The Day of Judgement seemed a fitter way of describing this drought than global warming or climate change. At least, to me it did, stabbed to childish shouts of anger by thorns, nauseated by the goat meat and harried by the wind: *someone* should be made to pay for this. But my Ruhhal were not distressed. Their faith made them strong, and told them that the world was meant to end in fire.

My illness had come as a shock, and I had not expected the climate or the terrain to change so suddenly. All in all, I felt cowed by the desert, fearful of the emptiness around us, and I said so.

'This is tough, even for us,' said Mbari. 'You see, Ruhhal usually travel very little, moving only a few kilometres every few weeks, just to find new pasture. They don't go far, like we're doing.'

'Not many of our youngsters could make such a trip. The young are becoming children of the schools,' said Hassan. 'Once they grow up in a town and go to school, they'll never know how to start a fire or care for the camels. They could never learn the trails. They couldn't survive. School spoils all that. It makes you weak.'

'Schooling is good, Hassan,' said Mbari.

'For some. Allah, the Day of Judgement is near.'

'Praise be to God!'

He and Mbari rose, cleared a spot of rocks, and brushed aside the thorns. In the wind and dark and blowing dust, dimly lit by the seething embers of the campfire, they began the prostrations and utterances of *salat al'isha'* (the evening prayer). Their lips moved but the wind drowned out their words.

After prayers I tried to prompt them to lament the

death of the world of their childhood, but I failed. It was preordained, they said – a prelude to the End of Days. I could not feel that way. I could not accept this death, knowing that it did not have to be.

I retired to my tent. The Qibli increased during the night. With the roar of an avalanche, sand squalls bore down on us, one after another. The wind now and then ripped my stakes out of the ground, the dust poured in through slits in my tent flaps. I slept in snatches, having to get up often to tend to the tent.

The evening of the next day of wind found us camped beyond the flats of Iriki on the basalt shelves, in Wadi Wunkil, a stretch of cement-coloured desert littered with dying acacias. We were somewhere near the Madwar, but its buttes were hidden by passing curtains of sand. I sheltered in my companions' tent, having been unable, owing to the Qibli, to set up my own.

Mbari had led the camels away to look for grazing. The oats we carried were not enough, it turned out, for them to live on; they needed a variety of pasture. Hassan was sifting semolina for couscous; I occupied myself with oranges and my pocket knife. I cut apart a couple of old oranges and squeezed what juice they had into a plastic mug, and then added gritty well-water and tossed in sugar, which I broke off a cone and ground with a rock. I couldn't stand the thought of another cup of Ruhhal tea. I wanted orange juice.

I raised the murky, flotsam-filled concoction to my lips. Just then, I spotted an enormous white spider creeping on the tent wall above Hassan's head, the two carapaced segments of its body the size of golf balls, its legs pencil-thick and several inches long.

'Hassan!'

He looked up and ducked, grabbed a sandal and thwacked the spider; it dropped to the ground and scurried for cover; he thwacked it again, and shoved the carcass into the sand. He went on with his sifting.

'A *bu siha*,' he said. 'Poisonous. If it stings you, your hour will come.'

I sipped the juice. It sent me into a delirium of pleasure.

Mbari returned with the camels, having found nothing green. He sat down and we waited in silence for the couscous to cook.

'Will the camels make it to Mghimima if we can't find grass?' I asked.

'If God wills,' they said. 'If God wills.'

MGHIMIMA

AT DAWN WE awoke to silence. The sandstorm had died away, revealing the shark-toothed buttes and jutting crests of Madwar mesa. Beneath it, Wadi al-Arjiliya ran a ragged course at the edges of a plain littered with volcanic tuff and ferrous rubble. It was now apparent that since leaving Iriki we had been trekking across a shelf some seventy metres above the rest of the valley. The sky was a radiant azure canopy; the sun showered the land in crystal light.

We emerged from our tent with our hair and clothes encrusted in dust; it had penetrated everything we owned. I found grit in the inner folds of my wallet, so I wrapped it in plastic and retired it to a pocket inside my pack. Mbari and I spent the better part of an hour shaking things out; Hassan took advantage of the calm to bake bread in the sand. As we loaded up our camels, they blinked at us from behind dust-caked eyelashes. They had weakened on their diet of oats and dry leaves. Hanan was still limping. Na'im bellowed louder than ever when we approached, and at first refused to rise with me aboard. Mbari delivered a swift kick to his haunches, which caused him to leap to his feet, nearly throwing me off, but then he grumpily couched again, so I decided to walk. Only Mabruk was in good cheer, but he too was developing a limp.

As we made our way down the highland on to the plain we set our sights on a distant dot of vivid green, Nakhl al-Madwar (the oasis of Madwar Palm) beneath the mesa. Once on the valley floor my Ruhhal broke into song, as much to celebrate the end of the sandstorm as to dispel the boredom the trek brought on and keep the camels going. Hassan performed Saharawi folk songs, lively ballads of yipping and yawing. Mbari slogged on to different rhythms, chanting, in a monotone that maddened me as the hours passed, '*La ilaha illa Allah!* [There is no god but God!]' and adding, at various times, '*La sharika lah!* [He has no associate!]' Singing has ancient roots among Bedouin, who cantillated to their camels to keep them moving when they became tired during long days of haulage. Proficiency at the *huda'*, the cameleer's song, thus became an essential qualification for caravan leaders; indeed, the lead cameleer came to be known as a *hadda'* (singer of the *huda'*). Mbari's chant resembled the *huda'*; Hassan's versified ballads reminded me that the first poetry in the Arabic language had probably been sung, if it wasn't the *huda'* itself.

We arrived at Nakhl al-Madwar — an idyll of luxuriant floppy grass called *zayyat* and stout, date-laden palms. The vegetation drew moisture from underground springs here and there accessible through yard-wide holes in the whitish, powdery earth. We let the camels drink but drew no water for ourselves, for it was brackish and we couldn't stomach it; the *zayyat* was encrusted with salt at its base. We didn't linger. Sweet water awaited us at Jbel Amsalikh (or so the Ruhhal at Hasi Biyyid had told us), where we would pass the night.

'Would the Nasrani like to buy a rock from heaven? God hurled it down most recently.'

I awoke at sunrise the next day to voices outside my tent. I crawled up to the gauze door and peered out. Beneath the sandy slopes of Amsalikh stood three bearded Ruhhal holding rocks, talking to Hassan. In the wadi below a herd of camels was wandering west, plodding their way among acacias.

'The Nasrani is sleeping,' Hassan said. 'I can't wake him, even for a rock from heaven.'

'But it fell just the other night.'

'I'm sorry.'

They wished Hassan well and walked on toward their herd.

'*What* were they selling?' I asked, stepping out of my tent.

'A rock from heaven. They fall all the time out here.'

'A rock from heaven? A meteor, you mean.'

'You see these rocks dropping out of the sky every night.'

'If you mean shooting stars, well, those rocks burn up entering the atmosphere. Very few reach the ground. I think they were just trying to sell an ordinary rock.'

'Oh no! You can tell they're from heaven because they're lighter than rocks from earth. The Ruhhal sell them all the time to tourists in towns. Unfortunately, Morocco doesn't regulate the export of these rocks, so you have them being sold all over Europe.' I raised my eyebrows. 'No, it's true. I know a Frenchman with these big glasses he puts on to see the markings on the rocks, markings that show a rock is from the sky. The rocks have marks because they're millions of years old, unlike the earth.' My eyebrows remained raised. 'Or so they tell me. By God, that's what they say. But who knows?'

We pulled up camp and set out toward the well from which we had drawn water the evening before. Now by the well we saw a wiry old man in a sirwal that bagged at the knee and stopped there (unlike the sirwals inland Moroccans wore which were wide to the knee but extended to the ankle). His huge nose jutted forth and his long ears protruded from beneath his turban; his chin came to a point – he looked inbred. Hassan and Mbari shouted greetings to him. He was, they said, a revered sheikh from Mhamid.

The well was equipped with a cement trough, on top of which the sheikh climbed and began waving his arms and yipping and yawing in much the same way as Hassan had sung the previous day. The camels passing near by turned and began lazily wandering toward us, lumbering along as if sublimely indifferent to water. His sons, the sellers of rocks from God, were walking amid them.

'By God,' the sheikh said, pouring bucket after bucket of water into the trough, 'we can take it no more. We're moving on to the Sous. There's grass there, they say.'

'God willing you will find grass!'

'God willing! If only God would bless us with rain! What's a son of Adam to do?' He yipped and yawed until the camels were near. They dropped their snouts into the trough and began slurping, the younger ones waiting until the elders had drunk their fill before moving in.

'Go in safety!' he shouted to us.

'May God keep you safe!' we replied.

Hours later, near noon, we caught sight of mountains of basalt and sand rising along the horizon like giant camel humps. They foretold Mghimima, a village about which neither Hassan nor Mbari knew anything except that it was roughly halfway between Mhamid and Akka.

'It's probably just some stone houses with a name,' said Hassan.

'We shouldn't stop there if there's no grazing,' said Mbari.

'Right. We should move on to Akka. Akka is a wonderful town with good grazing. But Mghimima? We know nothing about it.'

But Akka was still ten days away. If Mghimima proved a bust . . . I didn't want to think of what shape the camels would be in if they couldn't find good grazing soon. And I was tired.

That evening a crescent moon rose into view above the palms and blocky stone houses of Mghimima. Its oasis was richly endowed with moist grass and shrubs. We decided to spend three days there resting and foddering the animals.

'What do you think of our village?' Omar asked me. 'You probably find it beautiful.'

Omar, a young sharif with a handsome, intelligent face, was walking with Hassan and me through the oasis of Mghimima. It was ancient, judging by the great height of

the palms, and it was lush: *saqias* bubbled with clear cool
water; blue, red and yellow flowers rioted above plots of
limp alfalfa that were dappled by sun falling through
palm fronds; like wide-eyed houris (the virgins promised
by the Qur'an to the faithful in heaven), Haratin shepherdesses in black shrouds drove flocks of sheep and
goats along the embankments. After crossing so much
desert I told Omar that the oasis looked like paradise.

But the rest of Mghimima was less enticing than the
gardens. After arriving Hassan and I left Mbari to set up
camp and hiked up the banks of the wadi into the village.
The houses of Mghimima were square and solid while
most of the shops around its central square were boarded
up. Outside the one open shop gaunt Haratin men sold the
meagre produce of drought-depleted soil: shrivelled
carrots and egg-sized onions (but no potatoes or tomatoes;
it was too hot here). Inside, Berber boys, kinky-haired
and barefoot, snot-nosed and violent, passed around a
bottle of Fanta; they jostled one another until the bottle
smashed on the floor. Writing on his hand with a cracked
Bic pen, the shopkeeper took ten minutes to compute the
price of the olive oil, semolina and soft drinks we were
buying. This piece of simple addition taxed him greatly,
and none of the children present could help him: they
were all innumerate.

'Well,' I said to Omar, 'the oasis is beautiful, but I sup-
pose there's no work, and there are too many kids.'

'That's right. The only people who stay here are the
wives and children. The men go to Casablanca and Rabat
to find work.'

'But you're sharifs. You have ancestry,' Hassan said.

'Yes, but we also have drought. Agriculture is risky

here, and without that, what life can we have? And these villagers don't understand how to work together. They could form cooperatives and farm, and help each other. But that takes thought and planning, which is too much work for them. Instead, they go off to the cities and look for low-paying work. There's no organisation.'

Omar told us that the Arabs of Mghimima were originally Saharawi nomads from near Tan-Tan; they had long ago taken over the land from the Berber Haratin, who still worked the fields for them. A marabout had founded Mghimima (his whitewashed tomb and the tombs of his progeny stood on high ground over the oasis), but no one knew anything more about the village's history. 'There are no written records,' Omar said. 'The Ruhhal and the Haratin couldn't write.' Springs provided water ample enough for date palms. But the village had no telephone and no electricity, and this bothered everyone we talked to. 'Without electricity you can't have a life,' said one of Omar's brothers.

Pride in nomadic ancestry eventually brought Omar and Hassan together, and they talked disparagingly of the Haratin who were the majority in the village.

We stopped to greet a group of old Ruhhal sitting in a patch of shade. After the usual salutations came shouted enquiries from toothless mouths about tribe and family ('*Ay l-qabayil? Ay l-khut?*') These Ruhhal, as well as all the others we had met, greeted me last: a Nasrani with no ancestry, if an object of some curiosity, counted less in their eyes than a blue-blooded nomad.

Hassan told them that we had begun our journey near Mhamid ten days ago. They were not impressed.

'It took you so long to walk here?' they asked. 'Why,

our grandfathers could do that trip in three days, eating only dates and drinking only water.'

'We're nothing compared to our ancestors,' replied Hassan. 'God have mercy on our ancestors.'

They all agreed that the ancestors were stronger, faster and nobler than this generation. A sign that the End of Days was drawing near.

One of them turned to me and said, 'Well, by God, you did well in choosing 'Arib as your guides. A couple of years ago a Nasrani, a Frenchman I think, came through here. He bought a camel and set out for Sidi Abd al-Nabi. Our village chief guided him to Foum Zguid and then tried to find him a guide for the rest of the way, but he refused. "It's only a couple of days away," he said. A couple of weeks later they found his body on the hamada. Died of thirst.'

Hassan and I said goodbye to Omar and the old men and headed back to camp. On our way into the oasis three Haratin women in black shrouds, with babies strapped to their backs, stopped and stared at me, and then began a mime. '*Bébé! Bébé!*' they said, pointing at their loads. '*Kooh! Kooh! Duwa! Duwa!*'

They wanted medicine – there was no pharmacy in the village – but I had none to give them.

The next afternoon we were trying to nap in the shade, having lunched on brochettes. (Mbari and I had bought meat in the neighbouring village of Tissint.) A dozen Haratin boys had come out to the oasis to ogle us; from behind a cluster of palms, they laughed and giggled at me, now and then shouting, '*Donnez-moi un stylo!*' and ducking to hide when I looked at them.

'Go keep an eye on your things,' Hassan warned. 'Boys

here are spoiled and brainless. They can steal from you
and not even know they've done anything wrong.' I
dragged my blanket up to a palm near my tent and
stretched out.

A little while later pale feet in clean sandals padded by
my head and stopped. I looked up and saw peering down
at me a colourless but kind face that would have been
effeminate were it not for a trim moustache. I got up and
said hello. The man introduced himself as Hussein, and
asked what I was doing in Mghimima. I told him, and we
began to chat.

'You're American? America is a wonderful country. No
racism there, unlike here. Allah, Allah.'

No racism in *America*? I told him there was much
racism in America.

'There is racism here,' he went on to say, 'between
Arabs and Berbers. I've lived in Europe, so I know what
racism is; it's not quite as bad here as it is there. I've
never been to America, but I think Americans are very
conscious and developed. America is a land of reasonable
people, and reasonable people aren't racist. Unlike here.
Oh, and I'm not from here, from this village, that is –
God forbid. I'm just visiting for a wedding. I'm really
from the Sous. Does that mean anything to you?'

I felt silly doing so, but I repeated the popular wisdom
that Sousi Berbers were good at business. He was
pleased.

'That's true, but it makes sense. You see, we Berbers
and Native Americans are the same people, just like the
Chinese and the English.'

'What?'

'The early English kings. They were of Chinese blood.

I read it in a book. And Berbers and Native Americans are one blood, too. Are you a Native American?'

'No.'

He frowned. 'Oh, well, too bad. Because I would like to find out how Native Americans think, what they're like. They aren't like Arabs, I bet.' He looked out at the desert. 'Have you ever seen so much emptiness?'

'Well, this is the Sahara. What do you want?'

He lowered his voice. 'I mean, Israel has the same desert but they made it bloom. If Israel took over Morocco they'd make this wasteland bloom.'

This was an amazing statement; I had heard nothing like it in an Arab country before.

'We're the true inhabitants of this land.'

'We?'

'We . . . Berbers. And Jews. North Africa was Berber and Jewish before the Arabs invaded. Jews were here a thousand years before Jesus was born. Jews and Berbers have a lot in common. A sense of business, for one thing. This was prosperous land before the Arabs came. Now look at it. We're forgotten by our own government; our government doesn't plan anything or think of its own people. That couldn't happen in Israel. They're reasonable people in Israel.'

'I don't think Israel is paradise. Just look at the Intifada going on now. Doesn't that tell you something's wrong?'

'The Jews have a right to Israel. They were there two thousand years ago and they have a right to that land, more than any Arabs. But anyway, what do Arabs do? Instead of saying, "We need a strong Israel to help the economies of the Middle East, to make the Middle East a power like Europe," they talk about war. War, war, war. It's all the Arabs know. They're incapable of planning anything for the benefit of people.' He winced in disgust and rubbed his cheeks. 'But, to be fair, it's religions that are causing all these problems. Judaism and Islam have too many extremists. Being a Christian really doesn't mean anything specific any more, but being a Jew or a Muslim means a lot. To put it in as few words as possible, I think we're all human beings and religion just divides us when we should be able to live anywhere on this earth as citizens of the earth.'

'How do you know so much about Israel?'

'I . . . I've been there,' he said quietly. 'I have friends there. I've seen what they've done there. I . . . it must be terrible being a tourist here.'

'Why?'

'I've seen the way Arabs here treat tourists. Shouting at them and insulting them in the streets, and overcharging them. It's a disgrace. They aren't developed people. They're, they're little better than . . . I think I've taken enough of your time. Please, forgive me.' He stood up, shook my hand, and was gone.

The camels ate well in the oasis, munching away day and night on palm fronds, flowers and bush twigs. Mbari stayed with them, talking to them, watching them forage, tearing off the choicest foliage and hand-feeding them. Hassan and I spent much time with Omar and his brothers, whom we visited in their house; they treated us to tea and bread soaked in argan oil, which was something like olive oil, but thinner and yellower. It comes from a tree that grows mostly in the Anti-Atlas.

As it was everywhere, the drought was on everyone's mind. 'Rain!' they said. 'If it's going to rain this year, it has to rain now!' It was already the end of March; it would never rain in summer. *Shta* – rain in the local dialect – was the same word as 'winter'.

Just after noon on our third day in Mghimima we were amazed to see thunderclouds mass above Jbel Bani, to the north and east. The village square filled with spectators exclaiming, 'Rain! Rain! God grant us rain! God willing, it will rain!' The clouds were high, fulminating and blue-black; they had to be pregnant with rain. The air grew taut with the energy of a coming storm. There was just enough time, if rain fell heavy and long, to save the crops this year. If it rained, relatives away in the cities could return and work in the fields, and the year would be good.

Hassan and I stood with the crowd in the square, watching the sky. The clouds began dropping loads of rain on the mountains; each cloud trailed a lead-coloured skirt that curtained off first one ridge and then another. It was an awesome sight, as if God Himself were seeding the soil. When dust began stirring in the square children started dancing, women ululated and men muttered Allah-Allahs of relief.

We decided to return to camp and prepare for the deluge. We walked and then trotted as the wind rose and told us we had no time to spare. What an unexpected pleasure! Rain, moisture, mud and clouds! Anything but dust and heat and sun. Deliverance was at hand! 'God is most generous,' Hassan said. 'God provides.'

We reached the head of the trail leading down into the oasis. From there we looked out on to the desert and mountains again. The clouds were leaving the mountains now and heading our way, crossing over the desert through which we had passed days before. In those wastes the heat did its work: to our bitter astonishment, the luxuriant rain clouds metamorphosed into a horizon-to-horizon rolling bank of hamada dust and hot wind.

As we reached camp the sandstorm hit and roiled the earth and sky into a single swirling mass, ripping our tents from the ground, shrouding Mghimima in brown dust, bending double the ancient palms. By my tent, which only the backpack and gear inside kept from flying away, stood a Berber shepherd, his eyes smeared with kohl, who peered at me over a tightly wound firwal. He leaned on his walking stick and watched me struggle with my tent. Then he walked away into the brown. Their fouqiyas and firwals flapping in the gales, Hassan and Mbari struggled to reattach their collapsed tent to its stakes.

All night the sandstorm assailed us. Its ripsaw blasts and wild pummellings told us we were weak, vulnerable and puny. No wonder the Bedouin of Arabia and the Sahara felt the hand of God behind the wind that ruled their desert, the clouds that dropped their rain. There was no refuge save in God, said Hassan and Mbari, and cringing in my wind-blasted tent all night, coughing up dust, I found myself thinking they were right.

At dawn the storm ended. The sky the next morning was a brilliant blue, the air hot and still. Filthy again, we broke camp and set off walking single file toward the west. Between here and Akka, Hassan told us we must all look like Ruhhal, who walk in a line during their travels. We wanted to attract no attention. Ahead, somewhere, was the forbidden military zone.

THE GREAT SAND WALL

'*La ilaha illa Allah! La ilaha illa Allah! La*—'

Mbari stopped singing and halted to reach under a rock. Grunting and grimacing, he wrestled out a writhing, black-and-orange lizard a foot long and stout, with a mouth full of tiny serrated teeth. Its tail wound around his wrist.

'Dinner,' he said.

To kill the reptile now and eat it later would have violated Islamic law (which forbids the consumption of *mayta*, animals not freshly slaughtered) so he stuffed it into a fold in the blanket on Na'im's back and tied the fold with a short length of rope, forming a sack. Unfortunately, the blanket out of which the lizard then tried to squirm, claw and bite his way to freedom was one on which I was sitting. I protested, less out of compassion for the reptile than fear of its bite: it resembled the lethally venomous gila monster of the American southwest. However, the wind was strong and Mbari's firwal was wrapped around his ears, so he walked on, resuming his chant, oblivious to my cries, and eventually the lizard calmed down. We were ascending higher and higher into rocky foothills beneath Jbel Bani, hoping, within two days, to reach the restricted military zone and cross it under cover of darkness.

We had left Mghimima walking single file, but our discipline dwindled a few hours later when we came to Wadi al-Malih (Salty Wadi). There was much to the name: the wadi was a marsh of salt-encrusted muck, and we trampled through it in disorderly fashion, making squelching sounds that must have been audible a half-mile away. By noon we had climbed up and over the first foothill, and lunched at the bottom of another wadi, this one a nameless, crater-like oven. 'We should not be visible,' said Hassan, crouching and keeping his eyes on the ridges above. The wadi's walls kept out the breeze; its stone-strewn floor was infested with wasps and spry, silver-sheened ants; and when I dozed off after lunch magpies bouncing about on elastic legs swept down and made off with crusts of my ant-covered bread. The rest of the afternoon we spent traipsing up and down more hills, picking our way around waist-high boulders that looked black in the glare as we approached them, sand-stone-red as we passed. Colour in the desert depends on the position of the sun.

All day we walked alone, seeing no one. As the sun fell, we came within sight of the last looming ridge of Jbel Bani, on the other side of which, Hassan said, was a pass, the army post of Khinig al-Rezzoug, the military zone and the beginning of the Anti-Atlas range that would lead us to the Atlantic. We camped in the flat and sandy

upper reaches of a wadi that cut its way down a high
slope and expired far below on the basalt tableland of the
Drâa hamada, which stretched into Algeria. The view
and the fresh, cool air intoxicated me; the sky was glowing lavender; the moon and stars came out and turned the
rocks into shimmering boulders of mother-of-pearl.

After dinner we sat around the fire. Hassan stoked the
embers pensively. 'We must discuss our military operation.'

'Our what?' I said.

'Our infiltration. We have to infiltrate the restricted
zone around Khinig al-Rezzoug.'

'Hassan, just before we set out, Ali told me he spoke to
the head of the gendarmerie in Mhamid. He gave me the
gendarmerie general's name, and said we should tell any
military to contact him if there's a problem.'

'There will be a *big* problem. The gendarmerie has
nothing to do with the army. The army here is its own
law. The Algerian Reguibat cross into Morocco here and
steal camels and smuggle, and we're near the border with
the Western Sahara. Remember the war.'

I looked at Mbari. 'What do you think?'

'This is a bad post,' Mbari said. 'Have you seen any
Ruhhal around here? The military doesn't allow them. If
it catches them it arrests them and throws them out. It
doesn't want them to get to the sand wall.'

'The sand wall?'

Morocco managed to win the war in the Western
Sahara (or at least to expel the Polisario from its territory)
partly by constructing a series of sand walls, which it
mined and equipped with alarms. The combined length
of these fortifications was said to exceed that of the Great

Wall of China, and the Polisario guerrillas found it difficult to breach them. But I had never heard that the walls
reached into Morocco proper (they are not shown on any
map), and the Royal Gendarmerie had told Ali nothing
about them when he asked permission for my trip.

'The big sand wall starts here, at Khinig al-Rezzoug,'
said Hassan. 'We'll have to cross over it.'

'Is it mined?'

'I know the way across the wall.'

'How do you know the way?'

'I know the way.'

'But is it mined?'

'God forbid.'

'If God wills, it will not be mined,' Mbari interjected.

I pondered this evasiveness, which, combined with
their usual talk of God's will, could mean that neither of
them really had any idea of what we faced. 'Look,' I
asked, 'is it ridiculous to suggest that we approach the
post and request their permission to cross?'

'The captain of the post is . . . a scoundrel. He won't
listen to you. There's been a war on in the Western
Sahara, remember that, and Nasranis are not allowed
here. No Nasrani has ever crossed the wall. Like I said,
we'll have to conduct a military operation. We'll have to
infiltrate the zone, cross the wall, and get out, without
anyone seeing us. We should do this at night.'

Mbari sat up. 'We're too late now to make it through
the zone, so we should cross at noon, when the soldiers
are eating or taking their siesta.'

Hassan shot him a disdainful look. 'You know nothing
about military operations.' He turned to me. 'Mbari has
never been in the army, but I'm a military man. As I said,

it's too late to cross now. What I suggest is we cross at noon, when the soldiers are sleeping or taking their siesta.'

'I still wonder if it wouldn't be better to ask for permission from the captain. What if they take us for Polisario guerrillas or smugglers? What if they shoot?'

'We can't ask that captain. I . . . I was stationed at this post. They're . . . my division and I know that captain.'

'Ah! So if we're caught, you have some sway!'

'If we're caught, I'm done for! They'll say, "Oh, it's *you*! Showing a Nasrani our border! Giving away our military secrets!" God forbid!'

'God forbid!' echoed Mbari.

Their concern reminded me of something that should have been obvious to me: Hassan and Mbari were both Saharawis, sons of the desert people for whom the Polisario guerrillas claimed to be fighting for independence from Morocco. If we were caught, I might get away with nothing more than a bout of hard questioning, but they could pay a higher price, though exactly how high I didn't know.

'Okay, okay,' I said. 'We'll do as you say, Hassan.'

The next day we decamped and walked single-file down wadi after boulder-strewn wadi, running, cringing, mincing at times, and ducking to avoid being spotted by the (unseen) soldiers Hassan feared. But late in the afternoon Mbari and Hassan concluded that we weren't anywhere near the pass. The last time Hassan had passed this way was in 1987; Mbari in 1992. They would not say so, but I realised that neither had any idea where we were. Put simply, we were lost.

As darkness thickened around us in a nameless wadi,

and the cliffs of Bani stood jagged spectres of black against a sky of diamond stardust, we came upon a nomad tent. The lone Saharawi there, a hooded youth with dark eyes, gave us water and told us that the restricted zone was still three hours' hike away; there, he said, the sand wall ran along the bank of a giant wadi, overlooked by the post of Khinig al-Rezzoug. I would have advocated walking on and crossing in the dark, but we had so exhausted ourselves during the day that all we could do now was pitch our tents at the base of an escarpment a ways on and pass the night.

At camp, Mbari remembered the lizard, which he took out of the blanket, beheaded with his dagger, and roasted over the fire. He chewed the stringy white flesh, staring into the fire. We were all now nervous about the daylight crossing we would be compelled to attempt.

The following dawn, in rising heat, we set out into more boulder-strewn wadis, where palms clustered in ravines and waist-high spikes of dead grass snagged at our clothes as we walked. We could have hiked along the top of the ridges, but that would have made us visible. In the heat, which was becoming fiercer than anything we had experienced so far, I found walking newly difficult, with dizziness and a sweatless fever coming on.

Around noon we climbed out of the wadi on to a rise, and peered at a divide between two mountains a mile or two away: Jbel Bani and the Anti-Atlas, unsparing desert massifs, treeless and craggy, lifeless under a blazing white sky. Down the middle of the divide cut a deep wadi which passed beneath us and wound away into the heat haze hanging over the hamada. At the foot of the pass we discerned a small oasis, above which rose a red clay fort –

the army post. To the west a twelve-foot-high wall of
sand and rock ran from the far base of the Anti-Atlas
south into the desert, following the wadi, and, like it, disappearing in the haze.

'That's Khinig al-Rezzoug,' said Hassan.

'That?' said Mbari, raising his hand.

'Put down your hand! You want them to see us?' That
we had three bellowing camels loaded with gear that
might be more visible than one bony hand didn't seem to
occur to him. He turned to me. 'We'll have to hurry
across to the sand wall. Really hurry!'

'Hurry, in this heat?' I swayed and contemplated
whether it would be best to vomit and faint here or in the
relative seclusion of the wadi below. I checked my thermometer: it read forty degrees in the shade. Mbari, I
thought with some consolation, must have been right:
any soldier on duty now would be dozing in the shade.

I felt my cheeks turning fishbelly white and my palms
going clammy. Looking at me, Hassan's face registered
concern. 'What's wrong with you?'

'Nothing. Let's just get on with it.'

'Okay. Whatever you do, don't look at the post, and try
to be inconspicuous. *Tawakkalna 'ala Moulana!* [We rely
on our Lord!] *Yallah! Yallah!*'

With Hassan ducking and shouting nervous orders not
to tarry, we began the descent. His orders meant nothing:
there was no way to move quickly amid the boulders, and
anyway, the camels walked at their own pace. Feeling the
heat as strongly as I was, Mbari now and again staggered
and clutched at the side of his camel. Hassan, the oldest
of all of us, and presumably the least fit, thanks to his
pack-a-day Casa habit, was hopping from rock to hot

rock with the agility of a demented jinn. We reached the bed of the wadi and the shelter of its crumbling banks (which made us invisible to the post), but negotiating the trail through the boulder-filled bottom was treacherous, especially for the camels, who stumbled and bellowed with fear. We tried ascending the other bank several times before we made it.

'Come on!' Hassan whispered as we clambered up the last rocks on the bank to the base of the wall, once again becoming visible to any soldiers not dozing. We located a path leading to an eroded segment in the wall and fol-lowed it up and then down on to the hamada on the other side, dragging the camels. Even thoughts of landmines found no purchase in my nausea-addled mind, and, robotically, I slogged on.

It was noon now. Sun-infused heat haze blanked out the mountains, hiding the pass and the army post, leaving us alone on the hamada in a sweltering world of white. We walked as fast as we could for another hour, never looking back.

In a rockbound depression in the hamada, under a sky of nova-white glare, panting, all three of us now near fainting, we crawled into the meagre shade beneath runt acacias, each under his own separate tree, scratched amid the rocks to clear away the thorns and stones, and col-lapsed. We had made it.

Our days journeying along the base of the Anti-Atlas toward Akka began with the rising buzz of flies in a warm *sfumato* world of duns and greys and paling sky. At the predawn moment when the sky lightened enough to allow one to distinguish a white thread from a black thread –

the moment of *fajr*, when muezzins in towns would mount the minarets and make the day's first call to prayer – Hassan and Mbari would begin their ablutions, thrusting their hands into the thorn-spiked sand and using it instead of water to cleanse their faces, feet and forearms in preparation for prayer. (The Qur'an allows Muslims to wash in sand when water isn't available.) Then, they would stand and face Mecca, cup their ears and recite the Fatiha, between verses dropping to their knees and touching the earth with their foreheads, and rising to continue the process, adding other suras. Twenty minutes later, on their knees, they would mutter private prayers interspersed with formulaic addresses to God: '*Ya Rabbi, Ya Rabbi, Ya Rabb! La quwa wa la hawla illa billah! Ya Rabbi, Ya Rabbi, Ya Rabb!* [My Lord! My Lord! My Lord! There is no strength and no power except in God! My Lord! My Lord! My Lord!]'

There was, in their dawn prayers (and in my thoughts), the hope that the day would be cool, rain would come and travel would be easy – hopes that grew from the comforting sight of the slopes of the Anti-Atlas, still soft and gingery-looking in the early light, and the powdery grey sky, harmless yet. But then the sun would sear a path above us, scorching skin and wearying eyes; rain would not fall; the cantaloupe-sized rocks of the *harsh* made every third or fourth step an ankle-twisting stumble.

Faith allowed the Ruhhal to migrate when the well ahead might be dry, when the grass in the next wadi might be dead. Rational spirits such as mine, which wanted assurances and well-founded estimates, would quail under such prolonged uncertainty and peril. Despite the exemption from prayer that the Qur'an grants travellers, my Ruhhal would, one at a time, hitch their camels to mine and drop back, perform their ablutions in the baking sand, and then recite their prayers. No matter what happened, they praised God.

Now, as we moved toward Akka, I thought of the paradise the Qur'an promised to my Ruhhal. From this world of rock, sun and want, rare rains and certain death, they would one day ascend to 'lofty chambers of Paradise underneath which rivers flow', to 'Gardens of Bliss' where they would recline on sofas, 'a cup from a spring being passed round to them, white, a delight to the drinkers, wherein no sickness is, neither intoxication, and with them wide-eyed maidens restraining their glances as if they were hidden pearls'. Gone would be their tattered fouqiyas and flyspecked firwals; they would find themselves 'robed in silk and brocade', enjoying 'fruits and palm trees and pomegranates', sampling 'rivers of water unstaling, rivers, too, of milk unchanging in flavour . . . rivers of wine . . . rivers, too, of honey purified', gazing upon 'houris cloistered in cool pavilions'.

Believing in no such otherworldly compensation for the sufferings imposed by this vale of stones, I found my temper shortening, my strength sorely tested. The heat and chronic, sun-induced nausea and sweatless fever, which no amount of covering up seemed to cure, prompted me to withdraw into myself. I was soon filling the barrens with the image of my wife and verdant, dewy Russia; with the rancour and unsettled feuds of my past; and with, of all things, episodes of TV sitcoms remembered from childhood. By midday I was often traipsing across this Saharan inferno with an imbecilic smile on my face, answering Mbari's pious chant about the oneness of God with '. . . a story 'bout a man named Jed/poor mountaineer barely kept his fam'ly fed . . .'

Three days after traversing the sand wall, we ate lunch in an oasis of bayoud-afflicted palms and camel bones. While Mbari was out grazing the camels, I asked Hassan what the Qur'an suggests Ruhhal use to wash themselves after sex when they are in the desert, away from water. (Bathing after intercourse is obligatory in Islam.) Did they apply the same thorn-spiked sand they used before praying?

He got up and gesticulated as if scrubbing his private parts. 'No matter where you are, you must perform an ablution after sex with your woman to get rid of the *janaba*. You wash your—'

'The *janaba*?'

'The *janaba* – what you have to get rid of after touching your wife. You must clean yourself or you'll carry the *janaba*.'

Janaba, I recalled, was a state of ritual impurity associated with sex. It then occurred to me that, with the exception of Noureddine's harangue on the second night, not once in my trip down the valley had any of my companions mentioned sex. Not once had they let slip a bawdy remark. As far as I knew, not once had they spoken of their wives, even to each other. In this they contrasted strikingly with Moroccans in cities, who, male and female both, if the company is right, show a ribald sense of humour. I could only imagine that the thirst, heat and fatigue to which the desert subjected travellers left them with little energy for discussing sex.

Toward me, dime-sized camel ticks skittered across the sand, seeking blood. Forgetting my original question, I interrupted Hassan. 'Let's get out of here.'

Three hours later, as we dragged ourselves westward over *harsh* in unrelenting heat, a dense blue-grey mist fell over the mountains behind us. We stood transfixed for a minute by the vision of cool, which we disbelieved, and then marched on.

A wind hit us from behind, belting us with gusts of cool air; so cool I started shivering. The mist was gaining on us.

'Praise be to God!' Mbari and Hassan shouted, looking back. 'Allah! Allah!'

Two minutes later the sky above us darkened; rain struck us cold and copious, blown horizontal by the wind; water splashed and danced off the rocks, catching the glare of the sun still burning the desert just ahead. The camels began bolting and roaring; I jumped to the earth from Na'im's back, fearful of being thrown. Rain! As the sky dumped its load the temperature plunged. We were suddenly soaked and shivering.

Ten minutes later the cloud had passed. Around us lizards scampered and birds chirped, beetles scurried, all sparkling wet; steam rose in delicate wafts from glistening rocks. We inhaled the damp air. I mussed up my hair, working the water into the roots.

Soon the sun scorched the moisture away and the heat returned. We revelled in the memory of cool and wet, but such a shower could do little good: rain needed to fall for an hour to penetrate the soil deep enough to alleviate the drought. A soaking slow rain was better than a brief downpour.

But praise be to God, we had been granted relief. We would remember it during the treks ahead.

CUL DU DRÂA

THE SUN THAT had warmed us back to life at dawn in February now exhausted us by 9 a.m. with its fiery April resplendence. The acacias, which were in the Upper Drâa thorny but broad-boughed and wide-canopied, had shrivelled into runts that no longer provided enough shade for us to rest comfortably at midday. The rounded contours and soft hues of the Saghro massif had given way to the bleak escarpments and stark wastes of the hamada and the Anti-Atlas. I could now see why none of the early French explorers in Morocco had come this far, why their accounts dealt only with the *coude du Drâa* – the upper part of the valley that was as accessible as it was picturesque. The lower reaches through which we now marched were, I came to think, the *cul du Drâa* – a furnace, sparsely populated, in stretches lifeless from drought. And, to boot, this *cul* was a restricted military zone, terrain that the Moroccan military might have mined against the Polisario. As I stumbled amid the *harsh*

I wondered if my next step might blast me into the arms
of a vengeful Allah.

The previous day's downpour did more than soak our
clothes and give us the shivers. In granting us a reprieve
from enervating heat, it disrupted the balance of
repressed desire and wilful disregard that eased our passage down this valley. Every day, all day, we suffered
fatigue, boredom and fears about the state of the wells
ahead, but until the shower reminded us of cool and wet
we could ignore the discomfort and maintain our
humour. Now, tempers began to flare. Hassan's know-it-
all attitude, a source of chuckles before, became truly
irksome. Mbari took to blaming him for our every misfortune, denouncing the 'old dunce' to me whenever the
'old dunce' wasn't around, which I interpreted as base
and disloyal, given that the two were supposedly friends.
I found that my concerns – that there might not be water
at the next well, or that we roughly keep to our schedule –
intensified along with my sun-induced nausea and dizziness. All in all, I was falling far short of Thesiger, who
disparaged the amenities of civilisation and 'learnt the
satisfaction which comes from hardship and the pleasure
which springs from abstinence', and who, among his
Bedouin, found 'comradeship in a hostile world'.

Our course down the valley to the Atlantic ran west by
southwest, but my Ruhhal often looped north or veered
south, following circuitous *mijbids* regardless of the extra
distance they imposed. Irritated by this, and dissatisfied
with their explanation ('We follow the *mijbid* because
that's what we do'), I often headed straight into the *harsh*
and preceded them to one or another rock or dune, and
then sat down and waited for them to catch up, but they

paid no attention. When I overheard them multiplying
their per diem fees by the number of days we expected to
travel, I concluded that they might be zigzagging not out
of nomadic habit but because they wanted to extract as
much money from me as possible: the longer we took to
complete the trip, the more they would earn.

That suspicion visited me the afternoon after the
downpour. According to the map, we were only a few
hours' trek east of Akka – a village that promised me
every form of earthly salvation one could desire in the
desert: shade, soft drinks, sweets, perhaps even a restaurant or a café, and telephones. Along the base of the
mountains ahead the land was *harsh*, but it was flat; a few
hundred yards south the *harsh* began breaking into
steep-banked wadis that descended toward the hamada
and the Algerian border. Nothing appeared easier,
quicker or more logical to me than making a beeline to
Akka across the *harsh*, but Hassan was leading us up and
down the *mijbids* in the wadis. I protested; Hassan
ignored me. Mbari, when Hassan wasn't looking, made a
gesture of incomprehension, as if to say, 'The old
dunce!'

This way and that we followed the *mijbids*. Then, at
almost five in the evening, we took a sharp turn south
down a wadi that could only take us hours off course.
From my seat atop Na'im I protested again. 'Look,
Hassan, why are we turning? Akka is straight ahead!'

He shot me a look of overweening disdain. 'That *harsh*
is hard on the camels. I won't cripple our camels!'

'But there are rocks everywhere in this blasted desert!
Sticking to this wadi will add hours to our trip. Don't you
think that could hurt the camels?'

He said nothing, but kept negotiating the *mijbid* and heading south.

'Hassan, look! I demand to know why you're going the wrong way!'

Again he gave no answer.

'Hassan! I'm speaking to you!'

No response.

'Hassan!'

Nothing.

That did it. I leapt down from Na'im's back, pushed past Mbari, and set out due west across the rocks.

'Si Jelal! Si *Jelal*!' Hassan shouted.

Without looking back, I bounded over the rocks up the bank of the wadi. It would take me too long to reach the flat terrain at the base of the mountain, so, moving in a straight line, I climbed down into wadis and then up out of them, one after another, toward where my map and good sense told me Akka had to be. I had felt weak before; now a vengeful strength surged through my limbs. I would show *him*!

An hour later the sun began to drop, but I kept heading west, taking determined steps, at times jumping from rock to rock. As I did so I told Hassan off a hundred times in my head. I would stand for none of this shilly-shallying; he worked for *me*, and he was not going to rip me off by adding extra miles to our route.

I was mighty pleased with myself. The shadows lengthened, the sky darkened. The jackals started yelping, and Akka, for some inexplicable reason, failed to appear. Doubts began to intrude. What if I had misread my map and Akka was not straight ahead? On the *harsh* I was leaving no tracks. Who could find me if I got lost?

Getting lost in the Sahara, I knew from experience, could have grave consequences, and time would be short. In the desert a person can survive for three days without water. After that the skin darkens and splits, the throat constricts, the body temperature soars. Disorientation, hallucinations, gagging and liver failure follow, and then coma and death. One consequence of my showing Hassan just who gave orders to whom out here could be my ending up as dinner for the very jackals setting out on their nightly hunt around me.

Yet I trekked on. The chasms of the Anti-Atlas yawned empty to the north, the hamada spread vast and silent to the south, but in the failing light there was still no sign of Akka to the west, or anywhere else. My hands went clammy at the thought that the wadis around me were all deep enough to conceal three camels and two men; Hassan and Mbari could pass by me and I would never know.

But I kept walking. No, I could not have been mistaken about where Akka was. And I had seen a flat spot with acacias ahead where I knew my Ruhhal would want to pasture the camels and spend the night, so I made for it.

An hour later I reached the acacias. I sat down on a lozenge of stone and fixed my eyes on the gloom to the southeast, from which – I presumed – my Ruhhal would have to emerge. It was a moonless night, and there was no wind.

An hour and a half later ghosts rose out of a wadi, heading my way. It had to be them. All at once my fear disappeared and I wondered how I should confront them. Would they think me as temperamental and capricious as I had been? Since I was the boss, if not the leader, of the expedition, I decided it would be best to admit nothing and first calmly enquire as to just why we were taking such a long route to Akka.

One shade turned out to be Mbari; the others, the camels. 'Si Jelal! I'm happy to have found you!' he shouted, loping toward me. 'Praise be to God!'

'Where's Hassan?'

'By God, Hassan doesn't know what he's doing. I told him you would go west toward the acacias, and that we should just come here and wait. Why take the long road to Akka, anyway? But he shouted, "Si Jelal went the other way! I have to find Si Jelal! I can't let him run away!" So he took off heading north, for the mountains.'

North? Facing north and then east, Mbari and I took out flashlights and began waving them. He yelled, 'Aaa Hassan, yiii*p*! Aaa Hassan, yii*p*! *YIIP*!'

The chasms responded with a cacophony of echoes. Then the jackals resumed yelping.

'Could he get lost out there?' I asked.

'I doubt it. But then again he could keep going in the wrong direction, thinking you're out there somewhere, and he had no water. God forbid.'

'We've got to signal to him.'

We built an enormous fire with dead acacia timber. Mbari grabbed burning branches and waved them, sending sparks flying into the brush and nearly setting himself ablaze. 'Aaa Hassan! Yii*iip*!'

Only echoes answered, and the night deepened.

Two hours later there was still no sign of Hassan. The lights of Akka were now twinkling on the western horizon offered little consolation. We kept the fire going, and I periodically fed it brushwood to make it blaze.

Mbari could not keep silent. 'I kept telling Hassan, "Si Jelal likes to walk straight . . . *You*, however, always walk crooked . . . We must always do *exactly* as Si Jelal says . . . Si Jelal is our leader . . . We have to obey our leader."'

His toadying only made me feel guiltier. 'Well, I just hope he sees us,' I answered.

'It would serve him right if he didn't. He always thinks he's right about everything. He's old and stuck in his ways. Maybe he'll just wander out into the hamada. There are mines on the border. He could step on one.'

'Mbari!'

'I told him, "Si Jelal is our leader, and we *must* obey our leader, no matter *what* he says." So it would serve him right.'

We watched the darkness.

'It would serve him right. Also, he didn't take any water. He should have known to obey our leader.'

'Mbari!'

'Yes?'

'Please be quiet.'

I turned away from him. The flames of our fire leapt and danced and crackled.

An hour later, just as we were about to give up, a light flickered in the wadi below. It was Hassan, lighting a cigarette and walking our way.

He stumbled over the last rocks into the acacias and threw himself down on the blanket, burying his face in his firwal. '*Wallah*, I was afraid. They would say, "Hassan lost Si Jelal in the desert." It would be very bad for me, very bad.'

'You and your dumb ideas,' Mbari said. 'I *told* you, Hassan, Si Jelal is our leader and you *must* obey him.

I told you he'd head *straight* for the trees. I came *straight* here, of course, but *you* wandered all over.'

I felt terrible. Part of me wanted to apologise to Hassan, but the other part said such words out here might be superfluous. My Ruhhal often exploded at each other – a day wasn't complete without a good row. It would be better to say nothing and move on.

Hassan kept his face covered. 'I don't know the way any more. It's been years since I came this way. I just don't know the way around here.'

'I know the way,' said Mbari.

'Anyway,' I said, 'there's no problem. Let's just eat and forget about all this.'

The lights of Akka now shimmered as bright as Broadway on the horizon.

GOD COUNTRY KING. On a rubble-strewn brown slope of the Anti-Atlas, painted in four-storey-high white Arabic letters, these words announced Akka and the Alaouite sovereign who ruled the land from here to Tangier. The low cinderblock houses and swaying palms of the village quivered above the quicksilver flats of the midday mirage.

As we neared Akka and the mirage evaporated, we saw giant black rodents running south, endless swarms of rats on the move, rats as large as cats and dogs.

'Allah! Allah!' I exclaimed.

Hassan and Mbari said nothing and slogged on. As we neared them, the rats turned out to be discarded black plastic bags. The desert plains outside Akka were a dump for the villagers, and the wind was carrying their trash into the Sahara. Bags bounced along the earth, catching

now and then on shrubs, breaking free with new gusts
and then snagging on an acacia or hurtling off into the
empty hamada. We plodded through the skittering bags.
Soon the stench of excrement hit us. Littering the
ground were chicken bones, tin cans and plastic wrappers, sandals, torn firwals, shreds of nylon netting and
other rubbish, and, beneath bushes and acacias, dried
piles of human excrement.

Amid all this rubbish Hassan couched the camels.
Neither he nor Mbari seemed to notice the smell.

'We're not stopping here!' I said.

Both turned and peered perplexedly at me.

'I mean we're not stopping in all this filth!'

'The people of Akka have no ancestry,' Hassan replied.
'They dwell in ignorance.'

'You may be right. So let's not camp in their crap. Let's
move.'

'We must obey our leader,' Mbari said.

Smiling at yet another one of my puzzling caprices,
Hassan prodded the camels to rise. We moved on to a
place with less excrement, but the stench was close to
inescapable, and I knew I would not spend more time
here than necessary.

After we set up camp, Mbari put on a fresh white
djellaba, shook out his firwal and rewound it, and accompanied me to the village so we could buy provisions.
There, further disappointments awaited. Once a way-
station for caravans, Akka now consists almost solely of
bland cement *qaysariyas* painted shades of ochre to look
like adobe. There was no restaurant, only a couple of
cement cafés that sold scrambled eggs crawling with flies.
Every third person was a soldier from the border patrol;

a garrison was stationed there. The rest of the people were Berbers from the mountains and settled Ruhhal. North of town spread an oasis that led to a valley, up into which a dirt road wound to some of the most isolated villages in the Anti-Atlas.

We found Cokes, cigarettes for Hassan, cookies, semolina and spices. All this bought, we searched the stalls and stands of the souk until we saw a sign that read '*Jazzar*'. Butcher. The butcher turned out to be a tired old 'Abid in a grimy fez with a drooping tassel. His gritty hands clasped over his belly, he sat slumped on a stool in front of his shop – a cinderblock hovel with a linoleum-tiled counter overhung by hanks of fly-covered beef on rusted hooks. I didn't care: I was starved for meat. I hadn't eaten any since my last, nearly fatal, dose of goat in Sidi Abd al-Nabi.

We asked the butcher for meat. He climbed on to the counter, his sandals smearing crud over the tile, and then plunked a chunk of green meat on the crud. Flies exploded into a furious swarm around him.

'*Bagar* [Cow],' he said.

'Two kilos,' said Mbari.

The man asked for double what the meat was worth. Mbari grabbed the flesh and pointed out its flaws: yellowed bones, puzzling excrescences, suppurating white patches, a puke-green sheen – a nauseatingly effective demonstration of its inferiority, even lethality. This was, he insisted, rotten meat worth half – no, a quarter – of what the butcher was asking. The butcher countered that the pus and holes meant nothing, by God, and the bones were from God (how else would the cow have walked?); it was, he said, meat fit for the king.

Indeed it was not, replied Mbari; it was putrid offal. Both men called down the Almighty's wrath to back up their words. Voices were raised, chins were scratched, heads shaken and, finally, concessions made and a price agreed: half of what the butcher had asked. The butcher tossed the meat on a scale – and slipped a bone on the far side of the tray.

I protested. 'Take away the bone.'

'In the name of the Prophet remove that bone!' Mbari commanded.

He yanked off the bone – but left his pinky on the scale.

'*Shtara!* You're trying to rip us off!' Mbari shouted. The butcher slipped his finger off the scale. We had our beef.

We next looked for a Téléboutique to make calls home. We found one: another flyblown dusty cement storefront with high glass windows that let in enough sunlight to heat the premises to the temperature of a Bengali burning pyre in mid-July. I couldn't get through to Moscow and emerged from the booth dripping sweat, bluebottle carcasses mashed to my brow; Mbari got through to Mhamid, after a fashion, shoving coin after coin into the ancient phone, wiping his forehead with his firwal and shouting, 'Hello! I can't hear you. Can you hear me? I SAID, CAN YOU HEAR ME? FINE. HELLO? CAN YOU HEAR ME? *WHAT?* I CAN'T HEAR YOU! YES! HELLO? CAN *YOU* HEAR *ME*?' Then the line went dead.

He walked out of the booth. 'It was good to talk to my family,' he said.

We started back to camp. Along the way, we saw tall

Haratin women harvesting barley in the oasis, stacking their shocks in shaggy pyramids. The late afternoon sun gave their sweaty brown skin the look of glimmering gold.

AIT OUBELLI

I HAD ONE daily pleasure in the desert: bathing. We had one bucket – the black plastic one I bathed with. The day after we left Akka, Mbari threw it down a well.

He did this by accident. We had stopped for our noon meal by a palm that stood over a hole in the earth leading down to a sluggish spring of brackish water. Needing to draw water, Mbari picked up the bucket and the rope to which he thought it was tied, and heaved it into the spring. But the bucket wasn't tied to the rope. It bobbed for a minute, and then drifted away with the murky currents into the subterranean world.

'Oh, well. You can bathe in Assa,' he said with, to my mind, insufficient regret. 'There are buckets in Assa.'

'But I'd like to bathe this month.'

I tried to imagine how I would get clean using the cumbersome jerry cans. This problem concerned only me. Mbari had not yet bathed. Hassan had shaved and washed in Mghimima but then the sandstorm hit and dirtied him again. Anyway, their skin somehow didn't hold dirt the way mine did, and always looked fresh.

From the start, I had been in a nervous mood that day. The previous night in Akka three men in khaki uniforms had showed up in our camp, roused us from our tents, shone flashlights in our faces, and identified themselves as officers of the Royal Armed Forces. With them was the qa'id of Akka. They demanded our papers, and spent a long time scrutinising them and recording the details. They didn't ask how we came to be in Akka, but the commander, in a polite but grave voice, said, 'Look, we haven't had tourists here since before the Western Sahara war. We—'

'There was that Frenchman,' said his aide.

'Oh, yes. We saw him off to Mghimima. He had a camel and we made sure he was safe.'

I thought it better not to mention that his body had been found bloated in the desert a few days later.

The commander went on: 'Anyway, there are still a lot of mines out there placed by the enemy, so you've got to stay in the north part of the Drâa. Always. And don't forget, the Polisario are just across the border. We wouldn't want them kidnapping an American and causing a scandal.'

I thought, correctly or not, that I could handle the Polisario, but . . . landmines? His warning was the first official confirmation of my fears. If we knew the way exactly, if we hadn't spent days stumbling disoriented around the hamada in search of the military post, I might not have been worried. But we had and I was.

The next morning we got off to a late start, since Hassan had to send Mbari into Akka to get bread. (At my insistence, Hassan had refrained from baking bread in the faecally leavened sand.) My remonstration to Hassan that Mbari could have gone for bread yesterday, when he was loitering around camp with nothing to do, prompted neither of them to action: when something was broken they fixed it. Planning of the most elementary kind was foreign to them; they relied on God. Since God clearly had better things to do than worry about whether we had bread, our bread ran out. At first this negligence seemed natural, just something to be expected in Morocco, but then I reconsidered. Shouldn't those inhabiting the most resource-deprived land on earth survive by looking ahead and planning for the morrow?

Mbari came back with bread, and we set out on a trail around Akka, passing through more flocks of migrating trash bags, dipped into a winding wadi, and emerged into the blaze of the desert beneath the Anti-Atlas. Under the four-thousand-foot cliffs and ridges, basketball-sized rocks littered the eroded trail, and walking was a tiring and frustrating ordeal. To the south wended the Drâa, here and there passing through an oasis; beyond it, now blocking the Algerian hamada from view, rose Jbel Ouarkziz, a lump of sand and rock even more barren than the Anti-Atlas.

After a meal of green meat and a 'rest' on thorns by the spring that ate my bucket, we set out at three, our destination the village of Ait Oubelli.

Despite their meagre diet of dried grass and oats, the camels were faring better now. Hanan no longer limped, Mabruk was in fine form and Na'im's mood had improved (he had stopped couching without warning). Yet it pained me to see how two of them were treated. Mabruk was mature enough to wear an *aghaba* (a rope bridle looped around the lower jaw behind the incisors), but Hanan and Na'im, still young and wild, were subjected to the excruciating discipline and indignity of the *khurs*, or nostril ring. When they were little, their masters had pierced one of their nostrils and inserted a ring half an inch thick and a couple of inches in diameter, to which the rein was attached. Hanan had suffered this procedure twice. His left nostril had been permanently torn open, the result of too vigorous a pull by some impatient Ruhhal; his right nostril now held the *khurs*. The nostril ring ensured obedience, for a slight tug on the rope inflicted pain. Thus, Hanan and Na'im were led, grimacing, by their (tautly stretched) nostrils over six hundred kilometres of desert.

This was bad enough, but true misfortune struck that afternoon. Hassan had tied Hanan's *khurs* rope to Mabruk's saddle, and then gone off to pray. What exactly happened next we don't know – perhaps Mabruk had quickened his pace or maybe Hanan had couched – but Hanan's ring was torn out of his nostril. He hollered, shards of his split nostril flopping free and spraying blood over the sand; he thrashed his head, his tongue lolling and red with blood.

We all came running. Hassan shouted, 'Get me the bleach! Quick!'

Mbari obliged, and then grabbed Hanan's head and held it steady. Hassan poured bleach over the open wound. Hanan bellowed and thrashed his head wildly. Mbari and Hassan jumped away from him. But the bleach sterilised the wound and staunched the flow of blood, and within a few hours he was out eating oats and relaxing with his mates.

We stayed put to let Hanan recover; evening was coming on anyway. We pitched camp gathered around the fire. Hassan and Mbari took out a burlap sack of camel feed – dried dates of an inferior sort they had bought in Akka – and thrust their hands into it and began rooting around. They pulled out a couple of the crud-mottled fruits and popped them into their mouths, masticating the rubbery pulp lustily. In unison, they spat out the pits and crud, and reached into the bag again.

'You're eating camel feed,' I observed.

They went on chewing, their cheeks distended on one side.

'Why are you eating camel feed? We have plenty of human feed.'

'Dates are from God,' said Hassan as he examined a particularly filthy specimen. He bit into it and spat out the dirt.

'But you should at least rinse them.'

'What comes from God needs no rinsing.'

As Mbari chewed he took out the tea kettle and glasses. As on many occasions he 'cleaned' the glasses by pouring cold water in and using his fingers to swish it around, picking away gobbets of gunk left over from the last drinker. I had been suffering stomach upsets, possibly owing to my companions' poor hygiene habits. I watched the spectacle, feeling torn between accepting it as their way of doing things and taking an enlightened, if hectoring, stand.

Finally I couldn't resist commenting. 'Look, we had a talk about hygiene. About needing to clean glasses with soap and water.'

Mbari paid no attention. Hassan expectorated another

pit. '"Cleanliness is next to godliness," the Qur'an says. I know, I know.'

'Yes, so why do you still refuse to use soap and water? That's not Islamic. We have soap, and we have the fire to heat water. We agreed you should do this. It's not healthy otherwise.'

'We're healthy.'

'Well, *I'm* not. And for your information, the diarrhoea that kills so many children in Morocco comes from just such bad hygiene.'

'We have Danone yogurt to feed babies when they get sick. Anyway, God takes some children early, you know. In the Qur'an it is said—'

'I know what the Qur'an says about children going back to God. But you can't just shirk your responsibilities and put them all on God.'

'God writes every man's *ajal* [hour of death] in a book. We're Muslims and we submit to God's will. You can't change your *ajal*. What is written will be.'

'But you . . . I . . . oh, what's the use?'

I got up and crawled inside my tent and turned on my radio. In the past I would have accepted their habits, good or bad, as part of their culture, but here I had done just that and fallen ill. And I knew I was right about the hygiene. Why should I keep mum about bad habits that with slight effort could be improved? Why could we not reach a compromise? Whence their hard-headed faith in the correctness of their ways? Moreover, why did I feel wrong about correcting them?

Indeed, I felt bad: I indulged in quibbles partly on account of my fatigue with the trip and my irritation at spending so much time in such limited company. But there was even more to my discomfort than this. Repeatedly in Morocco I had seen poor people make their miserable lives even harder through ignorance. I stopped believing it was right and 'culturally sensitive' to keep silent, or worse, to follow their example out of a desire to show respect. On the contrary, in matters of health and hygiene, to raise no objection when people contaminated themselves (and their children) was little short of criminal, and implied a double standard: acceptance of filth and disease as 'part of the culture' for some people, but not for others. In hygiene, at least, certain ways of doing things led to good health and were right; other ways led to sickness and were wrong.

But I had neither the energy nor the disposition to make it my mission to change others. We all make mistakes, and every culture, including mine, has its failings, its totems and superstitions and stubbornly held but erroneous convictions.

I resolved to drop the issue of hygiene.

The village of Ait Oubelli hugs a curve in the base of the Anti-Atlas, protected from the desert by a small palm oasis. The next day, around noon, we arrived at the palms, hot and worn out from hiking over the unsteady rocks. Hassan asked me where I would like to camp, and I suggested we put down near the fields just ahead.

He pulled his firwal away from his mouth with portentous vigour. 'By God, those fields are of alfalfa and wheat! God forbid we should camp here and let our camels get into the crops!' He waved his arms, describing the scythe-wielding farmers who would come running; the days we would spend in court, if not in jail, for our transgression; the reparations I would have to pay; the disgrace that would befall them.

I cut him off. 'Look, why did you ask me where we should camp? *You're* the guide! *You* tell *me!*'

'*Yeah!*' shouted Mbari. 'Tell him!'

'Be quiet, Mbari! This is between Hassan and me!'

Hassan and I stood glaring at each other. Finally, he walked on a ways and pointed to a spot among the outer palms, away from the fields. We pitched camp there, knocking into each other as we unloaded. We set up our tents as far away as possible from each other.

After we had settled in I set off alone for the village, intent on finding anything to eat or drink that didn't come from a couscous bowl or tea kettle. It was 7 April. I had been trekking since 21 February and felt tired, sick of the trip. Hassan followed me across the sands, moping along with lowered head. Feeling bad for him, I let him catch up.

We walked into the village together and heard people speaking Shilha. Disdain washed over Hassan's face. Berbers. No ancestry. Yet progress of a sort had come to Ait Oubelli: there was a yellow cement storefront café by a gravelly square, a cracked tarmac road, and a sure sign of Moroccan civilisation: two gendarmes stopping mopeds and demanding bribes from their drivers.

Hassan and I collapsed in plastic chairs at the café. A gaunt man in his late forties came over with Cokes. Wearing a pressed green djellaba and a white skullcap, he introduced himself as Lahcen, the café's proprietor. He welcomed us to Ait Oubelli and invited us to his house for lunch.

'No,' said Hassan, stretched out brazenly in his chair,

only his eyes showing through a slit in his firwal. 'No time for that. We're here for supplies, that's all.'

'Oh. Well, God be with you, then,' Lahcen said, stepping back. 'I'm sorry to have bothered you.' He walked off.

I was shocked. 'Hassan!'

'These Ber—'

'I know, I know: they're Berbers without ancestry. Don't go into it. You should be ashamed for treating him that way.' I got up and followed the man inside the café. 'Excuse me, I'd be happy to eat lunch with you. My guide is tired. Please excuse him.'

'Oh, believe me, I understand the situation,' he said. 'There's no problem. Just let me close up shop.'

Lahcen and I said goodbye to Hassan and climbed the dirt lanes behind the café to an ornately filigreed green door – the gate to his courtyard. A mournful old woman sitting with a scarf draped sloppily over her head, Lahcen's mother, called out a greeting in Berber. He led me upstairs to a green room. There was a silver tea service on a small table, and a cabinet with glass-enclosed shelves on which stood heirlooms and photos glinting in silver frames. Rough woven red carpets covered the floor. More than any other house I had visited in the Drâa, this one seemed like a home. On the wall he had painted the words 'IN THE NAME OF GOD' in Arabic, and hung a Moroccan flag.

Lahcen washed his hands in soap and steaming water, and then broke bread for us as his son, Bilaid, brought in a tagine bowl filled with vegetables and chicken.

'You used soap to wash your hands,' I said. This was rare in Moroccan villages, where tepid water from the kettle usually sufficed for the task. It was also uncanny that so soon after my argument with my Ruhhal about dates and hygiene, a Berber villager would show by example the differences between nomadic and modern habits of cleanliness. I sensed he would enjoy the chance to elaborate on the subject, so I asked him why he didn't just rinse with tepid water from the tap.

'We must be clean. Soap is a necessity. Just to wash with water is never enough, though this is what our ancestors did. We're an old village, four hundred years old, but we mustn't look to the past to learn how to live, but to the future. You're a Nasrani, so you've been brought up in cleanliness. Here, so many of our children die of germs transmitted by dirty water and unclean hands. I've read about it.'

Another son, Ali, came in and sat down. 'You're the one who came with those Ruhhal?' he asked. 'The village is talking about you.'

Lahcen continued: 'My father was a trader who travelled every month by camel to Tafraoute. He brought back many goods, but never soap or bleach. People of his day hardly knew what those things were, before the road was built in '78. But we've learned since then.'

We said *bismillah* and dipped chunks of bread into the tagine bowl, scooping up vegetables and pieces of chicken. The Arab nomads have no culture and know nothing of the world, they told me. Lahcen blamed this on their illiteracy and stressed the value Berbers placed on education: 'We Berbers send our children, even the girls, to school. I have a four-year-old daughter who goes to the *madrassa*. That's only so she starts learning to read – it's the Qur'an she's studying now – but in three years she can go to first grade.' They told me about the history of the region, about how 'Arib raiders once extracted tribute from them.

Ali said, 'The 'Arib were bandits without culture. Even today we wouldn't want our daughters to marry them. We want civilisation for our children.'

It would have been easy to sit there lauding the Berbers as good and enlightened, and berating the Arabs as evil and primitive – easy but wrong, and not only because such stereotyping was inherently foolish, or because there has been so much mixing of blood between the two groups in Morocco, or even because when the Bani Ma'qil and 'Arib raiders went into decline in the sixteenth century a nomadic Berber tribe, the Ait 'Atta, took their place and ran the same protection rackets. The Berbers, if culturally and politically in the back seat in Morocco now, have had no small influence on their country's history; indeed, Berber dynasties ruled Morocco for most of the Middle Ages, and Berbers collaborated with the French and helped them subdue the Drâa. All this history colours relations between Arabs and Berbers in Morocco today, and I felt I should not be dragged into taking one side or the other on account of my fatigue with the trip or personal differences with my guides.

But to return to my hosts in Ait Oubelli and my 'Arib guides, the most palpable difference between them was that the former were settled, the latter nomadic (at least by birth and upbringing). Nomadic culture is unchanging, or changes little, and thus to town dwellers appears backward. To denizens of the desert the town dwellers look soft and inferior; worse, in their eyes, they have lost their tribal ancestry. These differences would be diminished or eliminated in a generation or two if the 'Arib continued to settle. Town culture – civilisation, in other words – always prevails.

We finished lunch and reclined on the cushions strewn about the floor. I enjoyed the cool and shade of the homey room as Lahcen and his sons told me about their lives. Everyone in the family could read and write. To follow the news they watched Al Jazeera, and though, on the basis of a puzzling rumour circulating in their region, they contended that Al Gore was an Arab, they were otherwise au courant with the world. They were profiting from the forty-year tax exemption for agriculture decreed by King Hassan II, and were taking credit from the state to farm. They were, in short, working to build their own future. I found myself inevitably contrasting their strivings with what I had seen among the Ruhhal, who never asked questions about events beyond the Drâa, and who relied on God for direction in their lives – which is to say, they accepted passively whatever befell them.

Lahcen's sons brought out mint tea, and we drank the customary three glasses before parting. With Lahcen and his family I relaxed for the first time on the trip; but this only made me painfully aware of how much of an outsider I was, and would always be, in the desert world of the Ruhhal.

Still, I walked back to camp that evening refreshed. Hanging above the horizon in the east, over the nearby hamada and the more distant Jbel Ouarkziz, was a belt of indigo melting into a sea of purple, wherein beamed an alabaster moon. I turned and faced the west, where we were headed: there, the sky was a paling azure, backlit by the sinking sun. I climbed into my tent to rest for tomorrow's journey and the return to the desert.

TO ICHT AND FOUM AL-HISN

THE NEXT MORNING, under an incandescent sky, we departed Ait Oubelli for Foum al-Hisn, traipsing south-west across the hamada, with Hassan taking long, determined steps, Mbari following close behind him, and me, much weakened by the heat, staggering along in the rear. They did not change their dress to accommodate the heat (though Mbari was now suffering increasingly from the sun): as before, over trousers and T-shirts they donned their firwals and fouqiyas. Their clothing served a purpose, however: to prevent the sun from hitting the skin and evaporating perspiration, the body's coolant. The black firwal cooled the head by retaining heat and creating a minor draught that rose between the fabric and skin. Since I could not adjust to Ruhhal clothes, I was doomed to suffer in my straw hat, cotton trousers and shirts, which failed to block the sun sufficiently. No matter how much water I drank it was never enough.

While travelling with Noureddine I always ate from

the common pot, as was the custom. But owing to the shrinking size of the acacias, my meal habits began to change when I hit the open desert with Hassan and Mbari. Now at midday I rested under my own tree, rotating my mattress around its trunk to keep within the shifting shade, until the food, which Hassan brought me on a separate plate, was ready. In the evenings, still queasy from the day's hike, I would usually retreat to my tent, listen to the radio, and wait for dinner. Eating separately, however necessitated by circumstance, further alienated us from one another.

But there was more to our alienation than a change in meal habits. Not surprisingly, most of my Ruhhal's talk concerned camels – our camels and theirs, camels present and camels past, the price of camels, the meat, milk, health, raising, accoutrements and breed of camels. I took part in this talk as best I could, but I could contribute little of value, and felt they held me in low regard as a result. In the beginning, to compensate, I told them about my family and asked them about theirs (within the limits of Islamic propriety, avoiding undue reference to wives and daughters), but I learned only that both Hassan and Mbari had a lot of children to feed and did not particularly want to be reminded of this. They asked me no questions in return about my family, nor had either of them, even once, enquired about my profession or hobbies. The world outside the desert and those who inhabited it were, at best, irrelevant to them.

Then there was religion. Although they couldn't read, Hassan and Mbari knew suras by heart; their first and last spoken words of each day came from the Qur'an. My own thoughts unavoidably turned to faith, but not only

because of my companions. On my short-wave radio I
found that chanting from the Qur'an and the sermons of
imams occupied just as much ether as did Christian evan-
gelical programmes, which were often transmitted (in
English) to North Africa from somewhere in the heart-
land of the United States. No doubt my Ruhhal and
Noureddine would have agreed with much that was said
on Family Radio, whose pastor, a Brother Harold
Camping, preached a fundamentalist creed: the Bible
(like the Qur'an for most Muslims) is the literal Word of
God, the sole and ultimate authority. Women are to be
silent in congregation and subservient to men. We are
living in the Final Days, during the Final Tribulation.
We are dirty rotten sinners, and Hell awaits us unless
we choose the Straight and Narrow Path (or *al-sirat al-
mustaqim*, as the Qur'an says).

Family Radio and the suras of the Qur'an brought to
mind the sermons of Jonathan Edwards, which I had read
during my teen years. We are, Edwards said, 'sinners in
the hands of an angry God'; 'the pit is prepared, the fire
is made ready, the furnace is now hot'; 'the flames do
now rage and glow'; 'God . . . holds you over the pit of
Hell, much as one holds a spider, or some loathsome
insect, over the fire'. Moved by such words, the members
of Edwards's New England congregation had pitched and
swayed in their pews, crying out with fear. I had seen
Muslim audiences cry out with wonder as they revelled in
the lyrical beauty of chanted suras of similar content.
Yet nowhere for me had words Qur'anic or biblical taken
on as much life as they had here in the Sahara, where,
apart from the Word, there was nothing but rock, sky
and sun. In the desert lurks the sere common spirit of

Judaism, Christianity and Islam – all doctrines of salvation, damnation and a single jealous God based on the Word, all as unsparing (at least in their fundamentalist interpretations) as the land in which they were born.

Here in the Sahara, which must have differed little from the desert of seventh-century Arabia, the Qur'an's desert imagery and metaphors sounded as relevant and modern as ever. But the commonalities among Judaism, Christianity and Islam were of academic interest to me and me alone, for my Ruhhal believed in their faith as the perfection of its predecessors, as a means of attaining salvation, not of exercising their intellects. They professed the right faith and would be saved; I adhered to the wrong faith and would be damned.

We passed our first night out of Ait Oubelli in a high *ragg* called Bou Marsal, under a low spotlight moon that gilded the dark camel-hump heights of Ouarkziz and gave the dwarf acacias around us long black shadows. We had pitched camp early after Hassan complained of pain in his knees and Mbari of a sun-induced headache; to boot, Mabruk was developing a limp. On the morning of the next day, the village of Icht should have come into sight, but a sandstorm erupted in the west and hit us head-on, browning out the sky. The camels bellowed in the hot wind. Once again we squinted into driving grit and walked blind, following the base of the mountain.

Just before noon we finally reached Icht. Its palms, mosque and blocky dun houses lay huddled beneath a rift in the Anti-Atlas so jagged and raw that it looked as if tons of dynamite had just blown a hole in the mountains. We needed to buy vegetables and meat here, and nothing else, so Hassan and I left Mbari in the oasis and set off

into the village. At first Icht appeared deserted, populated only by dust devils swirling in from the desert. We
followed an ashen dirt path between gardens until we
reached a small square, noticing the shards of broken
bottles stabbing out through the tops of walled houses –
protection against thieves. There were no shops open at
the square. A scrawny teenager with a caved-in lower jaw
and bug-eyes was loping by, and Hassan, shouting *salams*
over the wind, asked him where the main square was.
The boy didn't answer but kept on his way, giving us
frightened looks until he slipped through the gate to his
house and slammed the door.

We eventually found another square, where several
men were sitting on their haunches, oblivious to the
blowing sand. When Hassan asked them for directions to
a shop, two or three of them began screeching and snorting and making monkey gestures: they were insane or
retarded. But just ahead was a storefront.

'Vegetables are . . . are . . . Vegetables . . . are.' The
proprietor there spoke in a weirdly halting manner.
'Vegetables . . . come with the truck.'

Hassan spoke through his firwal. 'When does the truck
come?'

'The truck . . . the truck comes . . . sometimes. But it
might not have vegetables. Not today. But . . .'

Just then a gust of wind filled the storefront, and we
closed our eyes. We left this fellow in mid-sentence and
accosted an ancient man snoozing in his hooded djellaba
in the doorway of a concrete hovel with a Coke sticker on
the door. He appeared sober and sane. He would at least
have something for us to drink.

'We want Cokes!' Hassan declared.

'Cokes? In the name of God,' the old man said, righting his turban and standing up slowly, and then turning and moving even more slowly toward the back of his shop, limping, wheezing and coughing at every step. 'In the name of God, the Compassionate, the Merciful . . .' He picked up two Cokes. He looked as if he didn't know what to do with them. Then he seemed to remember. 'In the name of God,' he said, retracing his steps with the same limping and wheezing. I peeked at Hassan's face: his eyes were squinting in pure disgust. I knew what he was thinking: Berbers without ancestry, and inbred ones at that.

'Any vegetables on sale in this village?' I asked the old man.

He raised his eyes to mine and gave me a puzzled look.

'I said any vegetables on sale here?'

'Oh. Vegetables. There is one man. But with the drought, you see—'

'By God, just tell us where this man is!' Hassan demanded.

We found the vegetable man, who turned out to be quite sane. However, he only had a few puny tomatoes and walnut-sized potatoes to sell, plus some brown eggs. There was no chicken for sale in the village, and no meat. The drought, the drought . . .

'Your village is dying. May God bring you rain,' Hassan told him in lieu of a valediction.

We headed back past the lunatics in the square, into the gardens, and out into the sandstorm-whipped clearing in the oasis, where Mbari was squatting on the lee side of the camels, waiting for us. We gave him what we had bought and he began packing.

Hassan rubbed his eyes. 'I miss the mothers,' he said.
'The mothers?'

'My wives,' the two mothers of his six children. This
trip was almost as hard on him as it was on me, but he
would not say so.

The sandstorm ended a few hours later. That evening
we arrived in Foum al-Hisn, a grid of sun-scorched
streets lined with red concrete buildings (the new quarter), surrounded by warrens of stone houses (the old
quarter). It was also another military town. There hardly
seemed to be any civilians about, only soldiers, many of
whom wore sandals with their khaki uniforms. I remembered Akka and the late-night visit from the officers, and
wondered if we could be in for some trouble here with
the authorities.

We pitched camp on the mountain slope above town,
and I retired to my tent to rest. But soon Mbari and
Hassan came up. Mbari looked diffident as usual, Hassan
oddly bumptious.

'Si Jelal?' asked Hassan, peering through my door.

'Yes?'

'Si Jelal . . . ah . . .' He raised his eyebrows and cleared
his throat.

I climbed out. 'Well, what is it?'

'Si Jelal, we have a matter to discuss with you. It concerns money.'

'What about money?'

'We don't have any.'

He looked at the ground like a naughty schoolboy, but
then raised his head and peered down the bridge of his
nose at me. 'The money Ali gave us for supplies has run
out.'

Supplies were included in the fee I was paying Ali for the expedition, but we had agreed that if they ran short I would make up the difference and Ali would deduct the amount from my final payment when we met in Tan-Tan. This seemed to me a simple and straightforward matter.

'Well, okay, tell me how much you need.'

'Oh,' he said, much relieved. 'We don't need much. Let's see. We need a thousand rials for tea. Fifty thousand francs for olive oil. Four thousand centimes for rice. A hundred rials for flour, and fifty dirhams and six hundred rials for meat. Plus—'

'Look, just tell me the amount, and in dirhams.'

'What do you mean?'

'Tell me the total in dirhams.' It seemed reasonable to ask them the cost in the currency we would actually be using.

They gave me a grave, puzzled stare. 'Dirhams?'

Our exchange, as well as the bargaining with the teenager back in Sidi Salih, were examples of a uniquely Moroccan practice that perplexes visitors who venture into the country's south. The dirham (divided into centimes) has been in use in Morocco since the French left in 1956. Francs were the currency during the era of the French protectorate. Rials preceded francs and hark back to the eighteenth century. However, in the south of Morocco minimal rates of literacy and extreme stubbornness have combined to create a bizarre situation: most people, who cannot read, have to date not fully grasped that the franc left circulation almost half a century ago, and the rial died ninety years back. When the government introduced the dirham, southern Moroccans went on calling the bills by the names of the monetary equivalent in old notes. In urban Marrakesh, where I had lived before, people were educated enough to convert prices freely from rials and so on into dirhams, so I never bothered to learn the conversion rates. It had been a decade since I ran into Moroccans who could not convert one currency into another, and I was not prepared for their ignorance on the matter.

Hassan and Mbari exchanged baffled glances. 'We just told you what we need,' said Hassan.

'Well, what is the equivalent of all those currencies in dirhams?'

'A thousand rials plus fifty thousand francs and four thousand centimes and a hundred rials and fifty dirhams and six hundred rials. We could also use—'

I got out my calculator and interrupted him. 'Look, for me to total all that up, I need all of it in dirhams.'

'Oh.' Hassan pulled out a one-dirham coin. 'You mean how many of these?'

'Yes.'

'Fifty of these. Plus a thousand rials plus fifty thousand francs and four thousand centimes and a hundred rials and six hundred rials. And—'

I grabbed the coin. 'Look, how many rials or francs is this?'

He gave me the same look he had given the retarded shopkeeper in Icht. '*That* is a dirham, Si Jelal.'

Mbari stifled a giggle.

'I know it's a dirham. But it also has a rial value. What is the value of this coin in rials or francs?'

'Si Jelal, God grant you wisdom, that is not a rial.'

'Well what *is* a rial?'

He pulled out a five-dirham coin. 'This is a hundred rials.'

'Okay, okay. Now we're getting somewhere. Therefore, one dirham is twenty rials.'

'One dirham is this, Si Jelal.' He held out the one-dirham coin. 'But don't forget we need fifty thousand francs' worth of—'

'How much is a franc?'

'Let me see your money. I'll show you.'

I pulled out my bills – a half-dozen tens, some fifties, a two hundred-dirham note – plus an assortment of one-, five- and ten-dirham coins. All in all, about fifty dollars.

'You don't have a franc here,' Hassan said.

'What are you saying? I've got fifty dollars' worth of dirhams. You can't be telling me all this doesn't equal one franc, and we need fifty thousand francs' worth of—'

'Of olive oil,' said Mbari. Now I saw that he was thoroughly enjoying the berating he perceived me to be delivering to Hassan. Hassan by now had had just about enough of my obtuseness.

I pulled out a fifty-dirham note. 'Okay, how many of these—'

'That's fifty dirhams,' he said. 'This, Si Jelal, is a dirham,' pointing to the coin. 'And this is fifty dirhams. There are no other dirhams. Only ones and fifties.'

I began to understand. All these coins and bills carried different names and were, for my Ruhhal, without related values. We concluded that they needed twenty-five dollars' worth of supplies now, and would need another forty dollars' worth before the trip's end. I handed them the money and they headed for town, leaving me puzzled. It had once been impossible for

southern Moroccans to convert their ideas of francs and
rials into dirhams, but it seemed just as complicated for
me to conceive of transferring old names and values for
money on to bills with new names and values that also
bore different markings and colours. To do this, and
the resultant calculations among the three coexisting
currencies, required an agile mind. Doing things the old
way was by no means the same as doing things the easy
way.

A couple of days later we pulled up camp for Assa, a
four-day walk away. Hassan took the camels and headed
west; we would meet him by the oasis at the other end of
town. Mbari and I would take a detour through Foum al-
Hisn to buy bread (which they had forgotten again on
their supply runs). Cool weather and mists – 'air with
the sea in it' – were supposed to await us in Assa, so I was
in a good mood. Mbari was chanting from the Qur'an,
and I could tell he was relieved, too.

But not for long. At the edge of town a corpulent,
neatly shaven man in his forties, wearing pressed trousers
and a fresh madras shirt, strode toward us, sticking out
his belly. Trouble. Mbari stopped singing and his face
assumed a simpering cast. The man's wrinkled brow and
raised eyebrows communicated something like disdain,
and seemed to demand answers to the questions: '*Who
are you? What are you doing here? Why didn't you report
to me immediately?*'

Mbari veered toward him, wiping sweat off his hand
for a shake, adjusting his firwal for a bow. I walked on but
I knew it would be no use.

'*Monsieur!*' His eyes half-closed, he waved to me.

'*Venez ici, s'il vous plaît!* Where are you going and what are you doing here?'

I addressed him in Arabic. I knew he was from one of the security services, but he didn't say so: he held a position high enough to require no introduction, no presentation of a badge. I told him we were on our way to Assa by camel, and Mbari was one of my guides. I said that before departure I had informed the Royal Gendarmerie, and the chief had authorised my trip.

For some reason Mbari giggled at my words, which made it sound like I was trying to pull a fast one.

The agent heard me out, said nothing, and walked away. We walked on, but we sensed that that wasn't the end of it. Mbari left me to do his shopping. In a café close by I bought some mineral water and sat down to wait for Mbari.

I put the water to my lips. A Peugeot came screeching up, and a jackbooted, pockmarked young gendarme jumped out and made straight toward me, shoving aside the other patrons in the café.

He loomed above me and asked shrilly, 'Who are you? Show me your papers! What are you doing here? Who's with you?' The other people in the café turned and stared at me.

I showed him my passport and explained again what I was doing. He sat down next to me and began writing my details in French on a sheet of unlined paper. He first inscribed categories (name, date of birth, purpose of visit and so on). I noticed he left off diacritical marks and failed to double consonants where necessary, and I was seized by an irrational desire to point this out to him. Mbari walked in and, seeing this gendarme, looked suddenly ready to flee. I motioned him to come forward.

'This is Mbari, one of my guides.' I showed the officer Ali's business card. 'Mbari is working now for this man, who has a licensed expedition agency in Zagora.'

The officer grabbed the card. 'Who else is with you?'

I told him about Hassan.

'We must see this so-called Hassan,' he said, pronouncing the name as if it could belong only to a Polisario guerrilla.

'Well, we're going out to the oasis now to meet him.'

'Then show him to us.'

Outside the café the overfed agent was waiting behind the wheel of the Peugeot. At least they'll give us a ride to the oasis, I thought. But the gendarme got in the car and they drove off.

We started walking to the oasis. A half-hour later, as we neared it, they drove up behind us. They gunned the motor and sped past, spraying us with dust, and halted. They both got out.

The agent stood with his hands on his hips, looking pained. 'Where is this Hassan?'

Hassan was now walking briskly toward us; the camels were loitering on the sand behind him. He understood what was going on and pulled his ID card out of his fouqiya's inner pocket. This was a manifestation of the police state in which he took such pride, and he would gladly play his part in its rituals.

The gendarme looked at the camels. 'Got a licence for those?'

Hassan had some sort of papers establishing ownership and he produced them. (Ali had warned us that police might stop us and ask to see proof that we had not stolen the camels.)

The gendarme turned to me. 'What is your profession?'

'Bank consultant.'

The last thing I wanted to say was writer, which in countries like Morocco sounds a lot like 'spy–subversive–degenerate'.

'Ah ha. You work for the government,' he said.

'No. Banks are private in the United States.'

'Oh.' He turned to Mbari. 'You there, show me your ID.'

Mbari picked this moment to assert his indignation at being so treated. 'My card is packed. I'm not about to unload the camel to get it.'

'Mbari, get your card,' I said, puzzled at this surge in assertiveness after he had just shown himself to be so timid. This would only become complicated if we refused to cooperate.

'No!'

Hassan reasoned with him, and I again prodded him to obey. Swearing under his breath he stomped over to the camel's load and pulled apart his pack to find the card.

The jackbooted gendarme had got out his paper and pen again, and looked at Mbari and Hassan. 'Your professions?'

'Worker.'

The gendarme copied down the information. The madras man turned to me and put his hand on my shoulder in an annoyingly familiar way, but this signalled a change. 'Look, these camels won't die of thirst in the desert but you certainly can. You've got to have water

with you. The desert is a dangerous place. These 'Arib
are tough, but anyone can die of thirst around here. You
must rest in the shade from ten to four. Got that?'

'Yes. Thanks for your concern.'

'You're welcome. You know, one year we had this
French tourist come through here. He had his own camel.
We took every care to see that he was safe, and got him
safely to the next province. He was very grateful for our
attention. I'm sure he has fond memories of us. You see,
our only concern is your safety.'

The jackbooted gendarme was now standing by
Mabruk and trying to pet him. Mabruk roared, and with
bared teeth swung away his head. The gendarme jumped
back. He straightened his lapels and caught sight of the
bottle of mineral water I had just bought.

'That water cold?'

'No.'

He snatched it out of my hand and gurgled down half
its contents, returning me the bottle. A gob of his spit
glistened on the rim.

They wished us good travels and were off.

We walked into the desert for half an hour, but then a
dust trail signalled an approaching vehicle. Mbari began
simpering again. Hassan reached inside his djellaba
pocket for his ID.

The agent drove up, bouncing over the stones, and
skidded to a stop. The car frightened the camels, who
bucked and reared their heads, making their loads jingle
and sway.

The officer didn't care. He rolled down the window. 'I
just told the qa'id about you. He's very worried. He says
you have to go to that oasis just over there and wait until

four this afternoon before moving on. It's too hot to travel now.'

'Thank you, we'll do that,' I said.

'You must obey.'

'We will. Thank you.'

He drove away.

Hassan was high on all this interference. 'See, they're upholding order. Order! Beautiful, isn't it? We couldn't get away with *anything* here.'

Still, we ignored the command to halt at the oasis and set out on the *mijbid* for Assa. In the desert the words of city folk held no sway.

ASSA AND HOURIS
IN THE MISTS

HASSAN AND MBARI were spirited conversationalists. It was a rare moment indeed when they weren't praising the virtues of a prominent 'Arib sheikh, debating the vices of a controversial cameleer, or disputing the lie of the land ahead. I often found myself enraptured by the guttural music of their Hassaniya Arabic. I revelled in its rich interdental consonants, which, thanks to the isolation imposed on the Saharawis by the desert, had mostly retained their classical pronunciation (in contrast to the degraded consonants of the Moroccan dialect). I was intrigued by its vocabulary, which contained words (*witta* for car, *dashra* for city, *shidda* for drought, for example) that existed in no other dialect I had heard. And I relished the throaty 'ain and ghain sounds common to all forms of Arabic, dialectal and classical.

No other language enchants me the way Arabic does. *Sihr halal* (lawful magic) is what the Arabs call the effect their poetry produces on its hearers. The magic was born in the desert, among the Bedouin of pre-Islamic Arabia, who, though illiterate, were among the most accomplished poets of any age. Poor denizens of denuded earth, they had nothing but their tongues with which to make art; in a world where a cup of water and a handful of dates made for luxury, extravagant language took on heightened importance. The odes the Bedouin composed before the advent of Islam remain some of the greatest in Arabic literature. Even the words of simple orators like my Ruhhal companions held something of the poetic, and worked *sihr halal* on me. Their talk, pealing with locutions from the Qur'an and invocations of God, its Hassaniya inflections conjuring up the vast burning wastes of their homeland, made a description of camel fodder or sand dunes sound dramatic and grand. This was a matter of sound more than sense, to be sure, but here among the rocks sound was all we had.

Yet no enchantment with language could compensate for the physical and spiritual deterioration we suffered as we marched farther and farther down the valley. After we left Foum al-Hisn the rigours of the trip began wearing on all of us in ominous ways. We felt with each new day a fatigue more penetrating and, at times, disorienting; we suffered more and more stress-related ailments. Hassan's back now pained him as much as his knees; Mbari complained of spasms in his calves that turned each step into agony for hours on end; and the sun, growing stronger as summer came on, kept me light-headed, fever-stricken and nauseated for most of the day. Mbari and I tried to resign ourselves to silence about our growing infirmity: we knew it would not outlast the trip. But Hassan was volubly humbled. 'In the old days our ancestors walked twelve hours at a stretch without drinking water. They died strong. But look at us. We live weak.'

Could the desert defeat us, cripple us, prevent us from making it to the Atlantic? The closer we came to our goal, the weaker we became, and the more anxious I grew.

But good times were just ahead, Hassan kept saying. Refreshing blue mists would fill the air in Assa, which was just a couple of hundred kilometres from the Atlantic. As summer drew on and the heat increased we thought only of the mists of Assa.

The next day, in the distance, between Jbel Ouarkziz and the Anti-Atlas, the twin minarets of Assa's two main mosques wobbled rubbery in the heat under a fiery noon sky. There were no mists. We staggered, weakened from the sun, toward a pair of acacias that were more bushes than trees, the scrawniest we had seen so far. We couched the camels beside them and unloaded, moving slowly to conserve our strength.

I tossed my mattress under a square yard of acacian shade and collapsed – on thorns that stabbed through two inches of foam and punctured my back and elbows. I bounced back up in pain and impaled my straw hat on the branches. Smarting, for a moment I sat still and composed myself. After extracting the thorns I carefully cleared the ground and repositioned the mattress. This time I lay back slowly. Next to me was a hole in the ground, a burrow of some sort a few inches wide. Finally relaxing a bit, I peered into it, wondering what sort of animal would dig it. Not the palm rat, I hoped, whose bite was said to be fatal. I began to doze off.

From out of the rippling mercurial mirages in the east

whence we had come materialised three houri-like crea-
tures swathed in robes of black, blue and purple. At first
I disbelieved my eyes and strained to refocus them. But
there *were* three women gliding toward us through the
blaze, their dark milhafas fluttering with the hot draughts
rising from the stony earth.

'*As-salam 'alaykum!*' they intoned, making demure
gestures of salutation and pulling up their milhafas to
cover their chins.

We answered their greetings. Immediately I noticed
the striking beauty of the youngest one: oval-faced, she
had pale sea-green eyes, a regal arched nose and round
lips; tufts of unkempt hennaed hair were struggling free
of her shroud. Beauty was beauty, she had power, and I
found myself staring.

'*Shhalkum?* [How are you?]' I asked them.

'*Shi bes ma kain* [Nothing to complain of],' the oldest
one replied in a lilting voice; the other two kept silent,
smiling and bashfully averting their eyes.

Hassan, who was starting a fire to make lunch, made a
space for them on one of the rugs he had spread out.
Mbari, I noticed, looked away, too modest to confront
them. But only the eldest one sat down. She had a row of
crooked teeth; the skin on her face was crinkled white
paper; her hands were hennaed leather; her sandalled feet
were hennaed in elaborate geometric designs, as were the
feet of the others, who walked off a little ways and examined us, holding their milhafas over their mouths. Hassan
offered them tea, but only the eldest accepted.

She addressed me. Did I have medicine for the itch?
For the eyes? For the joints? I was sorry to tell her that I
had no medicine for any of these things. She was suffering

from rheumatism. Had I rheumatism pills? I hadn't. 'I'm just too old to live!' she said with a chuckle.

She and Hassan began exchanging news. She and her daughters lived in the white tent we had passed in the wadi an hour ago; her husband and sons were off tending their camels. Their talk ranged over the price of oats in Tata, the cost of flour in Fez, the flocks we had seen, the rain that, this year, was now certain not to fall. Her manners contrasted with those of Ruhhal men: she didn't slurp her tea, pick her nose, or shout at the top of her voice to those sitting a foot or two away; as she spoke she made graceful gestures with her hennaed hands. I could have watched her and listened to her lilting voice for hours. Lawful magic, if of another form.

The heat grew unbearable, the shade even scarcer. Hassan finished baking bread, and stew bubbled in our pot. They declined to lunch with us. The eldest rose and they all ambled away, their shrouds fluttering in the heat. The minarets of Assa had disappeared in noontime haze, and we sat down to eat.

'In Assa it's cool,' Hassan had kept saying. In Assa it felt like it was sixty degrees.

By any measure, however, Assa was modern. Unfortunately, modern in the Moroccan Sahara equates with concrete row houses where the plumbing backs up until people prefer to 'go' in the streets; where temperatures inside exceed those outside by a factor of ten; and where the screaming of one child echoes from house to house until it kicks off a crying spree among all the tots in the neighbourhood. Modern also means soldiers in sandals pedalling bicycles, plainclothes policemen, recognisable by

their crewcuts and urban dress, and a walled-off palace
with crenellated roof and white-trimmed windows for
the royally appointed governor. And modern of course
means electricity, much of which goes to illuminate the
governor's residence.

All this modernity impressed my companions. Assa
had become modern in the decade since they last saw it;
in those benighted times it had been a tranquil scattering
of adobe houses built around a mosque under swaying
palms. Yet there is still no hotel in Assa, and there are
only a couple of storefront dives serving grilled chicken
and French fries. This makes sense, for many of the
Ruhhal who live here do so only for part of the year (they
spend the rest of their time with their flocks), and have
no tradition of eating out, unless you count eating out in
the desert. I invited Hassan and Mbari to have lunch in
one of the restaurants, but they said no. Food from the
common pot was all they knew and all they wanted.

We pitched camp on the hamada a mile away from the
walls of the governor's palace. After doing our laundry
and hanging our clothes on thorns to dry, Hassan and I
sat and watched the sun go down, and the palace lights
come on. The wind was at our backs, wafting the latrine
stench of the nearby wadi away from us and into the
cement lanes. As in Akka, the outskirts of the town were
used as a dump.

'How beautiful,' Hassan said. 'The people here are all
Saharawis, all from one tribe. Their ancestry is grand.
I'm proud to see the city they've built. Before the
drought it was just a few mud houses. The sheikhs have
planned this city with the government.'

'Where do nomads get the money to buy houses?'

'Oh, money is no problem. A nomad will sell ten of his camels at ten thousand rials a piece [about five hundred dollars] and he can buy a house. A house with a floor and ceilings, made of concrete. If he wants, he'll buy a fan to make a breeze in the house.'

'And what happens to his camels?'

'He gets a cousin to look after them. Some of the people of Assa have three hundred camels. These are rich people. With ancestry. But living in a town like this changes people.'

'How?'

'I have relatives here. I saw them today, but they didn't even invite me for tea. Their manners are becoming those of city people. There are even drunks here.'

There was no reason to stay in Assa. We bought supplies, rested for two days, and prepared to move on. But by now we were too worn out to recover in so little time. Only the proximity of the Atlantic – the end of the trip – gave us the energy to get going.

Around dawn the next day baby-blue mists rolled in and cooled the valley. Nothing could have raised my spirit more, and I spent several minutes standing outside my tent taking deep breaths of the wet air – and listening to Hassan say, 'I *told* you so! By God, I *told* you so!'

But soon the sight of blood and gore and a bellowing beast spoiled my cheer. Hassan and Mbari decided that Hanan was still too young to be led with an *aghaba*. So, using a knitting needle, they tore him a new nostril and ran a rough nylon rope through the hole (his *khurs*, or nostril ring, having been lost along the way). The rope not only stretched the hole, it abraded it and added to the animal's misery. From then on, every morning, despite Hanan's protestations, they would rotate the rope in the hole (and rip apart the scab) to make sure his flesh did not grow into it.

Hanan, thus punctured, was the most obedient he had ever been. By now we knew the character of all three camels, which had developed to meet the challenges of the trip. Hanan had been a complainer who cried out whenever any of us approached him; now he was docile and stoic. As ever, his lower lip drooped and gave him a doltish look. However, he took his revenge on Hassan and Mbari by defecating whenever they passed by his rear end, from which green pellets would tumble out and bounce on to their sandals. Na'im was still petulant, but he had matured a little and come to understand his job; I couldn't remember the last time he had couched without permission. Still, he had a long way to go. He was a frequent belcher and avid urinater, taking advantage of any pause in our progress to spread his legs and pee. (In this he differed from Hanan, who dribbled as he walked.) Mabruk no longer stole vegetables, so we changed his nickname from Sinbay (thief) to Biyyid (the white one, on account of his colour). He was as cheerful as ever, and carried the heaviest loads without complaining. I humoured him and often brought him orange peelings, or gave him a carrot or two from the couscous pot on the sly.

None of the camels ever bit, kicked or otherwise threatened us, though they were powerful animals, and my Ruhhal cautioned me never to let my guard down around them. I grew dearly fond of all of them. They worked hard on this trip, harder than they had ever worked, and they suffered much − pulled muscles, stomach upsets, hunger and, most of all, debilitating fatigue, which was evident in their grunting gaits and belaboured, oft-aborted rises when loaded.

So we left Assa and headed into the mists, following a *piste* that led up a slope, with Jbel Ouarkziz and the Drâa somewhere to the south, the Anti-Atlas as ever a wall to the north. Our destination was the village of Âouïnet-Torkoz, two days' walk away. Torkoz was our last supply stop before we would enter the Anti-Atlas and face what my Ruhhal warned me would be our toughest trial yet – a week of trekking up steep mountain trails under a pitiless sun. This was a necessary detour. For a stretch the Drâa lacked wells, so we would cross the mountains and pick up the valley on the other side. Given our weakened state, I preferred not to contemplate entering the mountains.

Not an acacia or a tamarisk intruded upon the emptiness – there were only vistas of sweeping hamada ending in mist between the two mountain ranges. We breathed in the cool and walked. By midmorning we reached the zenith of the slope and began a descent, passing a dead jackal, who resembled a long-snouted dog, but with sharp ears, tawny fur and vicious, slit-opal eyes.

ÂOUÏNET-TORKOZ

BY NOON THE mists had evaporated. After lunch, Hassan grew oddly quiet. I asked him what was wrong.

He stood up. 'I cannot lie.' He stretched out his arms and shook his head; he closed his eyes, as if prepared to reveal the painful truths of a tormented soul. 'No, I can't say it'll take only two days to get to Âouïnet-Torkoz. God knows how long it will take. God knows.'

I got out the map and spread it on the ground. It showed that fifty kilometres separated Assa and Âouïnet-Torkoz – a two-day trip, given that we usually covered twenty-seven to twenty-nine kilometres a day.

'But—'

'Don't tell me what's on that map,' he said. 'Looking at paper isn't the same as walking.'

'Hassan, excuse me, but this map is accurate. We've seen that. I don't know what you're talking about. You just told me in Assa it would take two days to get to Âouïnet-Torkoz. You and Mbari *both* told me.'

'We never said that. I cannot lie. God alone knows—'

'Mbari?'

'Hassan said that, not I.'

This was not true.

'You *did* say that; both of you did. And why do you keep saying God knows and you can't lie? There are a finite number of kilometres between the two villages. The map shows it. It's not a question of words.'

Hassan spread his arms again. 'I cannot lie. I swear by God on high, we're three days away. At least. Maybe more.'

'That's absurd! We've walked half a day, and now we've got less than one and a half to go! It can't be otherwise! Think of how many kilometres we cover in an hour, and look at the map!'

Raising his forefinger and placing a hand on his heart, Hassan swore to God that he was truthful to a fault, a hater of liars, a straight talker renowned throughout the valley, nay, across the Sahara, for his honesty. His greatest fault was (it so happened and he would dare just this once to admit it) an overly zealous respect for the truth. In making such theatre of his honesty, he convinced me that he was trying to deceive me – in order to lengthen the trip and increase his fee. In other circumstances this might not have been a big deal: I knew he was poor, with many mouths to feed at home, and I sympathised with him. But we were all exhausted, our camels were weak and the heat now spoiled meat and vegetables so quickly that a delay would entail the risk that we might be caught out for several days or more with only rice to eat. I had no desire to slow our pace.

Seeking support, I turned to Mbari. 'Well, what do you think?'

'By God, Hassan speaks the truth.'

'Mbari, *you* are the one who knows this part of the route, remember?'

He muttered something inaudible and looked away.

That was it: they were conspiring against me. I told them to pack up – we were going to make Âouïnet-Torkoz by the next evening, and I would talk no more about it.

The heat returned and intensified: the next day at lunch it was forty-five degrees in the shade. Late that afternoon, after entering upon a stretch of valley rich with limestone and strewn with marble-coloured slag, we crossed Wadi Talh (Wadi Acacia), and dragged ourselves panting and bleary-eyed up a stony rise. From its height we saw, beneath a sun that burned straight into our faces, the village of Âouïnet-Torkoz (Little Spring of the Torkoz Tribe). Little more than a few dozen stone houses and a mosque beside a grove of stunted palms, Torkoz promised meagre provisions. Beyond it, following the base of Jbel Ouarkziz, the Drâa wandered away to the southwest, without wells, untrammelled by Ruhhal. Above the village towered the Anti-Atlas: crag after jagged crag cut into the sky, separating us from the Atlantic.

We made our way down to the village, with Mbari stumbling along sunstruck in the final half-mile.

We set up camp beneath the palms as the sun went down. After filling our jerry cans halfway at the well (we could not burden the camels with full cans in the mountains), Mbari and I walked into the village, needing a sack of oats or dates for camel feed, plus couscous, meat and vegetables. It was deserted (its inhabitants were out grazing their herds, or drought had driven them away, we didn't know), except for a few Saharawi elders crouched in the long evening shade of stone walls near the tiny central square. They set suspicious eyes on me; perhaps I was the only Nasrani to visit this remote settlement in years. In the one open shop there was no meat to be had and no couscous. The vegetables were scrawny and expensive, but we bought them. There were no oats or dates for the camels. Worse, Mbari said the camels might be squeamish about eating in the mountains, where the vegetation differed from that of the desert.

We returned to camp, ate dinner and assessed our situation. Between here and the Atlantic there were two small villages, but they would have few supplies, being basically Ruhhal settlements and therefore probably as deserted as Âouïnet-Torkoz. We had only rice and flour, plus three days' worth of vegetables, along with tea and some sugar. According to the map, and as the crow flies, Tiglite, the first village we would come across, was fifty kilometres away, but this was fifty kilometres through mountains, which inclined me to think that if we followed a trail, we could expect three days of strenuous travel at least. I asked them if they knew the trail; yes, they did, roughly. My map showed that we could pick up some sort of *piste* (winding down from the north) about halfway to Tiglite, but neither Hassan nor Mbari had ever heard of it. Did they know where the wells were? Not exactly, but there *should* be wells, and there *should* be Ruhhal to ask – or at least there *could* be: maybe the drought would have forced them north, to the Sous. In consideration of how much water we were going to lose in sweat hiking uphill in this heat, and given that the higher altitudes would make the sun harder to bear, increasing the likelihood of dehydration, their uncertainty about the wells made me nervous.

We stared at the map. Hassan and Mbari exchanged subtle glances. Mbari stood up. His voice shook with anger. 'It is not fifty kilometres to Tiglite but seventy! or eighty! By God, with these mountains it could be more. Maybe a hundred. God alone knows. The mountains are very hard. I'll not kill these camels with a breakneck pace! No, I will *not!*'

We had not talked of travelling at a breakneck pace. I sensed a continuation of their ruse.

'Mbari, *what* are you talking about?'

Hassan arose next. 'The camels must live! We must go slowly, *slooowly* in the mountains!'

I stood up and looked at them. We were all tired, but they had strength enough for more acts in their drama. I didn't. I said goodnight and walked back to my tent.

Mbari shouted after me. 'By God! I won't let these camels drop in the mountains! I swear it! I—'

Hassan asked him to calm down.

With the heat, which was not abating with the night, and with my nerves, which were fraying, I couldn't sleep, so I came out an hour or so later to sit with Hassan and Mbari by the fire. Soon after, strangers approached us. Two were young men in white djellabas, whose cheeks sported three-day beards (worn by some pious Muslims as a sign of humility; such beards cannot be groomed, and thus show a disregard for personal appearance); the third, who was older, wore the chocolate-brown 'abaya robes of the Saharawis who live in the Western Sahara. They were all from the village.

After the greeting ritual ended the older one asked us if we had come for the magic of the cave.

No, we answered. What was that?

'You leave flour in the cave up there and pray to the jinn. In the morning you find it changed into whatever you want, money or gold or silver. But it's deep in the mountains and many don't find it. You want to know the way there?'

We thanked him but said no, and asked him about wells. He explained where the first one was, but his directions were complicated, and I doubted whether a stranger to the region could follow them.

After that he looked up at the village. 'We're right on the border with the Western Sahara, you know. The Spanish were there' – he pointed to the south – 'the French here. When the Moroccans took over we built the village. We were all just Ruhhal till then. Anyway, good travels!'

He walked on. The others sat down with us. They were teachers at the school, and pleased to meet me; they got no foreign visitors here. After introductions we started chatting. They had never travelled to Tiglite and so couldn't help us plot a route there.

During our talk, one of them, Omar, called me a Nasrani. He meant no offence, but it rankled me. It was unpleasant being labelled, and it vaguely smacked of racism. Past experience had made me sensitive: while I was living in Marrakesh, no one called me anything but Nasrani until I adopted my Arabic name.

'You know,' I said, 'I'm not sure calling me a Nasrani is polite. I just told you my name.'

'Oh, I didn't mean any harm,' he said. 'But you *are* a Nasrani, a believer in Jesus.'

'How do you know? You have no idea what religion I am.'

His friend Samir cut in. 'To us, Nasrani means foreigner. Just like *gaouri*.' This was even less flattering: it derived from an old Turkish word for infidel, and was now often used in Morocco in place of Nasrani. 'Even some Moroccans call themselves *gaouri* now. Those who adopt Western ways are proud to say they're *gaouri*. It's not such an insult any more.'

'*Gaouri* reminds me of religious discrimination, of how in the Umayyad Empire and Ottoman Turkey non-Muslims had to cut their hair in a weird way, weren't allowed to ride horses, wear hats, or build churches or synagogues. In the Abbasid Empire they even had to attach wooden statues of devils to their houses and had to step aside when Muslims passed. So why don't we just call each other by name.'

Omar said, 'Well, it *is* natural that Christians were not allowed to do everything Muslims could do. There had to be some discrimination. After all, Islam is true, and privileges have to be given to those who follow the truth. We respect your religion but it isn't true. Christianity *is* incomplete, after all. Only Islam is complete. Isn't that so?'

Samir nudged him. 'Don't talk like that.'

'This Nasrani speaks Arabic. He should have read the Qur'an. Have you?'

'I don't ask you whether you've read the Bible. Religion is a personal matter. I respect that you're Muslim and I respect Islam, or I wouldn't be here. I don't ask you to explain why you believe in Islam.'

'I'll be happy to tell you.'

'There's no need to. All I'm saying is that religion is a personal affair. Even in the Qur'an it says this. And it says there should be no compulsion in religion.'

This kind of talk would only prompt him to lecture me about Islam, to do his sacred duty and try to convert me, so I changed the subject to language. The gendarmes who had questioned us recently had noted down all our details in French. When I was a Peace Corps volunteer in the 1980s the Moroccan government was Arabising its schools, phasing out French. This was a major shift, even though education had been in both Arabic and French during the colonial days. After independence government affairs and business still tended to be conducted in French; the educated middle class wanted to retain French, which allowed them to lord it over the Arabic-educated masses and the illiterate (more than half the population) who knew only their dialects. Many of Morocco's best-known authors write in French (and live in France, where they are free to write what they want). The Moroccan independence movement, led mostly by French-educated Moroccan intellectuals, issued its first demands in a French-language document. French politicians at times still praise Morocco's Francophone heritage, which certain nationalistic Moroccan politicians answer with anti-French rhetoric – in French. Morocco is Arab and Islamic, they tell them – in French. So what had happened to Arabisation? Why was there still so much French in official circles?

'Arabisation failed,' Samir said. 'The schools are Arabicised but not the universities, except in literature and history, which were in Arabic anyway. This makes it tough on the students who go to college because they

have to study French hard to catch up. All the university
textbooks in sciences and philosophy are in French, and it
costs too much to translate them. This is bad. We're still
stuck with the colonial mindset, even though our consti-
tution says we're an Arab and Islamic state. What we
really are is a Muslim state made up of two peoples. We
have three Berber dialects in this country and a third of
Moroccans speak them. Should Berber speakers be
forced to use Arabic? A lot of them prefer French because
they don't like the Arabs.'

He was right, but there was more to the language
question than failed government programmes or the
Berber–Arab divide. Perhaps more than any other country
in the Arab world, Morocco has developed a national identity that exceeds in strength the pan-Arab nationalism that
has so many adherents elsewhere in North Africa and the
Middle East. The simplest explanation for this lies in
Morocco's geography, and in its history of isolation: the
Turks, who unified most of the Arab world under the
Ottoman banner, never managed to conquer Morocco,
thanks in part to the Atlas Mountains. Later, competing
Great Power designs on Morocco resulted in a stalemate
that kept the country nominally independent until 1912. In
recent decades tension with Algeria (especially over the
Western Sahara) and a perceived threat to the Moroccan
monarchy from Islamic fundamentalism and radical Arab
ideologies, along with simple economics, have prompted
the Moroccan elite to look to Europe for alliances, cultural
exchange and trade: France remains Morocco's chief cred-
itor, investor, source of tourists and host of guest workers.
In 1984 the French-educated King Hassan II even offi-
cially requested membership in the European Union.

We discussed all this until midnight. Then the teachers told us that they had to get up early in the morning, and we had to rest before heading into the Anti-Atlas, so we all said goodnight.

I crawled into my tent worrying about the Anti-Atlas. The antics Hassan and Mbari had performed to convince me that God alone knew how long it would take to reach Tiglite made me wonder if they might not know the route. They knew the desert, but how could they know the mountains?

A wind began stirring. I hoped it would bring cool, which would greatly ease our travels. But it was coming from the east. Blowing in from the Sahara, the wind carried only more heat, more dust. It was a Shirgi, the same broiling, sand-laden gale that had once nearly cost me my life.

CROSSING THE ANTI-ATLAS

TO OUR RELIEF, the Shirgi died at sunrise, but it left behind stagnant, thirty-degree air that so early in the day boded ill for hiking. At eight in the morning we trekked out of Âouïnet-Torkoz in an effulgent bath of sunlight, passing around the rear of the village and up into a meandering valley formed by several abutting mountains. Sluggish from the heat, we walked slowly, saying nothing, dreading the terrain ahead.

We had begun the day in foul humour. I had deposited my gear in Hanan's saddlebag. Hassan came over and started working the nylon rope back and forth through Hanan's new nostril, abrading the hole and bloodying the rope. Hanan hollered and shook his head and tried to rise, spilling his load; Hassan cursed and pushed him down. I flinched at all this pain. Hassan saw my reaction and yanked the rope harder. He must be holding a grudge from our argument the day before, I thought, and he's taking it out on the camel. I glared at him, and thought of protesting. But an argument was the last thing we needed now, so I turned away. Soon we were packed and on our way.

An hour after leaving Torkoz, we came upon a *piste*, much degraded, here and there blocked by fallen rocks, but passable. Wanting to face the rigours of the land alone, I walked ahead of the group, but step by step, to my surprise and increasing delight, I found that we were entering a new world. Argan trees replaced acacias and clustered in low groves, their thick, holly-green foliage hiding acorn-sized fruit and sheltering squirrels. Manic butterflies and lazy bees attended rafts of crimson, purple and pale blue flowers. Patches of thyme began proliferating over the earth, which was turning from dust-brown to a pale limestone green.

We were leaving the Sahara! I walked faster and faster up the *piste*, breathing in air that was growing cooler, an unexpected elation rushing over me. Grasshoppers jumped about in thickening brush. Beetles with opalescent shells scuttled at the base of rocks. Red-rumped swallows darted against slopes of shale tinged with delicate mossy green. Martins and swifts cut through the pure morning light. Ahead a falcon dipped low and then ascended to an eyrie on a cliff shaded by a crag. The thick argan trees chased away any hint of drought, the dry or the dead.

We climbed higher and higher, sticking to the serpentine *piste*. The sun beat down but, breathing in the ever cooler air, I jumped ahead, quickening my pace and leaving my Ruhhal behind, feeling for the first time that I was nearing the end of my trip. I suddenly wanted nothing more than the caress of Atlantic breezes on my face.

I yearned to forget about the Sahara. The Atlantic, the Atlantic! I pictured myself crashing into the cold thrashing surf, as 'Uqba bin Nafi' is reputed to have done after leading the first Arab campaign of conquest into Morocco more than thirteen centuries ago.

At noon we stopped in a high valley and rested under a canopy of argans. The camels turned their heads away from the unfamiliar leaves and fruit, and they refused to eat the grass. This worried Hassan and Mbari, but they were pleased with the change in climate, if somewhat apprehensive: it was new to them, as were the mountain environs. We ate a salad and slept until three, and then moved on.

Nothing could dampen my joy at what I was seeing. The trail wound and rose and looped upwards, until finally we were trekking single-file atop a ridge, bathed in cool wind and light and the scent of wildflowers. But we didn't know where to find a well, and we needed water, having only half-filled our jerry cans in Âouïnet-Torkoz. Just as we realised our predicament, we spotted a nomad tent. A skinny youth in a blue and gold dara'a and an indigo firwal emerged, called out a greeting and waved for us to approach. After prolonged *salams* and enquiries about our health and provenance, he agreed to walk us to a nearby well, and we set out behind him. His long feet were jammed into kid-sized sandals; his toes appeared ready to burst like ripe grapes; and he walked with a limp.

We passed along a windy, slag-littered escarpment, with the sun hanging straight ahead of us. I shielded my eyes but the light burned into my brain, and something went wrong with me. My steps became tottery; a cold sweat ran over my forearms and dripped down my palms;

I felt hot and then cold; the rock- and argan-covered slopes of the Anti-Atlas flashed with pinpoint stars before my eyes. Mbari was staggering along, also sun-struck, keeping himself from falling by holding on to one of Mabruk's saddlebags. We followed a footpath down into an explosion of pink-blossomed reeds and sprouting palms set amid a tiny canyon of black rock. There was a well there. Two women, young, fleshy and pink-cheeked, wearing djellabas but no veils, were doing laundry in plastic tubs. I took wobbly steps to a sofa-shaped rock and collapsed on it; Mbari did the same. Hassan alone remained unaffected. The thin air of the mountains and the sun were getting to us, I thought: need to drink more water. I started dozing off.

'*Hak!*' a female voice said to me. '*Hak, khud!*'

I opened my eyes. One of the women was offering me a glass of tea. I sat up, took it and opened my mouth to thank her, but no words came out; my hands trembled as I raised the glass to my lips. But she kept smiling at me maternally. She was squatting over her tub, her djellaba pulled up, her floral-patterned sirwal covering her legs to her ankles. Her kohl-blackened eyes and aquiline nose, her dark hair glinting with tints of henna, her high-arched, dainty feet all marked her as a beauty. Contemplating her features, I sipped the tea and recovered. Hassan filled our jerry cans and watered the camels.

'The camels must eat,' Hassan told the boy, 'but they won't eat all these strange plants you have around here.'

'There is a wadi,' the boy replied. 'I'll show you.'

We thanked the women for the tea. Too weak to walk yet, I climbed aboard Na'im. Led by the boy, we left the oasis and travelled higher still, ascending the rumplike mountains into a realm of sea breezes and whirling mists that moistened my skin and brought on a delirium of pleasure. The Anti-Atlas spread to every horizon, wild and pristine, like the surface of a forgotten planet.

We left the heights and descended into a valley, Wadi Mhijjiba, still led by the boy. A wind from the west ripped through the palm- and argan-studded slopes, bringing billowing mists and even, now and then, drops of water large enough to be called rain. But the sun was shining, slanting toward the horizon, turning the mists reddish gold. I found myself shivering as we reached the spot where we were to camp: it was cold enough that I almost needed a sweater. There were many herds of camels there. The valley resounded with the bellowing of adult males, the nasal complaints of foals and the groans of pregnant females. Their Ruhhal masters, all in brown Saharawi 'abayas, greeted us; they were heading for the Sous. The boy said goodbye and left.

We pitched camp. Incredulous of the change in climate, I sat down with Hassan as Mbari made tea.

Hassan was grinning: he was happy with the cool. Our mood lightened. 'That girl at the well invited us to spend the night in her tent with her and her friend.'

'Are you serious?'

'I'm not joking. But I wasn't sure if you would permit it, so I said no. After all, we want to stick to our schedule. We can't take any extra days to fool around with houris.'

I looked at Mbari. 'He's joking, right?'

'By God, I don't know.'

'I'm not joking. Not at all. By God!'

He had to be joking about the woman: we had been

together at the well and I had heard no such talk. Still, it was odd to hear him speak of sex in this light-hearted way, after both he and Mbari had shown themselves so reticent on the subject. I could only ascribe it to the intoxicating effect the cool was having on us all.

The night was cold. I slept with my sleeping bag zipped to my neck, waking up now and then to wonder at the sound of the wind soughing in the trees. Around dawn a raucous chirping of birds awoke me for good. The temperature hovered at ten degrees. The sun shone through crystalline air; the breezes carried hints of pomegranates, grasses and other vegetation – the scents of life. The Ruhhal were already on the move, herding their camels north into the mountains.

Hassan and Mbari had thrown on every piece of clothing they owned and were already packing when I came out. We picked up a *piste* that wandered out of the valley, climbed up and around a succession of low ridges, and then led on to a mesa where the wind played and sheep grazed – there was grass enough here for livestock. Now round leafy shrubs dominated the land, increasingly mixed with low, round cacti. Even at noon it was only twenty degrees here (I kept checking my thermometer), but the wind made it seem colder. With a feeling of new-found gratitude I pulled my sweater out of my pack, shook off two months of Saharan dust, and put it on. I walked, hugging the wool to my body, enjoying the comfort of wearing a warm sweater in cool air. We stopped for lunch beneath a bower of argans. I grabbed my foam mattress and threw it down in the sun. Luxuriating in the warmth, I slept until the food was ready.

By late afternoon the *piste* had left the mesa and led us

into rolling mountains. We would not make Tiglite that evening, that was clear, but Mbari said it was close. We stopped for the night in a valley, and I took my tent and hiked away with it to a secluded dell of argans and cacti, needing solitude. The foliage in the landscape reminded me of something familiar and made me feel at home; I relished this half-formed sensation. Selfishly, I did not want my companions to intrude. They seemed to understand, and took no offence.

Iron-grey clouds hung low over the valley, sifting shafts of failing sunlight over the mountains, and rendering the dusk lonely and mournful, reminiscent, somehow, of death. The night fell truly dark, without stars. Bundled in my sleeping bag, cold, still somewhat weak and nauseated, I ate a couscous and tomato dish in my tent. The camels soon couched around me and began munching on argan leaves; they were adjusting.

In the middle of the night a pellet-like rattle awoke me, along with gusts of wind. Rain was hitting my tent. The camels, I heard, were still chomping argan, and the rain was washing the dust off their hides.

We awoke to a bizarre sight: a dawn without a visible sunrise, the first such since we departed Tizgui Falls in February. I climbed out of my tent and hiked up the small mountain above us. The cactus-covered slopes, the tawny, ancient earth, the sheep, goats and leaden rocks filled me with nostalgia, and I tried to think for what. As I studied the scene I felt strongly that I had been here before. Then it struck me: this was the landscape of Crete, these were the hills of the southern Peloponnesus. In truth, this was once the Roman territory of Mauritania; could the ruins of Volubilis be far? This was the Morocco

of classical history, not the Morocco of tribal wars and
Ruhhal.

I sat down entranced. It became February 1984. I was
riding a rusty old Icarus bus across the craggy, mist-
sodden mountains of Crete, beneath Gero-Psiloritis
under thunderhead skies, heading for the village of
Sphakia on the island's southern coast. A raven-haired
young woman sat opposite me. Her melodious wild
banter in Greek with the other women aboard filled the
bus. She was perhaps only five years older than I (which
made her about twenty-eight) but of a different world.
Her black dress, black stockings and black scarf told me
she was a widow; she would wear black for the rest of her
life and never remarry.

We trundled out of the mists and the road wound
down toward the Libyan Sea, a rainbow breaking over its
azure swells. After arriving in Sphakia I never saw the
widow again. The next day I set out walking down a dirt
road for Frangokastello ('Castle of the Franks'), passing
through mountain villages: Vouvas, Komitadhes, Agios
Nektarios. Villagers on donkeys rode by and said
'*kalimera*' to me, but others stared in silence. Some of
the young women were widows in black scarves that covered their faces almost as much as a veil or firwal, a
tradition that the Ottoman Turks had brought to Greece.
The Mediterranean was one world.

Firwal. The word woke me up, and I was back in
Morocco. It seemed newly wonderful that a country
could be both on the Mediterranean and in Africa.

Hassan was ill, stricken with an upset stomach and
exhaustion. This I learned as we were packing up. We
hiked for three hours down the *piste*, with him lagging

behind. Where three shale-covered mountains met we saw
white stone houses with smoking chimneys, heard the
barking of dogs and the bleating of sheep: Tiglite. Berber
shepherdesses in pink and black robes and tinselly head-
dresses stood leaning on staffs, examining the strangers
walking out of the mountains. Here houses stood far apart,
one to a slope; farther on they clustered under palms.

'*Hooa! As-salam 'alaykum!* Where from?'

A tall Saharawi in a dark grey djellaba and white turban,
his high-browed face handsome despite its pockmarks, was
coming down the road, followed by a long-faced Berber.
Hassan and Mbari stopped for them, and I had the sense
that the turbaned man was a little too direct, too effusive,
to be a common resident of Tiglite.

Abundant greetings followed, along with lengthy handshakes. God have mercy on our parents. How were we?
What might bring us here? Where might we be headed?
By God, we were on our way to the Atlantic. For the first
time Hassan admitted our destination.

'Well, all that sounds fine,' the man said. 'Welcome to
our village. I'm the sheikh. I invite you to tea. We can
take care of the formalities a bit later.'

'The formalities?' I asked.

He smiled broadly. 'Every visitor to our modest village
is obliged to leave behind his story. Words on paper.'

'Such as?'

'Passport number and date of issuance, date of birth,
purpose of visit, profession, father's full name, mother's
maiden name. The sort of information that lets us understand who this man is, and what he's doing in our region.'
His eyes hardened. 'We're close to the Western Sahara,
you know.'

Hassan perked up and winked at me. The beauties of the police state.

'In fact, would you like to take care of business now?' the sheikh asked.

We said we would. We left our camels with some children called over by the sheikh and set out after him. He and his friend walked up the hill ahead of us, looking back to make sure we were following. Both Berbers and Saharawis lived in this village, which was nothing more than stone houses scattered around various converging slopes. They were heading for a pink concrete building that was the headquarters of the village. Hassan whispered to me. 'See, no troublemaker could get away with *anything* here!'

'Hassan, we're not troublemakers.'

'We could be Algerians.'

'But we're not.'

'They wouldn't let an Algerian get away with *anything* here. Algerians are crazy. They kill children. Listen, they're afraid here. They have to take measures. Any Moroccan passing through here would be questioned, too.'

We entered the headquarters. The sheikh led us to a door marked 'Communications Room'. Next to a radio transmitter a short, beetle-browed man with mussed-up hair sat beneath a portrait of King Hassan II and the Crown Prince Mohammed; he was behind the times in his royal portraiture.

The man looked as though he'd just woken up. He took my passport. 'An Englishman!' he pronounced, with a smirk.

'I'm American.'

He rolled his eyes. 'You were colonised by the English. You speak English.'

'We haven't been English since the eighteenth century.'

He glared at me and shook his head. He set about writing down the information in French.

Up at the sheikh's stone house, in a chilly and Spartan stone room, we sat around a bowl of couscous piled high with vegetables and meat. It was a succulent meal, and Mbari and I enjoyed it; Hassan ate little, still feeling sick. The sheikh poured out his woes to us. It was hard getting by on a sheikh's stipend – a thousand dirhams a month, about a hundred dollars. (In the 1960s the government began appointing village sheikhs, who became state functionaries.) He reported to the president of the community, who reported to the governor, who reported to the head of the region, who reported to the king. He never said what all these people spent so much time reporting, but Hassan found the arrangement very reassuring, and he nodded at each mentioned rung in the ladder, repeating the ranks for me to make sure I was following.

Looking around me, I suddenly felt depressed. We were in a land of rock and shrub and sheep and poor people, sitting in a stone room that could have been a prison cell. I fleetingly sensed exile, which no doubt would be what affluent Moroccan friends of mine in Rabat and Casablanca would consider life in Tiglite. They dwelled up north in a pseudo-European country within a country where people talked of reforms and constitutional monarchy, of winning rights for women and freedom of the press. They wanted these changes for their own reasons – for themselves, that is – but they spoke of the good of the people. But what would the people say about these rights? What would Hassan and the sheikh and all the Ruhhal and villagers we had met in the Drâa think about such changes, about democracy? Always in Morocco the people – the masses – have stood behind the king and Islamic traditions. In any case, when more than half the population is illiterate and under the age of twenty, when millions live in tin-shack slums, what would democracy lead to here? If I objected to the police-state order of which Hassan so approved, what would I replace it with?

After the meal the sheikh and his aide led us back to our camels. We thanked our hosts for the meal and the hospitality – it had chased away my nausea and revived Mbari and me (but not Hassan, who still looked ill). Unfortunately, the sheikh said, they could offer us nothing else. The village had no real store; for supplies people here travelled to Guelmim, a five-hour drive by four-wheeler.

They pointed out the *piste* winding up the mountains. We said goodbye and began the trek up steep switchbacks, toward the sky, which raced with clouds and now and then spattered us with chill rain. We clutched our clothes tight against the cold and wet, and climbed higher.

Late that afternoon, high on the plateau to which the *piste* had led us, amid the low, scrubby, golden hills of Wadi Ghumman, Hassan collapsed. I ran up to him. He had vomited; his cheeks were drawn and pale. He rolled over on to his back and shut his eyes, and a frigid wind blew sand over his face. We waited for Mbari and the camels to catch up. Aside from nausea, he complained that his knees and shoulders were aching so much that he could no longer sleep at night. He had pushed himself so hard that he had ruined his health; he had done his best to live up to his soldier's standards, and his strivings had taken their toll.

The camels looked worse than ever. Hanan was irritable, his jowls caked with dried blood from his new nostril; Na'im was bellowing, urinating and releasing dung at the slightest provocation; Mabruk was fatigued and walked slowly, his limp almost crippling him.

I sat by Hassan, rocking back and forth to fight the chill. Eiderdown clouds rolled swiftly across a low, turquoise sky, the sky of cold climes. My wool sweater and long-sleeved shirt did not keep me warm. The change in climate, so welcome at first, was now proving hard on us all, and the cold made the fatigue tougher than ever to bear.

We would go no farther that day.

After the sun set luminous lavender light poured from a band of sky above the horizon and filtered through gunmetal clouds marching in from the Atlantic. The wind blew in wailing gales across the golden, coarse-grained sand, over the cacti. We were about a thousand metres above sea level. Wadi Ghumman was an isolated place to stop, but we were not alone. A Saharawi shepherdess, thirteen or fourteen years old, wearing manifold robes of wool and cotton, and white wool leggings, drove a flock of goats our way, tossing stones at stragglers, uttering little sounds to keep them going: 'Chit-chit, kh-kh, utch-utch, tsud-tsud, click-click, ay-ay!' Her dishevelled russet hair was stuffed under a black scarf; her skin was fresh, if sunburned. We asked her where she was from. She pointed to a white tent barely visible at the end of the wadi, and kept on her way, making her sounds. This wadi was her home.

Rocking back and forth on his haunches, Hassan watched her walk away. 'We need whiskey.'

'We do?' I asked.

'It would warm us up. We used to drink it in the army.'

Mbari said he had never tried alcohol, and he praised God for that. He was also sick to his stomach, and had curled up by the fire.

A couple of hours later, under a cold black vault bejewelled with stars, a young man came from the direction of the shepherdess's tent and sat down by our fire. He wore a heavy wool djellaba and sandals, but had an imitation gold watch on his wrist. None of us had the strength to make conversation, and he seemed to understand our fatigue. We fed him some couscous. A little while later he consulted his watch and bade us goodnight.

Lying in my tent that night, I reflected on what I had seen since leaving Tizgui Falls. Most of the Ruhhal I had met, like the young man and the shepherdess, possessed an innate dignity. They suffered every caprice of weather, from heat to rain to sandstorms, but did not complain. They cared for their animals and did not abuse one another: crime is unheard of among them (now that raiding belongs to the past; but then raiding was never considered a crime). The dignity of the Ruhhal was commanding. At times a regal silence seemed to hang about them, making polite enquiries – or any speech at all – sound frivolous. They led an ancient way of life that harmed no one, and they were content with it.

I thought of Omar, my old Saharawi cameleer of 1998.

Looking at the dunes of Shgaga, he had told me then, 'Desert life has no equal. What a pleasure it is to lie down at camp at the end of the day, your camels watered and fed next to you. They rest and you rest. You sip your tea, you eat your dates, you look at the sky. This is pure. And the children of the desert are brought up pure, with no narcotics or alcohol or brothels. In the cities children are born sick. Here you're healthy from birth and your mind is clear.'

Every Ruhhal to whom I mentioned the cities of the north expressed a distaste for them. Here they differed from Moroccan villagers, who often wanted to move to the nearest town, or preferably cross the Strait of Gibraltar and make their way to the tenement conurbations surrounding Paris or Marseilles. The Ruhhal were convinced that the nomadic way of life befitted them more than any other, and saw the same humiliation that I saw in the bidonvilles in which more and more Moroccans, driven off their land by drought, are seeking refuge.

But the Ruhhal's world is changing, and the bidonvilles and other slums are spreading and becoming inevitable. In the past twenty years the anticyclones from the Azores that once brought Morocco rain have rarely come ashore. Eight of the thirteen major droughts that have struck Morocco since 1940 have occurred since 1980. Of the fifty-three million hectares of land suitable for pasturage (three-quarters of the surface of the country), eighteen million have been severely damaged by drought. To be of use, rain must fall between planting season and the harvest. Morocco's scarce rain now often comes at the wrong times of the year, and simply washes dried topsoil into rivers and reservoirs (the latter are now two-thirds empty) and silts them up, worsening the country's chronic water shortage. Overpopulation aggravates everything: at independence in 1956 there were eight million Moroccans; now there are thirty million, and the population keeps growing.

The climate and the earth have been altered, and the Ruhhal are suffering as a result. They are fleeing the sands, and the bidonvilles are filling up. In the tin-shack slums of the north, the ancestry of which Hassan spoke so proudly means nothing, tribal identity dissipates, and the Sons of 'Atta and the Daughters of Yahya take their place in the bread lines. Many turn to theft, smuggling or prostitution. There are no reliable statistics, but roughly out of every hundred Ruhhal who roamed the desert a decade ago only two or three remain. Drought, in short, is killing the Drâa and a way of life; its parching winds are eroding the casbahs, the most authentic architectural vestiges of North Africa's long, glorious Islamic history.

More rain fell during the night. I awoke shivering, my sleeping bag failing to keep me warm for the first time since Tizgui. At dawn I crawled outside. Hassan and Mbari had been too fatigued to set up their tent; they awoke soggy in their 'abayas and wanted to move on quickly. The camels had feasted all night on argan fruit. I walked over to Mabruk, patted him and fed him the remnants of my couscous.

Hassan looked at him. 'You like Mabruk, don't you?'

'Yes.'

'Well, he's going to die, the poor fellow.'

'What?'

'He's about to die.'

His face was overcast and his eyes dark; he threw his gear together in an aggressive manner. I asked him how he was feeling; he was obviously much improved to be in such a bad mood.

'Oh, my brain is deranged today. I'm disturbed. Let's just get going.'

I watched him finish packing. I sensed he must have been frustrated at having failed to slow the pace of our trip. He knew Mabruk was my favourite camel and he just wanted to upset me.

After eight hours of walking we reached Âouïnet-Ait-Oussa, the last village of the Anti-Atlas before the Atlantic. It consisted of a few houses beneath a lump of rock called Jbel Guir. There was a telephone there but little else. I called Ali and we agreed that he would wait for us either at the bridge over the Drâa at nine o'clock on the morning of 23 April (in which case he would hike the last day with us to the ocean), or at the village of Foum Oued-El-Drâa (Mouth of Wadi Drâa) on the Atlantic that evening. We would rest here for two days, and try to recover our strength for the last days of hiking.

I walked back to camp sensing deliverance. The trip was ending, but I felt an emptiness coming on – the emptiness that follows the fulfilment of a cherished dream.

TO THE ATLANTIC

'*THIS* IS THE Drâa bridge?'

I hopped off the bridge into the Drâa and back on to the bridge again. The 'bridge' was a six-inch-high, two-lane rutted blacktop (otherwise known as the Rabat–Laâyoune highway) that stretched about half a mile from one sand dune to another over a series of cement conduits. Through the conduits ran a six-yard-wide channel of water – the Drâa.

Hassan waved his arms and ducked as though under fire, just as he had during our 'infiltration' of the sand wall. 'This is no time for jokes! Keep moving! Keep moving! We don't want the gendarmes to catch us!'

I ignored his exhortation. In the middle of the bridge there was a gendarme post, but its officers were too busy stopping trucks and inspecting freight to bother with us. We were all strangely irritable and anxious, aware that the end was near. It was nine in the morning on the 23rd. Ali could be around here somewhere. If he wasn't, we were to push on to meet him at the Atlantic. Scanning the dunes to see if he had shown up, I crossed the bridge at a leisurely pace.

Two days had gone by since we had left Âouïnet-Ait-Oussa, suffering from continuous pains and fatigue that had weakened our spirits. Encountering not a soul, with the cold wind and dark clouds as our only companions, we had dragged ourselves over a succession of high, rumpled, sandy plains, passed a ruined *zawiya*, and, in the lower reaches of the Anti-Atlas, emerged at the edge of the plateau, where mountains began again. From the edge, in the sombre blue light of a sunless late afternoon, we saw Jbel Ouarkziz looping north and west, as if coaxing the Drâa, somewhere far below, toward the Atlantic.

We made our way down the rugged slope of the plateau, heading toward the valley along a switchback *piste*, and came upon a white Saharawi tent in a gorge. A stout woman who might have been in her thirties and two teenage girls whom we took for her daughters were puttering around in front, and goats bleated from the lower branches of acacias. We exchanged greetings with the woman and asked directions to confirm that we were on the right path. She smiled and came out to meet us. 'You're going the right way, but why hurry? You're welcome in our tent. We'll feed you and you can spend the night. Please, spend the night with us. My husband's away.'

'God requite you,' said Hassan. 'But the Nasrani is in a hurry to see the ocean. God bless you.'

We left them.

'So were those women making advances to us?' I asked him later, half-joking.

He appeared to have forgotten what he had said about the woman at the last oasis. 'Why?' he snapped. 'She wasn't offering to sin with us. She was just being hospitable.'

'But wouldn't the husband have minded us sleeping in her tent?'

'No, women and men both must offer travellers hospitality – that's Ruhhal tradition. There's nothing unlawful about it. The women would never expect a travelling man to think of sin.'

The *piste* wound back and forth on its way down the mountainside, here sparsely strewn with cacti, and we followed it until we emerged at the Drâa a couple of hours later, around sunset, with the bridge, my Ruhhal said, just ahead. Watered by underground springs, this manifestation of the Drâa was a stream running between grassy clay banks and lightly forested knolls. There were willows, egrets and thousands of mosquitoes. Saharawis were grazing camels, and their bellows and roars reverberated off the valley's steep stone walls. From rocky perches above, eagles launched themselves into ponderous flight and circled over the water, set against the glowing grey canopy of dusk.

We pitched camp at water's edge. We would walk the final couple of hours to the bridge in the morning. Hassan and Mbari had said little the previous days, and would not explain their low moods. But we were near the end, and it was cold, and I was not inclined to concern myself.

After crossing the bridge the next morning we set our eyes on the last stretch of the Drâa. Here the valley widened, becoming a sandy plain dividing cacti-speckled mesas. The Drâa wandered capriciously through the middle of the plain toward a stormy sky – presumably above the Atlantic. We halted in a wadi of shrubs to look for Ali, but he was nowhere to be seen.

'*Nhattu hoon?* [Should we put down here?]' Mbari asked.

'Looks fine here,' Hassan said.

'*Nhattu?*' I said. 'What do you mean? We're not stopping here.'

'We're camping and waiting for Ali.'

'What?'

'I told him we would meet him by the bridge,' Mbari said, making reference to a conversation he said he had had with Ali when we telephoned from Akka. I had heard of no such promise until now, and in any case I had confirmed our plans with Ali from Âouïnet-Ait-Oussa.

'*You* told Ali?' I said. 'I just spoke to him. He said if he wasn't here he'd meet us at the coast this evening. It's only a day's hike. We're moving on to the Atlantic. Ali will be waiting for us.'

Mbari and Hassan set about couching their camels. '*Nhattu hoon,*' Hassan repeated, ignoring me.

They began unloading. I sensed I was in for trouble: for the first time, they weren't bickering with each other. Mbari raised his eyebrows in a puzzlingly self-assured way; Hassan's face bore an expression of saintly disregard. With bizarre gravity, as if performing some religious ritual, they took everything out of the saddlebags, item by item, and marched it to spots around us, forming a broad circle of supplies and gear. We were eight hours' trek from the Atlantic. If they couldn't find a way to delay the trip now, they never would.

'Stop unloading,' I said. 'We're moving on.'

'It's two or three days to the coast,' Mbari said. 'Your map is wrong. We need to rest and wait for Ali.'

I glanced at Hassan, but he paid me no attention, his look of saintly disregard now verging on an expression of pity for me: this time, he gave me to know, I had no choice but to submit. He had renounced his role as guide and become Mbari's accomplice. He squatted on his haunches and prepared to knead dough for bread of the sands, fixing his eyes on the sky.

'Reload your camels. Please.'

Wrinkling his forehead, Hassan moulded his dough as if sculpting a miniature David. Mbari began slowly tapping Extra Gunpowder into the teapot. Tap. Tap. Tap.

'I said we're moving on. We're too close to the end to stop.' I began to seethe. I was exhausted and eager to be done with the trip. Who were they to decide to halt? 'Listen, we are moving *on*!'

Mbari looked up from his tea. 'We are staying *here*. I won't break my word to Ali. By God, I won't. *By God!*'

Hassan's face assumed an unbearably pious expression, and he cocked his head and regarded me through half-closed eyes: I would have to accept their decision as the writ of God, or at least as the fatwa of Ruhhal without whom, he must have assumed, I wouldn't take a step in this desert. He kneaded and kneaded, and returned to examining the sky, the dunes, his dough.

'I order you to pack up those camels. I *order* you! *Now!*'

'We will *not* break our word to Ali,' Mbari said.

I threw down my bag. '*Your* word? Who's paying you to make this trip? *Who?*'

'Ali.'

'You know very well I'm paying you. I arranged this expedition with Ali, not with you. Now get up and pack your camels!' He poured water into his kettle and slowly swished it around. Swish. Swish. Swish.

I turned to Hassan, who was now humming a Saharawi folk song. 'Hassan!'

'Yes, Si Jelal?'

'Hassan, I'm shocked!'

'Oh, please, Si Jelal, we'll get to the Atlantic. If not today, then tomorrow. If not tomorrow, then the next day. Or a few days from now. If not—'

Mbari cut in. 'Si Jelal, I will *not* break my word to Ali. I'm staying here.'

'Mbari, if you don't pack up now you're fired.'

'I must keep my word!'

'You're in my employ! If you don't pack up you're *fired*!'

'Oh? Oh? You can't fire me – I quit!'

He tossed his tea water aside, stood up, and tore his backpack off the sand. He looked both ways, and then started walking back in the direction of the bridge.

I turned to Hassan. 'Hassan, look . . . *Hassan!*'

Hassan went on kneading his dough, humming his tune. 'Sit down, Si Jelal. For God's sake, what difference do a few days make?'

'Hassan, I've been hiking since February. We're eight hours away from the Atlantic. It's not for you to tell me it makes no difference.'

'Sit, please.'

'All right then, you're *both* fired!' I tore my pack off the sand. 'I'm going to hitch a ride to Tan-Tan, where I'll call Ali. Knead your dough. I'm walking to the end alone.'

I stormed off, heading for the road. This was certainly an ill-considered move. I didn't want to go to Tan-Tan (which was ten miles south – the wrong direction) and call Ali. I'm not even sure why I said I would do so, and I had even less desire to finish the trip alone. I recalled my berating of these poor Ruhhal and it sounded like the ranting of a madman. But I had reason to be angry. Not only was I burned out, fed up with Ruhhal life, exhausted and sick; most of all I felt the divide between us (differences in faith, culture and upbringing – everything that distinguishes people from each other) widen into an impassable void. I was not their equal: I was not Muslim or Ruhhal or Arab, and they would not listen to me. I was in their eyes, however, rich, and they would extract their tribute. My legs made long steps as if of their own accord toward the road. When I reached it I raised my hand, as if to flag down a truck. But there was no truck, or any other vehicle.

From behind me I heard a plaintive voice. 'Si Jelal!' Hassan was calling out and loping toward me, his fouqiya tangling between his legs. 'Si Jelal!'

I turned around. Mbari was walking back to the camels.

Silently, we packed up and set out west, up and down the mesas along the Drâa, toward the ocean.

The next morning, under scudding, tufted clouds, a smoky-blue ridge of oddly flat mountain appeared on the

western horizon, beyond the sandy mesas we were crossing, over the last bend in the Drâa: the Atlantic.

We walked on to where the mesa gave way and looked
down at the Drâa, which was flowing silvery green into
the ocean: deep blue and rippling with the whitecaps of a
rising gale.

'The . . . the end?' asked Hassan, in a small voice.

Mbari stared transfixed. He had never seen the
Atlantic before.

'The end,' I said.

We all tried to smile at one another, but it was tough;
we shook hands and embraced feebly. Our last argument
was forgotten, we seemed to be saying with this gesture,
but it was really too fresh to forget, and we were too tired,
too sore. We were not Thesiger and his Bedouin, but
lesser mortals who had walked a long way, suffered a lot
and exhausted ourselves. Still, we had done what we had
set out to do. Here beneath us was the *bahr al-zhulumat*,
the Sea of Darkness, as the Arabs once used to call the
Atlantic. When 'Uqba bin Nafi' reached the *bahr al-zhulumat*, neither he nor anyone with him knew what lay
beyond it. Morocco would later become known to the
Arabs as al-Maghrib, the Land of Sunset.

We stared at the water, listening to the waves. But soon
we heard the ominous putt-putt of a moped intrude on
the crashing of the surf.

'*Messieurs! Messieurs les nomades!*'

We turned around to face a man in khaki bobbing
across the mesa atop an ancient moped, waving at us and
clutching his cap and waving again, as though we could
somehow fail to notice him. He sputtered up to us and
braked, having some trouble with his balance. He had a

beanpole build, and he was grinning with a mouthful of blackened teeth.

'*Bonjour, les nomades!*'

I quickly explained in Arabic who we were, and got ready to show my passport; Hassan and Mbari reached into their fouqiyas for their papers. But he pushed back his cap and began shaking our hands, switching to Arabic. 'Oh, until I got close to you I was afraid you might be escaped prisoners or something. Or illegal immigrants. You see, criminals are always trying to escape here. Convicts and illegals. They follow the valley to the water and the boats wait for them down there. Anyway, it's not easy being cooped up in my post all the time. Day and night, night and day, I guard the border here. Come, let's have tea. I've also got a friend coming with a fish, so we can eat, too.'

His name was Mohammed and he was a Berber from Agadir. We walked toward his 'post' – a stone hut at the edge of the mesa overlooking where the Drâa flowed into the ocean. He and his fellow border guard had built the hut themselves. It was, he said, at least better than living in the collapsed watchtower that stood next to it.

We ducked and entered the hut and sat down on heavy wool Berber carpets spread over the sand. 'From here it's a day or two by boat to the Canary Islands,' he said over the crash of the surf below. 'We find their shoes washed up on the beach after storms.'

'Whose shoes?'

'The immigrants. The illegals. You can go all the way to Spain from here. Once they're in the Canaries they're in Europe. Every day they try to cross.'

A few minutes later I remembered Ali. We had agreed

to meet at the village of Foum Oued-El-Drâa. Foum Oued-El Drâa had been abandoned, Mohammed said, and no road led here. Worse, he told us we were a two-day hike to Tan-Tan. As we listened to all this I noticed Hassan and Mbari exchanging covert glances. Two days more of hiking! They had won!

'Wait. Does this Ali drive a Land Rover?' Mohammed asked. 'Maybe one of the two guys in a Land Rover on the other side of the river is Ali.'

I raced outside. There was indeed a Land Rover parked across the river, here quite wide, atop the opposite mesa; beneath the vehicle two men had rolled up their pants and were trying to ford the currents to cross to our side. I waved and they waved. Hassan and Mbari commenced signalling, too. We were too far apart to be sure who they were, but I had no doubt one was Ali, the other his driver.

Hassan divined grave and succinct instructions from the man gesticulating with his pants rolled up. 'Ali says there's no road so he can't reach us, so we should start hiking to Tan-Tan. We're not to hurry. He'll meet us there, and all previous plans are cancelled.'

Mohammed tugged my sleeve. 'Does this Ali have a cell phone? Come on, let's call him!' He pulled a mobile phone out of his pocket and handed it to me. 'Dial!'

I dialled.

The man far below pulled something out of his pocket and put it to his ear.

'Ali!'

'*Ahlan*, Jeff! You've made it! Wait for me, I'll be right over!'

'I'm waiting.'

Ali and his driver began slowly turning around in the water, and headed back to the Land Rover.

The fisherman friend of Mohammed's, a youth in dreadlocks and a blue djellaba, walked up with a huge silvery mackerel. Mohammed invited us inside his hut for fish tagine. The breeze was salty and fresh; we would eat the fish with bread of the sands that he had just banked. Five pounds of fresh tomatoes, carrots, onions and potatoes had been simmering for hours in the pot. Dreadlocks began cleaning the fish.

Mohammed looked at Mbari.

'So, you're from the Western Sahara?'

'No! What gave you that idea?'

'Your dialect, your robes, your firwals, your faces and your camels.'

'Means nothing. We're from Mhamid.'

Hassan went further. 'We're from Ouarzazate!'

'Oh, so you're Berber?' (Ouarzazate is a Berber town.)

'Berber? Oh . . .' Hassan looked oddly abashed. 'Well . . . no, we're not Berber.'

'Don't tell me lies,' said Mohammed, mocking a police investigator. 'You're both Saharawis.'

'No! We're from Ouarzazate,' repeated Hassan.

'Look,' he said, lightening up, 'what do I care? Welcome! Drink your tea! Relax!'

Two hours later, as the top was being removed from the tagine pot and we broke warm bread, we heard a Land Rover crashing and banging over the mesa. We went outside. Ali jumped out, barefoot and in jeans but still wearing his firwal, and we all embraced. Mohammed invited them in for tagine.

They had been delayed by the rising tide, which filled

an otherwise shallow crossing point. Tides? Mbari looked puzzled.

'All salt water has tides,' Mohammed said.

'Salt water? That water is salty?' Mbari asked. 'The camels! They could drink from the sea and die!'

Holding his firwal tight to his head, he ran outside, stumbled his way down the mesa slope, and dragged the camels away from the ocean (in which they had shown no interest). We watched this and laughed, and went back to our tagine – the first meal of something other than rice and bread Hassan, Mbari and I had tasted in a week.

After the meal, Ali announced that someone would have to walk the camels three days to Guelmim, and there put them on a truck for Mhamid. Who would undertake this onerous task? His gaze fell on Hassan. Looking like a condemned man, Hassan bowed to his fate and arose, picking up his pack. We walked out to see him off.

Since our falling out at the bridge I had been wondering how I would say goodbye to him. I didn't want to part on bad terms, and I had truly appreciated his work. He set about loading our things into Hanan's sack. While we were all discussing the trip, he whipped the camels to their feet and started driving them ahead. He would leave us all without even saying goodbye.

'Hassan!' I called out.

He stopped and turned to look at me. The wind played with the ends of his firwal. He smiled weakly. We shook hands, and I handed him a wad of bills as a tip. 'Thanks, Hassan. It was a pleasure. May God keep you safe!'

He smiled weakly again, turned and continued driving the camels onward, heading northeast. As a Ruhhal he was too practical for gushing displays of emotion – if he even felt anything other than relief at the end of the trip and displeasure at beginning another hike. Moreover, God had willed that we meet, reach the Atlantic and then part. I was not choked up, as I thought I would be, but for other reasons. The tension of the past ten days or so was still running through me. I couldn't fully believe in our deliverance; and fatigue dulled my senses.

Ali and Mbari went on talking about the trip. I turned and watched Hassan, Mabruk, Na'im and Hanan grow small on the mesa and then disappear over a rise. I felt a painful sense of bewilderment: for the first time since Tizgui, I had nowhere left to go.

Later, as the tide was ebbing, Mbari, Ali and I said goodbye to Mohammed and his friend and thanked them before boarding the Land Rover. We bounced back across the mesa, speeding through landscape across which we had so laboriously trudged. Scrub barrens, rock and sand flew by my window. We drove down a slope, turned toward the Drâa and splashed through it. An hour after that we were pulling into the adobe-coloured cement warrens of Tan-Tan, where Saharawi children kicked soccer balls, where Saharawi men in brown 'abayas and women in batik milhafas ambled down gravel streets. We stopped by a hotel and I got out.

Mbari got out with me.

'*Al-musamaha! Al-musamaha!* [Forgiveness! Forgiveness!]' he pleaded, his tired eyes smiling over the dusty folds in his firwal.

'Mbari, I want to ask *you* to forgive *me*!'

We laughed and embraced, and I slipped bills into his palm. I knew one day I would return to the Drâa and see him again. We had, after all, accomplished a difficult mission together, and I did not want simply to abandon him (or Hassan), whatever our differences had been over the last weeks. Life is too short to hold grudges; and we must do good to others. Bad deeds always come back to us.

Grabbing his sack, still smiling, he pulled his firwal tight around his head and hailed a taxi for an uncle's house. Ali and I said goodbye and arranged to meet the next afternoon.

Recently settled Ruhhal made up most of Tan-Tan's inhabitants. Straight streets, rudely paved, ran up and down a patch of land near an oasis; row upon row of cement houses stood in the sun, which, reflected off tar and gravel, felt hotter here than in the desert. There were stores and barbers, auto repair shops and cafés and pharmacies. The town had one claim to historical fame: in 1975 King Hassan II launched his Green March from Tan-Tan, and thereby began the Moroccan occupation of the Western Sahara, just to the south.

I took a room at the Hotel Al-Rimal Al-Dhahabiya (the Golden Sands). Up in my room I examined my reflection in the mirror and barely recognised myself. I had lost fifteen pounds and my cheeks were drawn; my hair had been bleached by the sun; my forearms and face were patchy brown; the soles of my feet felt like corrugated iron. I unpacked. Most of my gear now wore a patina of reddish dust that would never come off. I took out my city clothes – I had packed them in plastic, and by a small miracle they were still clean – and put them on. My jeans were two sizes too big, my shirts loose.

I went down to the lobby café and sat in a chair for the first time in a long while. The hotel was noisy, stuffy and hot, and I would not sleep well that night.

The next morning I hired a Land Rover to take me back out to the mouth of the Drâa, and I invited Ali to come along. I had been so excited to arrive at the Atlantic that I had not gone down and put my feet in the water. Our driver, a portly Saharawi who shouted his every word, drove us out to the strip of land on which he and Ali had arrived the day before, across from Mohammed's hut and the crumbling watchtower. We got out, made tea and talked about the trip. Between us there was no divide.

Ali told me of the tourists coming from Europe to travel through the Mhamid area; the guide business wasn't going great, but it was coming along. A survival trait of the Ruhhal is adaptability. When we met he had goats and camels; later, prompted by the drought, he had sold his goats and set up his expedition company. There might appear to be something distasteful in the arrival of tourism in the Upper Drâa, but the people of the valley need to eat. I like to think that Ali and his Ruhhal will teach visitors the humbling and salutary lesson I had learned, the lesson of the Sahara: there's still a very big place in the world where people, without their gadgets and armour, are fragile animals indeed.

Finished with my tea, I got up and started down the mesa toward the Atlantic, slipping in the warm sand.

The ocean foamed silver and white. There was the roar of the breakers, the sheltering grey clouds; there were the cliffs of the mesa, mottled with the shrubs on which our camels so loved to graze. The dunes down by the water were frosted with salt. I took off my shoes and waded into the surf. It was cold and there was something autumnal about the bleak windy scene.

We drove back to Tan-Tan, and there Ali and I said goodbye. I watched him get back in the Land Rover, and the brown 'abaya of our driver reminded me that there was one last thing I had to do before leaving Morocco.

EPILOGUE:

In the Homeland of the Reguibat

THE NEXT DAY at the road station in Tan-Tan I hired a sullen Saharawi and a lopsided, blue-and-white Mercedes taxi to take me the 230 kilometres southwest to the town of Smara, in the Western Sahara, in the heart of Reguibat territory, where Mbari had spent much of his childhood. I wanted to meet the Reguibat, and not just to set eyes on the Ruhhal whom Paul Bowles had portrayed in such terrifying detail. Hassan and Mbari had described them as heroes of the sands, as men almost equal to the fabled ancestors who could walk a hundred kilometres in a day, surviving on a few dates and a little water. Was there truth to any of this? How were they faring after more than twenty-five years of Moroccan occupation? Was drought driving them off the sands, as it had the Ruhhal of the Drâa?

We shot out of Tan-Tan on to the road for Laâyoune, which was tolerably smooth, but then we took a turn dead south for Smara and bumped and rattled our way on to a narrower, cracked tarmac that in places was covered in sand. At first the surrounding hamada resembled that of the Drâa, slightly undulating, with acacias here, a camel or two there, but soon it degenerated into expanses of utterly flat sand and ashen gravel, which gave way to ashen sand and black gravel. This was strip-mine desolation, quarry bleakness, a sterile blazing sun and burning sky, with no sign that there had ever been rain.

We bounced past a sign announcing the province of Smara and drew up on a few brick hovels designated as both Abetteh and Abtih, depending on which sign you read. Another sign shouted, 'HALT! POLICE!' Beneath it, a belt studded with black steel spikes stretched out into the road. We slowed and a young, grey-uniformed gendarme stepped out of one of the hovels, correcting the slant of his visored grey cap. He made an irritated wave for us to stop, and we did.

He leaned into my window and, snatching my passport from my hands, demanded in French to know what I was doing in the Western Sahara. I answered in Arabic, saying I was on my way to Smara for a short visit. He thumbed my passport. Where was my residence permit? Did I have a work permit? What was my nationality 'before becoming American'? He assumed, owing to my Arabic, that I was originally from somewhere in the Middle East, and that I had to be working with the United Nations to set up the referendum on Saharawi independence (which would have made me an unwelcome guest he would have to tolerate). It took me a while to disabuse him of these notions, but eventually he handed me back my passport. He lifted the spiked mat and tossed it aside. We drove on.

Soon after, the road began breaking up, and DANGER became a familiar word on signs: 'DANGER! ROAD DIVERTED!' 'DANGER! CAMEL CROSSING!' 'SPEED IS A DANGER!' 'PASSING IS DANGEROUS!' The last warning provoked a smirk from my driver: we had seen only a couple of cars on the road all morning. The black gravel and ashen dust started rolling slightly, in suggestions of *hidban*; in places wadis with stunted acacias cut through the wastes. Then two signs written in Arabic introduced Smara: one said, 'Asmara', the other 'Al-Smara'. After stopping for two more checkpoints, we entered a concrete slum jutting up into the fiendish glare. A banner by a military base at Smara's edge proclaimed in Arabic, 'A century of struggle by the glorious Alaouite throne for the unity of Morocco.'

I took a room in a hotel and asked the desk clerk if he knew anyone who could take me out in the desert to see the Reguibat.

'*I'm* a Reguibat,' he said, smiling and standing up from his desk. But then, as if frightened by the sound of his own words, he began lowering his gaze. 'But . . . but we're settled now. There are some tents, but seeing them, getting to them, is . . . *contrôlé*. Very *contrôlé*. I can't help you. No, there's nothing I can do. No, I'm sorry.' He looked at the floor and sat down again. 'No. Everything here is *contrôlé*.'

I walked outside and wandered around town. I had seen few places fouler. In the 'centre', sand-blasted cement *qaysariyas* stood painted in peeling ochre; the Café Paris and Café al-'Ahd al-Jadid (the New Era) were empty except for clouds of flies; a trash-strewn administrative district built of basalt bricks covered half a dozen blocks, but there were no officials about. Away from the main street, avenue Hassan II, the stench of sewage lingered by shabby concrete row houses, all of the same Moroccan faux-adobe design. (There could be no indigenous Western Saharan architecture, since Saharawis had traditionally dwelled in tents.) Fat Saharawi women wrapped in milhafas of black and yellow or blue and yellow sat slumped in doorways; lean Saharawi men pulled their firwals to their faces when I passed, as if fearing recognition.

I walked out of the alleys and back on to avenue Hassan II, hoping to meet someone with a Land Rover whom I could hire to take me out of town. But most of the people about appeared to be either soldiers or plain-clothes police, the latter betrayed by their clipped hair, Western dress, efficient demeanour and northern dialect. Now and then UN Land Rovers rumbled by. The shop-keepers also appeared to be northerners. Perhaps the most lucrative concessions went to settlers from Morocco proper, who were said to enjoy tax incentives for moving here; or perhaps only northerners could do the reading and writing necessary to run a business.

By late afternoon a Shirgi filled the sky with brown dust that glowed with the glare of the sun. I gave up my search. Caked in dust and holding a firwal to my nose, I returned to the hotel, but I saw a Land Rover near the entrance. By it stood a Saharawi wearing a white firwal piled high around his head; his bearded face was almost black. I approached him and told him what I wanted.

His name was Sma'il, and he said, shouting his words, that he was a Reguibat. 'We have a camp outside town. I'll take you there. But we have to leave from a back alley to avoid the police. They're rough on us. They don't want us showing foreigners around, and they'll demand to see a permit from you to leave town. Go down that alley and wait for me. I'll drive up in a few minutes.'

I did as he asked and he appeared as expected. We pounded down alleys and bounced on to a *piste*, nothing more than two tyre tracks so faint as to be almost unnoticeable, that led on to the hamada, into the sandstorm, toward the setting sun. Chunks of basalt trailed wavering wakes of sand over corrugated earth. Sma'il lifted a handkerchief tacked to the dashboard and popped a cassette into the radio it covered: a wailing tenor sounded, at intervals punctuated by the fervent strumming of a lute. Reguibat music, simple and haunting. The wailing lyrics and the bleakness around us, which exceeded in desolation anything I had seen in the Drâa, unnerved me, made me feel as though I were visiting the desert for the first time. Shouting through his firwal, Sma'il talked at length about the valour of the Reguibat and his love of wandering the desert as far south as Mauritania. While he spoke, to make points, he now and again hit my knee or my shoulder with his callused hand, which was jarring.

He lurched left off the *piste*, and we rocked over shards of shale and basalt. In the browned-out dusk, a half-hour later, we came to a wadi with a few blackened acacias bending in the blasting wind. There were no camels.

'The well has gone salty,' Sma'il said. 'There's been no rain, you see, only *shidda*.'

We came upon a mess of cinderblock huts and halted.

'These are my friends. Come!'

Six or seven elders crouched on their haunches behind a cinderblock wall that protected them from the wind.

They shouted greetings to Sma'il and asked us to sit with them. 'No thanks,' Sma'il replied. 'I want the Nasrani to meet the sheikh.'

The cinderblock house near by offered no surprises. The floor of its one room was bare cement; its roof was straw and wood; there was a smell of sewage. We entered and the two women inside nodded a greeting, and then betook themselves to the other side of the room to chat in low voices. The sheikh sat in a dirty grey 'abaya with his knees pulled up to his chest. He covered his mouth with his firwal when he saw me and did not respond to my greetings. From what I could see, his face was handsome, with a regal nose and high cheeks, but his eyes were bleary, his lashes fringed with dust.

'What people are you from?' he asked.

'I'm American.'

'Ah. Foreign.' He turned to Sma'il. 'How did you bring him here? Did you pass through the checkpoint?'

'Don't worry. No one saw us.'

'I don't want any problems with the authorities.'

'No one saw us.'

'No police followed you?'

'By God, Sheikh, no one saw us.'

'I don't want any trouble.'

I apologised but the sheikh said nothing, nor would he look at me.

Sma'il had brought with him a box of tea and a cone of sugar. He grabbed a Buta burner near by, turned it on and lit it; a weak blue flame quivered in the dusty wind that blew in through the glassless windows. 'The sheikh's happy to see you. But it's this drought that upsets him. Seven years it's lasted. This is the longest drought we've ever had. The wells are drying up and the animals are dying. There's no grass left any more.'

'How do people survive?'

'The sheikh gets a pension. Most of us do odd jobs. Here and there we try to find work, but it's getting harder and harder. Moroccans from the north come and get all the jobs, and government officials steal the food Rabat sends us. The king doesn't know, you see. But God be praised, we are getting by. God be praised.'

Sma'il offered the sheikh tea but he refused; the women came over and handed us a steel bowl of chunky milk. I declined; Sma'il accepted, and downed half the liquid in a few loud slurps. I had wondered if it might be a local treat (milk from camels or goats), but there was a Nestlé Nido can in the corner; it was powdered cow's milk. There was no longer any water for flocks out here; the family had sold its animals long ago.

Then the sheikh set his eyes on us again, asking Sma'il which *piste* we had followed to get here, and repeating his earlier concerns about the police. I felt terrible: my visit had obviously disturbed him, and I decided I wanted to leave him in peace and go back to Smara. I leaned against the wall but quickly pulled away: it still held the heat of midday, and cockroaches were skittering up and down it.

We finished our tea. As darkness fell the wind began screaming. 'This house is much better than a tent,' Sma'il shouted, knocking me in the shoulder with his hard palm. 'A tent blows down in the wind, but not a house like this!'

I got up and thanked the sheikh, who nodded a farewell and turned to face the wall. We left him and drove out into the night, heading back to Smara. I found myself longing for the time when the Ruhhal, fearsome and proud, had ruled their land, when notions of climate change and cinderblock houses would have seemed absurd. I thought back on what I had read in *Arabian Sands*. Thesiger had returned to the Arabian Peninsula decades after his wanderings to discover an 'Arabian nightmare' of Bedouin with televisions and Land Rovers. I found, in the Drâa Valley and the Western Sahara, not modernised Bedouin but future residents of tin-shack slums, proud sheikhs humbled by the politics and police of nation-states – the future of the Ruhhal across the poorer countries of the Arab world.

The headlights cast shafts of yellow light through the sand blowing over black rock and ashen earth. Sma'il turned on his folk-song tape and looked at me. 'You see, we Reguibat could once walk a hundred kilometres a day without tiring, drinking only a litre of water and eating only a handful of dates. By God, our ancestors were strong! Why, in the old days we walked all the way from here to Mauritania!'

The twin ruts of the *piste* swerved into view, and we turned left to follow them. The lights of Smara now glowed ahead, dimming and then brightening, dimming and then brightening again behind flickering curtains of Shirgi-driven sand.

EYUKI FURUHASHI

hin the story, the events
this single, gloomy, very
bad night continue.

nwhile, in the real world,
re still struggling to find
e exit from the COVID
ndemic. Keep standing
firm, everyone!

BETTEN COURT

We're celebrating
100+ chapters!

Each chapter, I start ou
wondering how on earth
going to fill all those pag
but somehow the work g
done. It's a marvel that I
now gone through tha
process over 100 time

VOLUME 13
SHONEN JUMP Edition

STORY: HIDEYUKI FURUHASHI
ART: BETTEN COURT
ORIGINAL CONCEPT: KOHEI HORIKOSHI

Translation & English Adaptation/Caleb Cook
Touch-Up Art & Lettering/John Hunt
Designer/Julian [JR] Robinson
Editor/Mike Montesa

VIGILANTE -BOKU NO HERO ACADEMIA ILLEGALS-
© 2016 by Hideyuki Furuhashi, Betten Court, Kohei Horikoshi
All rights reserved.
First published in Japan in 2016 by SHUEISHA Inc., Tokyo.
English translation rights arranged by SHUEISHA Inc.

The stories, characters, and incidents mentioned in this publication
are entirely fictional.

Printed in Canada

Published by VIZ Media, LLC
P.O. Box 77010
San Francisco, CA 94107

10 9 8 7 6 5 4 3 2 1
First printing, September 2022

viz.com

MY HERO ACADEMIA
VIGILANTES

13

Writer / Letterer
Hideyuki Furuhashi

Penciller / Colorist
Betten Court

Original Concept
Kohei Horikoshi

【anonymous】

adjective | anon • y • mous
: not identifiable by name, having no known name
noun
: one who uses an assumed name, such as an author

CHARACTERS

[Vigilantes]

WANTED
POP☆STEP
(REAL NAME: KAZUHO HANEYAMA)

A self-styled freelance idol who gives impromptu live performances without the proper licensing or permits. Primary suspect in the Naruhata serial bombing case. Currently unconscious and receiving medical treatment for her grave condition.

WANTED
KNUCKLEDUSTER
(REAL NAME: UNKNOWN)

A middle-aged man of mystery who became the master Koichi never asked for. Though Quirkless, his fighting prowess is on par with pro heroes. Disappeared after the Sky Egg incident.

WANTED
THE CRAWLER
(REAL NAME: KOICHI HAIMAWARI)

A college senior and good-natured young man who started out his vigilante career under the moniker "Nice Guy," while making use of his Slide and Glide Quirk. Material witness in the Naruhata bombing case.

[Allies]

MOYURU TOCHI

Soga's friend. His family runs a motorcycle shop.

RAPT TOKAGE

Soga's friend. Excitable member of the peanut gallery.

SOGA KUGISAKI

Leader of a trio of ruffians in Naruhata.

MAKOTO TSUKAUCHI

Detective Tsukauchi's younger sister.

STORY

What is "justice" anyway? Get ready for a PLUS ULTRA spin-off set in the world of *My Hero Academia*!!

Heroes. The chosen ones who, with explicit government permission, use their natural talents, or Quirks, to aid society. However, not everyone can be chosen, and some take action of their own accord, becoming illegal heroes. What does justice mean to them? And can we really call them heroes? This story takes to the streets in order to follow the exploits of those known as *vigilantes*.

MIDNIGHT
THE SEXY, R-RATED HERO.

PRESENT MIC
THE VOICE HERO, WHO MAKES DECIBELS HIS WEAPON.

ERASER HEAD
THE ERASURE HERO, WHO APPROACHES EVERYTHING RATIONALLY.

ALL MIGHT
THE NUMBER ONE HERO AND SYMBOL OF PEACE.

INGENIUM
THE TURBO HERO BOASTS GODLIKE SPEED.

EDGESHOT
THE ENIGMATIC NINJA HERO.

BEST JEANIST
A SKILLED HERO WHO CONTROLS ALL FIBERS.

ENDEAVOR
THE FIERY NUMBER TWO HERO.

[Police]

EIZO TANUMA
A DETECTIVE UNRAVELING THE BIG PICTURE BEHIND THE DRUGS AND VILLAINS.

NAOMASA TSUKAUCHI
A DETECTIVE WHO'S FRIENDS WITH ALL MIGHT.

CAPTAIN CELEBRITY
A TOP HERO FROM THE U.S.A.

FAT GUM
A ROUGH AND TOUGH BRAWLING HERO FROM NANIWA.

[Villains]

UNKNOWN
???????

KUROGIRI
A VILLAIN WHOSE BODY CAN TRANSFORM INTO MIST.

MYSTERY MOB
VILLAINS WHO APPEARED IN NARUHATA ONE NIGHT.

NUMBER 6
THE SCARRED MAN WHO SCHEMES IN THE SHADOWS OF NARUHATA.

MY HERO ACADEMIA VIGILANTES

13

EP. 99 - FACELESS INVASION

ANONYMOUS

This mob of villains are sort of the culmination of what good villains in *Vigilantes* have to be. First, they operate off of All Might's radar, and second, that means the people already on the scene have to cope with them somehow.

—Furuhashi

In a way that's appropriate for these interchangeable guys, I let my mind go blank and work in silence while drawing them. But the fact that my mind goes blank doesn't make me a Nomu (literally: brain absent).

—Betten

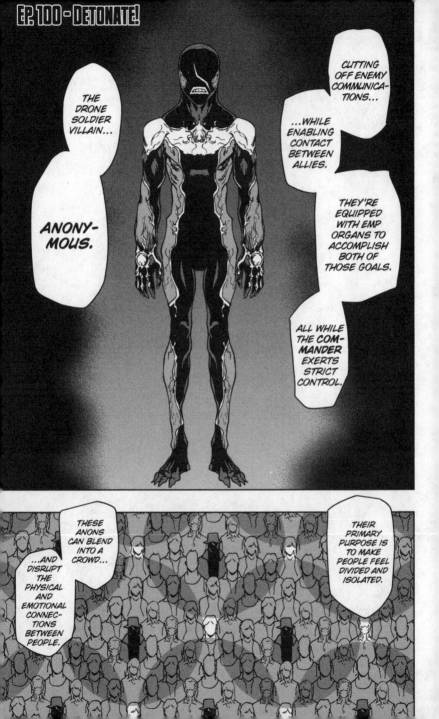

EP. 100 - DETONATE!

AT THE MOMENT, THE HEROES ARE FIGURING OUT WHAT'S GOING ON!

TAKE SHELTER INSIDE A BUILDING!

EVERYONE, PLEASE KEEP CALM.

*SIGN: NARUHATA STATION

BASED ON WHAT I COULD SURMISE FROM THE AIR...

*SIGN: STATION CHIEF

AND BECAUSE THE RAILS AND ROADS ARE EFFECTIVELY CUT OFF...

...THEY'RE HAVING A HARD TIME RESTORING POWER.

...THE BLACKOUT EXTENDS SEVERAL KILOMETERS IN EACH DIRECTION AROUND NARUHATA STATION.

THE ANONS WORKED HARD TO MAKE THE POPULATION FEEL ISOLATED...

...BUT NOW THE PEOPLE'S FAITH IN HEROES IS REPAIRING THOSE CRACKS.

HELP!

THE HEROES RACE OFF TO FIX THINGS AND END THE DEADLOCK.

YUP, HEROES NEVER FAIL TO IMPRESS.

CAN'T HELP BUT ADMIRE THEM.

JEANIST'S DAY OFF

I love thinking up minor Jeanist-related content. Whatever he happens to be doing, he's always cool and kind of funny. But a key element of the character is that he remains super serious about everything.

—Furuhashi

I can never seem to get the balance quite right when drawing Jeanist, so I've taken to shortening his neck—oof! (LOL)

—Betten

Ep. 101 - Soar into the Night

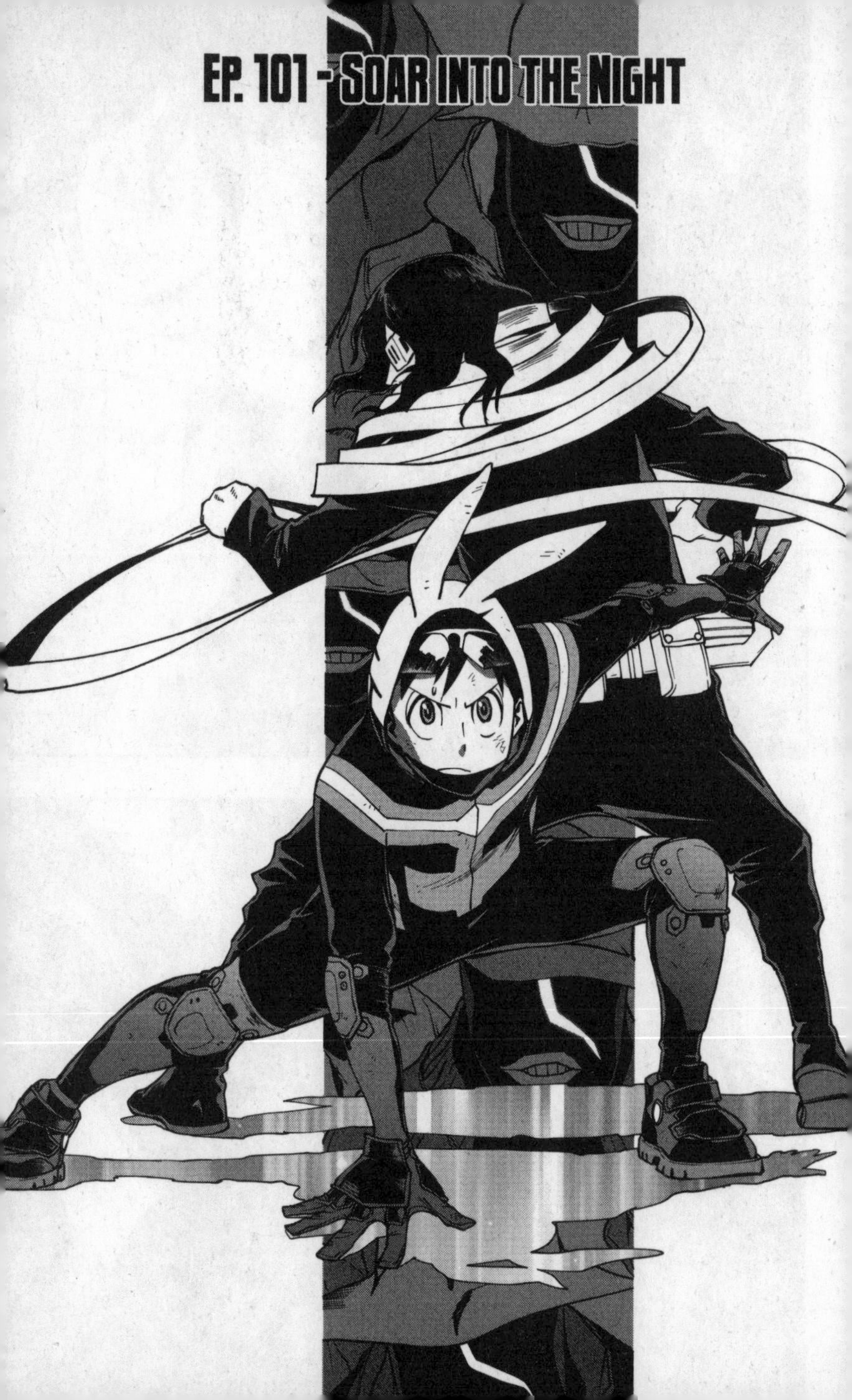

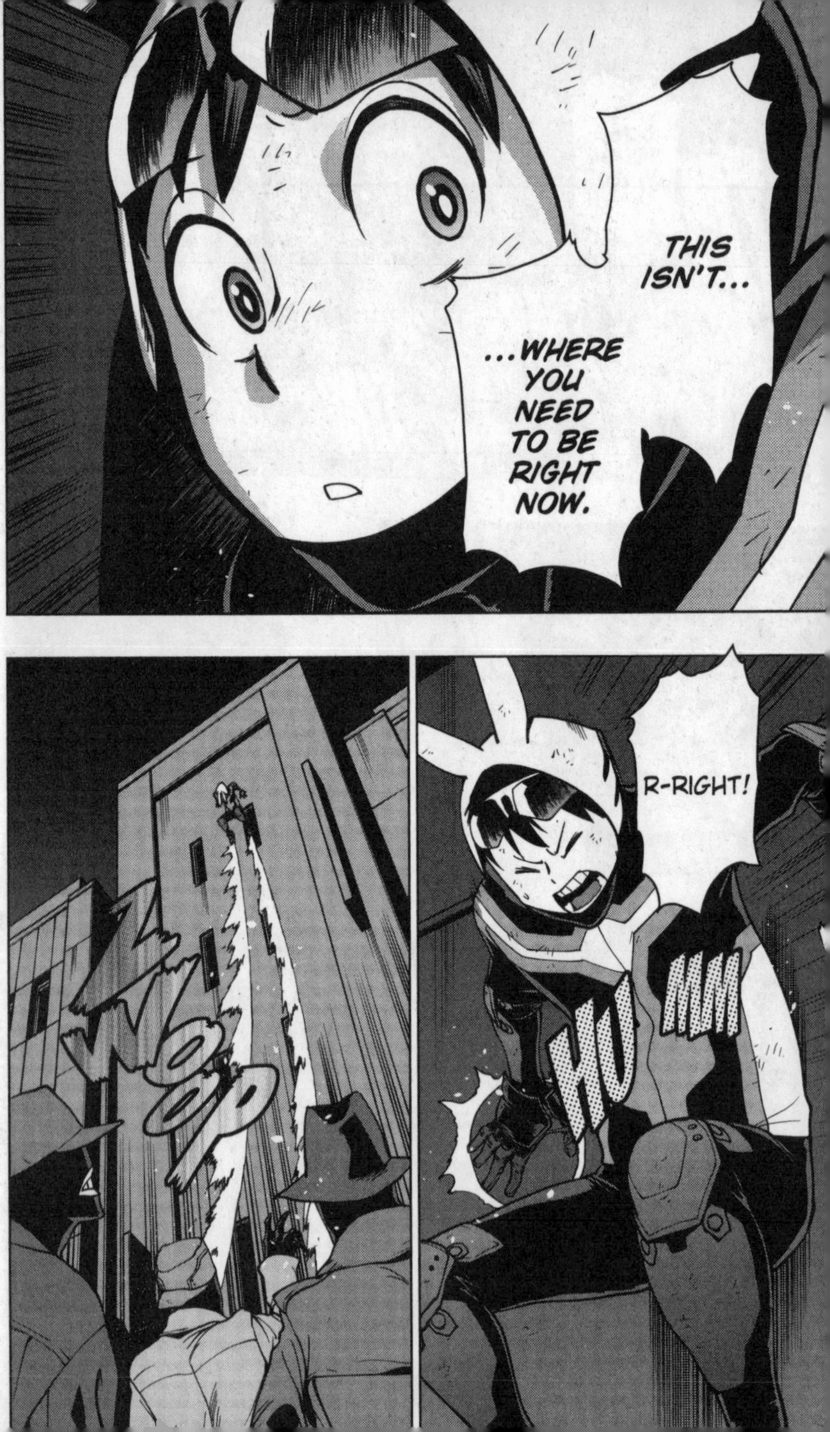
THIS ISN'T...
...WHERE YOU NEED TO BE RIGHT NOW.
R-RIGHT!
HUMM

THE HOSPITAL!

THERE IT IS!

?!

KABOOM!

AIZAWA SENSEI

He's been through a lot, and while ol' Aizawa was kind of careless and apathetic during his Naruhata days, he's got his act together more now that he's a teacher…

That was the vibe I was going for when writing the scene where he sends Koichi off to do his duty.

　—Furuhashi

Even after over 100 chapters, Aizawa Sensei is still pretty hard to draw. Hmm…

　—Betten

SOGA THE VIGILANTE

Soga's probably done the most growing as a person out of everyone in this story. Koichi will always be an airhead, but Soga uses his vigilantism as a way to come to terms with his own ideals and past sins.

—Furuhashi

From the very start, I subconsciously pictured Soga's hair as red, but when it came time to produce a full-color drawing of him, the red hair made him look too much like a carbon copy of Kirishima. So I hastily changed his hair color at the last minute... (Yikes, huh!)

—Betten

EP. 103 - SHOULD'VE AIMED FOR THE HEAD

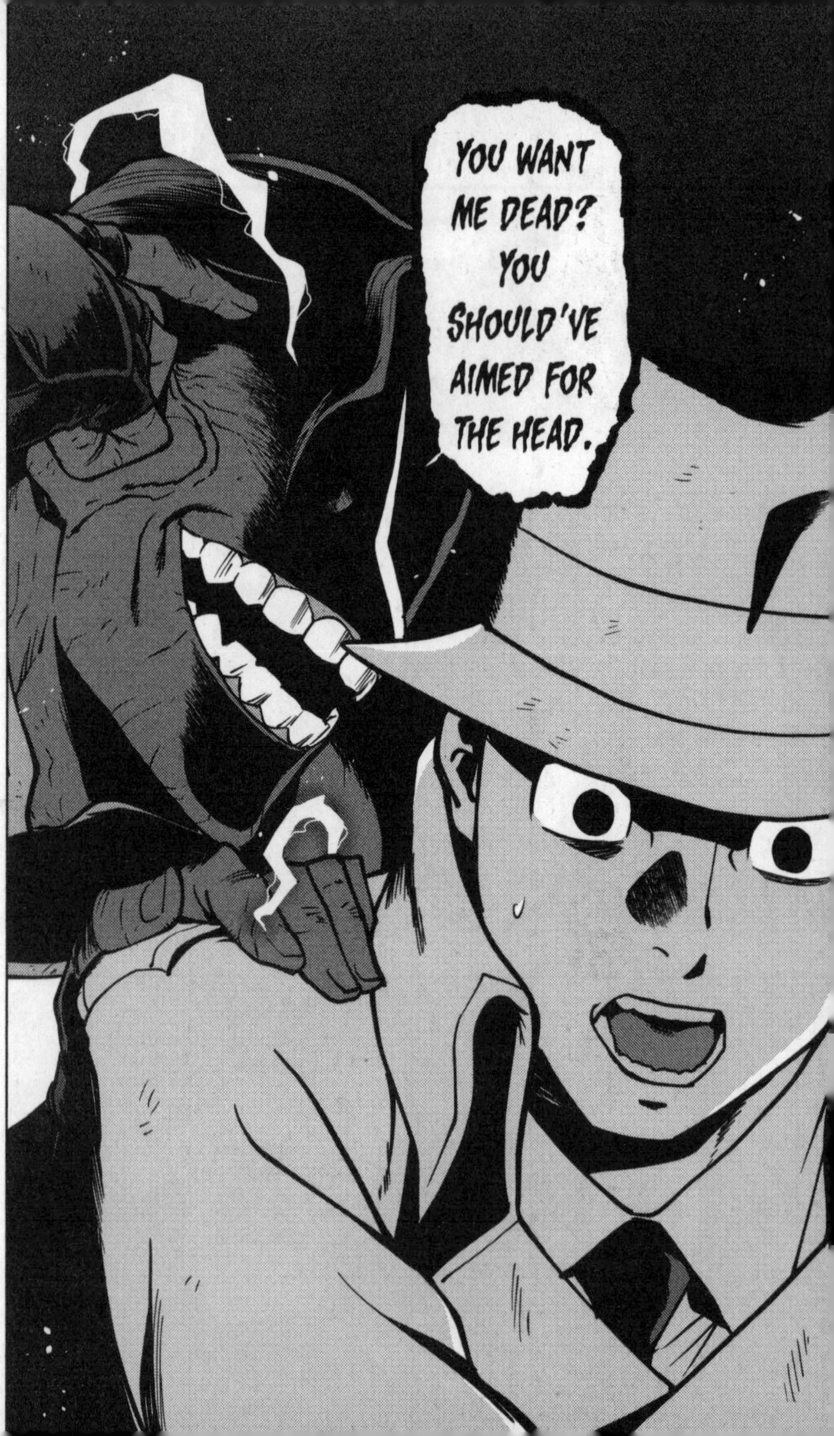
YOU WANT ME DEAD? YOU SHOULD'VE AIMED FOR THE HEAD.

THE FACELESS MAN

Whenever I'm writing the character of Rock, a.k.a. Number 6, I never want to really nail down his true form. I make a point of having him exude this almost yokai-esque, intangible creepiness. He flaunts his lack of an identity while really just seeking recognition and acceptance. Truly a walking paradox.

—Furuhashi

Weirdly, I like faceless Rock. He's fun to draw.

—Betten

EP. 104 - THIS FACE

A HEAD-TO-HEAD FIGHT WITH A NASTY VILLAIN? NOT IN MY WHEELHOUSE.

THE BEST I CAN DO IS SNEAK ATTACKS AND DIVERSION TACTICS.

THAT'S WHY FLYING OFF TO GET ALL MIGHT IS THE RIGHT CHOICE HERE.

EP. 104 - THIS FACE

IN A FAIR FIGHT, YOU DON'T STAND A CHANCE.

WE'RE UP AGAINST THAT SCUMBAG SPEEDSTER.

FOR WHATEVER REASON...

...THAT ONE'S A REAL TALKER. JUST LOVES TO RUN HIS MOUTH.

IN THE WORST CASE...

...THERE'S ONE TRICK THAT COULD WORK.

?

MAYBE IT'S HIS PRIDE DOING THE TALKING.

OR MAYBE HE'S TRYING TO GET SOME RESPECT WITH ALL THOSE SPEECHES.

OH...

KOICHI'S ATTACKS

For this chapter, at first I wasn't sure whether to have Koichi use Shooty-Go-Blam (standard version) or Shooty-Go-Kablam (high-velocity, piercing version), but I realized that Koichi would never purposely shoot a bunch of what are basically bullets into someone's face, so I settled on Shooty-Go-Blam (max power version). Each of those shots is about as strong as a no-holds-barred punch, but Pop would probably still get mad about that.

—Furuhashi

When this chapter was released, a lot of people saw Koichi zipping around in a kowtow position and thought that he was responsible for smacking off Rock's leg...

But no—Rock blew up his own right leg (I should've drawn that in a less confusing way...)

—Betten

EP. 105 - COMMENCE OPERATION ESCAPE

GUESS MY LIMIT'S THREE PUNCHES IN ONE BREATH?

A HIGH-SPEED FLURRY, WHILE MY FIST WAS LOADED UP WITH *BOMBIFY*, *DETONATION*, AND *REGENERATION*...

ZRM

SHLRP

FWP
FWP

THOUGH HE WAS DEAD AFTER THE *FIRST ONE.* ♪

SHAA

...RUNNING AWAY IS MY FORTE.

AND NOW, TO ENJOY MY DINNER AT LAST.

PHEW. THAT TAKES CARE OF THAT.

THERE WAS A NAMAHAGE PROBLEM IN AKITA PREFECTURE, BUT ALL MIGHT BROUGHT THE INCIDENT TO A SWIFT CONCLUSION!

ALL MIGHT

"THAT'S THE LAST STRAW!"

WHAAT? NOW IT'S THE AWA ODORI DANCE IN TOKUSHIMA?!

AWA ODORI

ALL MIGHT'S DISPATCHES

Having All Might get caught up in a variety of incidents at Japanese cultural events is mainly a way of showing that he's always zipping around the entire country, solving problems. I'll be scraping the bottom of the barrel with these gags soon enough.

—Furuhashi

All I could think was how the waitstaff at the cafe must wonder where this guy's always running off to without eating what he ordered. (LOL)

—Betten

EP. 106 - CRAWLER CHASE

EP. 106 - CRAWLER CHASE

NUMBER 6:
CRAWLER STYLE

HE BLOCKED WITH HIS QUIRK?!

The HERO TEAM in WORLD "WHAT-IF"

ILLUSTRATION:
BETTEN COURT

EP. 107 - HUNDRED-HIT RUSH

IT'S LIKELY THAT A LARGE PORTION OF KOICHI HAIMAWARI'S ACTIONS FALL UNDER THAT SUBCONSCIOUS UMBRELLA.

VERBAL GAFFES

DODGING

GRACEFUL FALL

NOW AND THEN, THE HUMAN BODY WILL TAKE ACTION WITHOUT WAITING FOR A CONSCIOUS DECISION TO BE MADE.

WHILE IT'S TRUE THAT *YOUR BRAIN* CAN PROCESS THOUGHTS FASTER THAN ANYONE...

...IT SEEMS THAT HIS BODY CAN ACT EVEN FASTER THAN YOUR THOUGHTS.

ABANDON THE MISSION AND RETREAT AT ONCE.

THIS FACTOR TROUBLES ME.

...THERE COMES A MOMENT WHEN HIS MOVES OUTSTRIP YOUR FORESIGHT.

ONE COULD DOWNPLAY THIS AS AD HOC REFLEXES ON HIS PART, BUT...

VIGILANTES
13

THE CLIMAX!
MY HEART'S
POUNDIN'
AS I READ!
KOHEI HORIKOSHI

Messeage from KOHEI HORIKOSHI

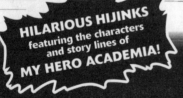